On Our Backs

guide to

LESBIAN
SEX

On Our Backs
guide to
LESBIAN SEX

alyson books
los angeles

© 2004 by Alyson Publications. Authors retain copyright to their individual pieces of work. All rights reserved.

Manufactured in the United States of America.

This trade paperback original is published by Alyson Publications, P.O. Box 4371, Los Angeles, California 90078-4371. Distribution in the United Kingdom by Turnaround Publisher Services Ltd., Unit 3, Olympia Trading Estate, Coburg Road, Wood Green, London N22 6TZ England.

First edition: February 2004

05 06 07 08 09 a 10 9 8 7 6 5 4 3 2

ISBN 1-55583-805-7
ISBN-13 978-1-55583-805-8

Library of Congress Cataloging-in-Publication Data
On our backs guide to lesbian sex. — 1st ed.
    ISBN 1-55583-805-7
    1. Lesbians — Sexual behavior. 2. Sex instruction for lesbians.
3. Lesbianism I. Title: Guide to lesbian sex. II. Title: Lesbian sex.
III. On our backs.
HQ75.51.O5 2004
        613.9'6'086643 — dc22   2003062819

Cover photography by Michelle Serchuk.
Cover design by Matt Sams.

CONTENTS

[Chapter 12]

On-Screen Sex: Videos to Get You in the Mood

INTRODUCTION

Rereading the last 20 years of *On Our Backs* magazine in order to gather this collection was like having sex again with all my ex-lovers. I have fond memories of everyone who has ever taken up space in my bed, my heart, and my pussy. And I feel the same way about all the articles I've ever read in *On Our Backs*. I remember reading much of this stuff for the first time and having my little budding lesbian head blown off. But this collection was more than just a horny trip down Memory Lane; it provided empirical proof that dyke sex has come a long way, baby.

Deciding what to include and what to exclude was the most difficult part of this process. *On Our Backs* published its first issue 1984. Every issue of the magazine has been sexy and exciting and smart. And though the older stuff in the magazine was incredibly hot and interesting, some of it seemed dated—and not just because of the hairstyles. I wanted this collection not only to be useful for all lesbians, but also to speak sexually to the way we are now. Most of us are over arguing whether or not porn is good for us. And we pretty much agree that strap-ons are fun, not tools of the patriarchy. *On Our Backs* no longer needs to take the proselytizing stance it once did. Our main concern now is how to do it better and more often, rather than whether or not we should be doing it at all. I believe that *On Our Backs* does a great job of celebrating our sex lives without politicizing the hard-on out of them. No matter how vanilla or kinky or butch or femme or top or bottom, I hope this book will provide examples of hot dyke sex and inspire readers to go out and fuck as gleefully as they can.

I included a few articles from the early *On Our Backs,* such as Carol Queen's "The Ins and Outs of Fisting," in which she playfully acknowledges the perceived no-nos of penetration while explaining in explicit detail exactly how to do it. It gives us a wonderful sense of the state of lesbian sexual culture at the time. Obviously, we were all fucking our brains out in all sorts of naughty ways but still feeling we had to justify it. Compare that to Tristan Taormino's 2003 piece on anal fisting in the butt-play chapter and you'll get a good sense of how much the terrain of our sex lives has changed over the past couple of decades.

On Our Backs magazine completely changed my sex life. In the early 1990s I moved to San Francisco, ready, willing, and able to get laid by women. I was a randy and open-minded girl who made up for her lack of experience with the ladies with sheer enthusiasm. But dyke sex, I mean real dyke sex, was foreign territory to me. All the girls I had fooled around with looked just like me, fucked just like me, and provided little challenge. I had no idea what I wanted or how to talk about sex with a partner. I didn't even know how to get off most of the time. Sex was a big fun game, but I knew there had to be more to it. And if my lovers weren't going to teach me how to have sex, where was I going to learn?

At that time, sexual information wasn't easy to find. Even now it's not so easy. And our imaginations and fantasies are limited by our experiences in the same way that our thoughts are limited by our vocabulary. I didn't know what it was I wanted in bed because I had no idea what was out there. I was completely oblivious to butch-femme desire, power dynamics, and BDSM. Flogging? Cutting? Water sports? Needles? I didn't know lesbians did all that. If a woman had asked me to call her "Daddy" I would have just looked at her confused.

The photos and articles in *On Our Backs* opened my mind to a whole new world of fucking that I had previously been left out of. I remember seeing my first image of a packing butch dyke getting her cock sucked and thinking, *Hey, that's what I've been looking for.* Finally, I not only knew what I wanted sexually, but I also knew who I wanted to do it with. *On Our Backs* was like a blueprint for the amazing sex life I now have. And the more I read, the more I experienced firsthand and the more I fell in love with being a dyke.

And now, more than 10 years and a whole lot of dyke sex later, I understand that *On Our Backs* plays that kind of role in the lives of many of its readers. This magazine teaches us about ourselves. It makes our desires visible, and by doing that it normalizes them. I'm excited that all this information is now collected in this book for all of us to read. Whether it's merely a reminder to you or it's the very first time you've seen this material, I hope you enjoy these articles and images and that they inspire you to fuck well and often.

It's important to thank all the contributors to this book. Many of the women whose work is included here have worked hard for many years because they love what

x

they're doing and believe that *On Our Backs* magazine serves a purpose in the community and in our bedrooms. They share my belief that creating images and stories of hot dyke sex is going to keep the rest of us fucking and banish any chance of lesbian bed death. And that this magazine also helps show the rest of the world who we are and what we're doing—because there is power in visibility. Associate photographers Michele Serchuk and Phyllis Christopher have provided *On Our Backs* with gorgeous photos of lesbian sex for many years, and *On Our Backs* thanks them so much for all their hard work. Every writer in this book has worked very hard and inspired me, and most of them have taught me new tricks. Also, I owe many thanks to dedicated interns Myriam Gurba, Cara Herbitter, Marie McAllister, and Gina de Vries, who've all spent countless hours transcribing old articles, digging through archives, and helping to brainstorm new topics to cover. A big thanks goes to the editors that were here before me, especially Susie Bright, whose work has inspired me for years and without whom this book would not have been possible.

On Our Backs will be celebrating its 20th anniversary when this book hits the stores. That's two fabulous decades of turning on dykes, pushing buttons, and generally encouraging lesbian hedonism. In a market where few publications have that kind of staying power, I'm pretty impressed that we're still going strong. I hope you enjoy reading this book as much as I enjoyed putting it together. Here's to many hot hours of pleasing your lovers and yourself!

—Diana Cage
Editor, *On Our Backs*

ONE

UNLEASHING DESIRE : CRUISING AND FLIRTING

How Do You Get a Woman Into Bed?

On Our Backs Readers Share Their Tips for Getting Laid
compiled by Diana Cage

"My current girlfriend is a stunning 5-foot-10 femme, rocking the straight sorority girl look. I met her at a play party. After three minutes of small talk, I asked her what she was into. She said she was new to the scene and didn't really know yet. So I used my best line ever: 'You like to get fucked, don't you?' She nodded enthusiastically. 'I'll go get my gear,' I told her. 'Why don't you find someplace to lie down.'" —*Sadie*

"'Are you wearing space pants? 'Cause your ass is out of this world.' I've learned that girls can get away with using cheesy, obnoxious guy lines and not get slapped. But you have to deliver the line with the appropriate self-referential corniness." —*M.P.*

"I invite them over for homemade sushi and *The Matrix* on DVD. I don't have a couch in my studio apartment, so we have to lie on my bed to see the screen. When the movie's over I just ask them if they want to make out. It's worked every time." —*Y.T.*

"I sing in gay clubs, and I've learned that the more skin I show the more money I make. I scope out the hottest butch stud I can find in the audience and then make my move. Perhaps it's the spiked heels or maybe it's my ass on her lap. But before too long, I've buried her face in my tits and she's on her knees in front of me! Afterward, I reward a good sport with a wild (yet safe) night of fucking." —*Bella*

"Make it your job to convince your prey that she's hotter than you. Think of why you want to sleep with her, then compliment her on that. Compliment her in front of other ladies, and get them to agree with you. Learn what she's passionate about and start a conversation on that topic. Get her riled up in conversation, agree with her, and learn from her, but don't be afraid to debate a little. When she's at the peak of her excitement and talking a mile a minute, interrupt her and say, 'God, we would make great lovers!'" —*Brandy*

"If it's a first date and the vibe is promising, I take a woman out for ice cream cones and innocently let her witness a sampling of my deft mouth." —*Naughty Dred*

3

"First I explain that my Leatherman Micra tool on the ol' key chain could easily fix that broken zipper of hers. Then I use the aforementioned tool to open the next dozen beers. The rest is herstory." —*Devina*

"Find an excuse to use your fingernails. If you're butch, and she's wearing a sleeveless shirt, compliment her on it, then ask her if she's cold while tracing down her arm with your deliciously scratchy nails. If you're a yummy femme and she compliments your manicure, smile devilishly, thank her, and ask her if she would like to feel those nails on the back of her neck." —*Miss Kitty*

4

Michele Serchuk

How to Cruise Women

by Midori

There she is, across the room. The woman that makes your throat tight and your mouth dry. But your feet are nailed to the floor. So how do you go about cruising her? Are you feeling shy or uncertain about how to flirt with women? Although there's no surefire pick-up line, there are some tricks that can seriously improve your chances. Here are a few of the highlights from my class "Approaching Venus: Cruising Women."

Make Friends First—With Everybody
Friends are your greatest allies when it comes to good cruising. So when you go to an event, make friends, even with people who aren't your type. He or she may be that cute gal's best friend. Ask a mutual friend to introduce you to your heartthrob; that's a really smooth transition. When you go out cruising, take your friends. It makes it easier to break the ice.

See Eye to Eye
A slow gaze with a soft smile that lingers a beat or two longer than usual…that's quite seductive. It lets her know that she is captivating and desirable. But don't stare. That makes you look loony.

You Are the Bait!
Don't underestimate the physical message you send out. Present yourself in a way that says, "I like myself." You'll get bonus cruising points for having good posture, neat grooming, a nice smile, and clean nails. ("You want to put those fingers where?") Be careful with scented products. Think of it this way: You're drawing her in closer, not knocking her out. Only people intimately close to you should be able to smell your perfumes and colognes.

Exude Confidence and Competence
Nothing's as sexy as a confident woman. Leave your insecurities at home when you're going out cruising. And remember, your shy streak was cute until you were about 21. After that, leave it at home too. Instead, emphasize the good stuff: Are you a fine

Popping the Question: Use Tools

When you ask a woman for a date—and you will—present it in a way that allows both of you a graceful way out. Try something like: "Should there be an opportunity to have dinner with you some time, I'd be delighted." Or, "I'd be thrilled if you'd let me take you dancing some night!"

Then hand her a personal card. This is a card made just for flirting. Include your name or nickname, E-mail address, and maybe a phone number. Always remember to carry a pen with you so you can add notes to it. As for her number, let her give it to you. Don't ask for it. But if she does offer, you'll have that pen handy.

dancer? A musician? A mechanic? An athlete? Share it. Women are drawn to those who gracefully display their competence. Liquid courage, in contrast, only gives courage to look foolish. Don't date drunk.

Be Direct, Not Pushy
Unless your lust object is a mind-reader, she'll never know you think she's hot unless you tell her. But just let her accept that fact; don't expect or push for a reciprocal answer. Give her some personal physical space when flirting with her, but make sure to turn your body and fully face her.

Compliments Will Get You Everywhere
Let her know she sparks your interest. Sometimes it's as simple as "I find you very attractive."

Give Good Ear
Listen and pay attention to her. Stuck for conversation? Ask her open-ended questions about herself: "What kind of music do you enjoy?" or "How did you get into skydiving?" Don't ask yes or no questions. That'll lead to another verbal dead-end. You'll learn a great deal about her while you make her feel interesting. Everyone wins!

Leave Her Wanting
Leave before she wants you to leave. Don't overstay your flirtation. Let her have a chance to miss you. It's generally a good idea to keep the first couple of cruise attempts short and sweet.

Identify Your Niche

The long gaze is more likely to get a good response at the big dyke dance in town than at nonqueer events. The same goes for the Ani DiFranco concert. Places known as dyke hangouts are a good bet. Volunteering at local LGBT clubs and organizations is another great way to increase your cruising success ratio.

Talk Trash—Later

Gossip, dishing your exes, and general negativity isn't going to get her hot to trot. Keep your attitude positive and adult so you can get X-rated later.

Handle Rejection With Grace

She said no. Smile and thank her. If she's open to your offer some other time, your graciousness will be remembered fondly.

Phyllis Christopher

Flirting Tips for Fat Girls

by Mama Sutra

Never Self-Deprecate

Don't make excuses for your size or body weight. Never make comments about being on a diet or recently having gained weight. Do not try to beat people to the punch regarding fat comments. It shows you fear those comments and gives them undue power. Do not laugh at jokes that disrespect large people. Pythagoras said, "Let no man entice thee to say or do whatever is not profitable for thyself."

Use Fat-Positive Language

We need to learn fat-positive language, because we have learned fat-negative language our whole lives. Think of words to describe how sexy you are, like Rubenesque, voluptuous, succulent, ravishing, goddess-like, etc. It's important to refer to yourself with positive, sexualized words. Fat women need to assert a sexual identity through the words they use as much as through their body language.

Pamper Yourself

Make dates with yourself. Buy oils and massage your own legs or thighs or butt or arms or chest. Purchase nice-smelling bath salts and sensual clothing. Sometimes I feel fabulous in a vinyl mini-dress, wild tights, and Doc Martens. Take time to perform rituals for yourself. Do yoga. Commune with your body in a warm bath. Get up a half-hour early for work and drink tea and read. Meditate. Light candles and listen to music. Go for a walk and pick flowers. Slow down and treat your body and mind like royalty.

Learn to Be Erotic for Yourself First

It's essential that you get a handle on your own sexuality before you go out looking for sexual partners. Dance erotically, solo. Seduce yourself. Collect pictures of people you find sexy and figure out why you find them sexy. Make an altar to your sexual energy/body parts. I used to make slips of paper with sexual things I could do with myself, put them in a box, and draw one. Paint or draw a picture of your genitals looking at them in a mirror. Become a friends and lover of your own body.

Seek Out Fat-Positive Community

Find places where fat is not an issue, or fat-friendly environments. Groups I have found to be fat-positive include pagans, the S/M community, and more (Wagnerian Opera circles, for example). Another strategy is to *create* an erotic, fat-positive community. Some of my friends and I started a group called the 201 Club last October in Seattle. To be included, you must be a woman who weighs more than 200 pounds. (If you weigh slightly under 200 pounds, you may wear heavy jewelry to tip the scales.) We have organized clothing exchanges and a dessert-a-thon, made berry cordials, and discussed everything from sex and lovers to food and life. We meet at a different member's house every month and keep in touch through an E-mail list we created.

9

Surround Yourself With Fat-Positive Imagery

Create an altar of images that reflect your body type. We are inundated with images of thin = beautiful; we need to reinforce to ourselves that our body type is also beautiful. Whenever I see anything that looks like my body, I grab a copy for my altar. I have Xeroxed pictures from *Women En Large,* a fabulous book of lots of different types of fat women, naked and erotic. I get old *National Geographics* and cut out pictures of large international women. I hang Annie Sprinkle postcards on my wall, because her breasts are big and they hang instead of having that duct-taped, gravity-defying look. You can also collect art objects. I have seen Venus of Willendorf beeswax candles and fat woman candleholders. Just as we need new language for a fat-positive environment, we also need new imagery for self-confidence.

Use Intrigue and Mystery
Do unusual things to set yourself apart from the crowd. Exploit your talents and wear them on your sleeve! Dare to be creative and different. Allow yourself to take up the space you deserve. I once knew a woman who was fat yet exuded sexuality. Did I study her! She wore sexy clothes in exotic cuts as well as fabrics and suggestive jewelry that dangled into her cleavage. She always smelled intriguing, with earthy, sensual scents. I was astounded by her sexual confidence. I suggest we all take more risks of visibility as fat lovers, and accentuate our features, tastes, and talents, rather than trying to cover up and hide our bodies.

Remember Your Fat Lovers
Once I was driving to a fair with a fat-phobic Seattle performer who said to me, "How would you like to date a fat person?!" He said it as though it were a fate worse than death. I retorted, "I've had fat lovers! And they're wonderful!" Their fat was not something to overlook. And then I realized that perhaps *my* lovers felt the same! A lot of fat insecurity is in our heads. Remember the fat people you love and find sexy, and apply the same standards to yourself.

Revere Your Belly at All Times
It seems that bellies are vulnerable on practically everyone. What is it that makes even people who aren't fat freaked out about their bellies? I don't know, but I do know that I've met few lovers who were completely at home with their naked belly. So I recommend belly adoration for all. I adorn my belly with watercolors or face paints and massage it with sweet-smelling oils. I wear temporary tattoos and body glitter. You never know what's going on with my belly underneath my clothes! Your lover probably could use some belly adoring also. Break the belly taboo. Touch a belly today!

Cyber Hell

by Michele Tea

After spending—no shit—five solid hours staring into the life-sucking glow of my computer screen, it's hard to relate to the thing as an object of sexual pleasure. But being noble enough to try all sorts of stunts in search of a cheap thrill, I logged on to the virtual suburbia of America Online in hopes of finding myself a perverse lesbian, or a manipulative straight man masquerading as a perverse lesbian, to get dirty on the computer with me.

My first snack on AOL's Gay Romance chat menu was, of course, "Lesbian Butch." I was actually pretty thrilled that such a category even existed, and felt a moment of real excitement that temporarily dislodged the microchip on my shoulder. But fantasies

"What do you think about when you play with your pussy?" I typed, thinking that some storytelling or role-playing would get this party started.

of being seduced by a sleazy hunk of rough trade evaporated as stark lines of type began slashing across my screen, and I felt oddly shy at the thought of bursting in on the boring chatter with the suggestion of sex. Chat rooms really lack ambience. I think their real-life equivalent might be institutional cafeterias. Another friendly note: Typing in all-caps is not sexy. It is abrasive. It looks like you're yelling at everyone.

I clicked over to "Lesbian Femmes." It was definitely more lively. I spotted a chick who was "looking to chat private" and quickly sent her an Instant Message with a request for some serious dirty talk. "Do you have any pictures?" she asked. Now, I had thought that one of the scant good things about having sex via computer was that you didn't have to see what the other person looked like; you could let your own aesthetic fill in the gaps and create a grand fantasy of whoever you were about to simulate sex with. I was pretty sure we would each be repulsed by the other's fashion choices and the lifestyles they signified, and besides that, my archaic computer can do nothing as esoteric as trade photos. I cutely typed back that I could barely turn my computer on. She responded, "Oh." Everyone in this cyber hell seemed strangely monosyllabic.

Finally, I hooked in a fellow prowler, the 45-year-old "sweet and sensuous" "Mary," large-breasted, freshly out of a lame hetero relationship, and looking to experiment with the ladies. After assuring her I wasn't a guy, Mary told me all about how her black slip was yanked up above her smooth shaved pussy, how she was sucking her own enormous tits, and already had three fingers working up inside her wet cunt. While this information sloooowwwly cranked out onto my antique machine, I smoked a cigarette and listened with sympathy to the cat in heat howling outside my window. I like sex that has the immediacy of an unexpected smack across the face, so this trickle of smut rankled my patience and triggered my *Sesame Street*/MTV–borne attention deficit disorder. "What do you think about when you play with your pussy?" I typed, thinking that some storytelling or role-playing would get this party started—right. Turns out Mary thinks about young girls…really young girls…and lactating mothers. Maybe I should have asked Mary to promise me *she* wasn't a guy. I felt bad for suddenly suspecting her gender, since taboo stuff turns me on as well, but something about the lactating mom bit just seemed really male. And why had she been so concerned that I might be a guy? It really didn't matter so much, since all the talk of underage girls and milky tits had at last gotten my cunt all throbby like that unfortunate alley cat yowling in my backyard.

And how was poor Mary to know that I wasn't really a guy? I felt like a guy, or at least more like a boy than normal as I slapped at my keyboard, telling Mary how I was groping the fresh tits of the teenage girl next door, her hard little nipples poking through the thin fabric of a summer tank top. I typed about sucking the milk from the swollen tits of a new mom as I slid my hand up into her slick cunt. Purely fantasy, Mary assured me as she responded, which lessened but did not relieve the icky twitch that I could possibly be emboldening a pedophile. At the fantasy's absurd climax, in which the two kinks merged into a lactating adolescent, Mary's communication abruptly stopped, which makes me think that she really was a he, since any self-respecting lesbian would certainly need some closure at the end of such a vulnerable confession of perversity.

Feeling like I'd been kicked off the futon without so much as cab fare, I bounced through some other lesbo chat rooms asking for ladies to IM me with their fantasies.

Dirty fantasies, I kept having to clarify. One chattee involved me in an excruciating conversation about her mother's Bay Area nursing home. I clicked away. The women in "Lesbian Support" were—I swear—having an actual argument about who had the most brutal childhood. Not wanting to traumatize them further by soliciting perverted sex acts, I signed off.

Darlene Weide

And thus ends my sad foray into the cold and illusory world of cybersex. It served only to illuminate my poverty—my rotten, incapable computer and my recently shut-off long-distance service, which prevented me from calling my girlfriend in an area code far away for some serious guilt-free trash-talking. With a creative, quick-thinking, and fast-typing cybertrick you could no doubt conjure up some hot back-and-forth action, but I just think that computers are for work, not for fucking or anything that requires the exchange of earned sweat. There are other machines out there built to get you off, so learn from my pain and plug in that Hitachi.

Cruising the Web

by Cara Bruce

You look like a librarian. Your appearance says prim, proper, and vanilla all the way. Yet you're dying to be tied up and degraded. You long for a big strong butch who will make you suck her cock and lick her boots. But frustratingly, every girl that picks you up treats you as if you could break at any second. So you put an ad online: "Librarian-looking lesbian seeks daddy to spank her, punish her, and fuck the hell out of her." Two nights later you're tied to the bed begging and pleading for daddy's cock. You're in heaven.

After a hot fuck session she tells you she's seen you around but never dreamed you were that type. The next day you've got another ad on Craigslist. You've never been happier.

It's hard to pick up girls in real-time. You can cruise the dyke bars—if there are any in your town—but even then you run the risk of hitting on the one straight girl out for a thrill, or picking up a lesbian whose idea of a wild night is rubbing against you fully clothed, when you just want to flip her over, pull down those jeans, and spank the little slut.

Thank God for online personals.

"Online it's easy to identify a girl who likes chicks, so there's none of the horribly awkward 'does she or doesn't she' thing," says Belle, a sweet, funny dyke who's been using online personals for about four years. "There's quite a long list of women I'd like to spend the night with. But I look straight, so no girls ever ask me out. Even when I stare at a butch all night and flirt heavily, I never get taken seriously."

Online dating is also great if you're shy. "I had a crazy crush on this girl," says Dani, a 27-year-old bike messenger, "so I put up an ad on a local personals site. About six girls that weren't her responded, but then the right girl finally saw it. She was so flattered. Especially because I wrote in my ad how much I wanted to fuck her! Our first date ended up with me getting fisted in the back of her truck. Talk about hot."

These days dykes are flocking to online personals in droves. Mainly because they offer a more selective way to cruise for potential sex partners. Instead of heading straight to the bar and making eye contact with every hot chick in leather pants, you

14

can place a very specific ad on a local personals site and then arrange for her to meet you at the bar once you've established a connection. In addition, online ads are anonymous, and this allows many dykes to act more aggressively than they normally would in person.

"I'm a very social person, so I have no problem approaching people in bars or clubs," says Maya, a cute 20-something dyke. "But the results of online searches are more favorable because you get a chance to get to know the person before you meet. There are no awkward moments, and the conversation flows better."

The number and variety of women online are what make it such a successful alternative to bars. And the convenience of cruising for a sex partner from your home can be seductive. Many women find the process of searching through so many ads arousing.

"My girlfriend and I often look online together," says Irene, a butch from the Midwest. "I remember one night she was under my desk eating my pussy while I surfed for a cute little femme to join us."

In fact, some women stated that online personals were maybe too tempting. The easy availability of so many lesbians looking to get laid can be a major distraction.

"My girlfriend and I had a fight, and I was so angry I posted an ad. Within hours I was E-mailing back and forth with what sounded like a pretty hot butch. But when I came to my senses, I realized I wasn't ready to start up a new fling. Plus, my girlfriend apologized later that night and I had to explain to the butch that I wasn't really single. I felt really bad about leading her on," explains Annie, a Boston-area femme who works as an exotic dancer.

With personal ads, honesty is the best policy. Many women express concern about being led on or lied to via E-mail. And more than one dyke has complained that straight girls often post ads looking to play—although not everyone cruising the Web feels so proprietary about lesbian space. "As long as they're outright about it, who cares? You don't have to call them. But if popping a chick's dyke-cherry turns you on, well, there you go," says Dana, a butch top who says she met her last girlfriend online.

One of the most popular places online for girls to pick each other up is Craigslist (www.craigslist.org). It began as a Bay Area phenomenon but in recent years has spread to major cities across the U.S. The "women seeking women" section of Craigslist functions as a community bulletin board. Dykes promote their clubs, dish the bar scene, and post messages to one another.

"I'm addicted to Craigslist," gushes Jenny, a 30-year-old graphic designer living in Fremont. "Every day I read 'women seeking women' and the 'missed connections.' I have fantasies about someday reading one for me. I've posted plenty looking for other people."

In addition to searching for that perfect partner, Jenny also uses Craigslist to see what clubs, parties, or events are going on. "It's kind of cool seeing so many girls in one place. Now we all know what's going on and where. I think it's made the community tighter. When I first moved to the city [San Francisco]," she says, "I didn't know where to meet girls. I used Craigslist to find a job and started checking out the personals. I put up a post for friends—a little embarrassed and a lot nervous—but I got a bunch of responses. Two of my best friends and my girlfriend are from that first ad. But I'll tell you, five years ago you couldn't have paid me to put up a personals ad."

This is not an uncommon sentiment. Many women state that there used to be a stigma attached to using personals: If you had to answer an ad to find someone, you must be desperate. But with the ubiquity of the Internet, that idea has disappeared. Online ads run the gamut from women seeking friendship, life partners, three-ways, ass slaves, daddy's girls, someone to worship, and the bi-curious girl who wants to experiment, with or without her boyfriend. So not only do you know exactly what you're getting into sexually, you also know whether she expects you to be cohabitating next week or to be out of her bed before the sun rises.

Looking for a girl who will enjoy your riding crop collection? There are sites that cater to specific audiences. Alt.com is a BDSM site, Butch-femme.com is self-explanatory, and Nerve.com attracts women who read. (Try and find a bar for that.)

"I'm really into BDSM," says Rex, a kinky femme-bottom. "I don't want a monogamous relationship—all I want is to play. I'm a femme and I'm attracted to femmes. I can't even tell you how many times I struck out trying to get a femme to top me. The day I saw an ad online that read 'Femme Top Seeks Femme Bottom.' I nearly came right there."

So are dykes having more sex? You bet your sweet ass.

"The U-Haul on the second date thing is such a myth," says Rex. "Dykes like one-night stands just as much as the next guy or girl. As far as one-night stands go, I've had the best sex of my life with girls I've met off of Craigslist. One night I even scheduled two dates by accident and all three of us got lucky!"

Lesbian Online Hook-Up Sites

On Our Backs (personals.onourbacksmag.com)
PlanetOut (www.planetout.com)
Craigslist (www.craigslist.org)
Nerve (www.nerve.com)
Butch-Femme.com (www.butch-femme.com)
Match (www.match.com)
Swoon (www.swoon.com)
Curve Magazine (www.curvepersonals.com)
The Advocate (personals.advocate.com)
Yahoo Personals (personals.yahoo.com)
Girlfriends (personals.girlfriendsmag.com)

17

TWO

TUNE IN, TURN ON: MASTURBATION AND FOREPLAY

Get Yourself Off!

Dykes Tell Us How They Do It
compiled by Lindsay McClune

"My favorite masturbation technique is to use an electric vibrator right on my clit. I like to feel something inside me too, so I use a soft seven-inch dildo and a three-inch battery vibrator up my ass. I love that all-over vibrator feeling." —*Susan*

"I take out my vibrator, turn it on, unzip my pants and place it between the folds of my pussy to rest on my swollen clit. I kneel down and lean over the bed to imagine a beautiful large woman sucking me off. I begin a rhythmic motion fantasizing about this woman, hearing her moan with each thrust. Faster and faster my hips move until I feel my orgasm explode, letting out a yell—as my fantasy becomes a reality." —*Lola*

"I love to fuck my blow-up doll with my big dick. I fuck her in the ass, in the mouth, and in her pussy. I imagine shooting my come in every orifice." —Barb

"I started masturbating early, around age 6, when I still feared my vagina. I have crushing orgasms by squeezing my legs together and fantasizing about power roles; it doesn't require me to use my hands. I sometimes use dildos or household objects, but once I used a glass bottle and didn't realize that it can produce enough suction to bruise your cervix and vaginal wall. Ouch." —*Deirdre*

"She stripped me naked, slapped me down in a vinyl chair, and carved her initials in a heart on my chest. For days afterward I could feel the blood rushing to that spot and I had to touch myself each time I saw the mark in the mirror. The secret thrill of her mark on my body kept me hot for days. The memory itself sends me to my bed with the vibrator she left when she flew away." —*Tramp Kitty*

"First, I take my favorite dildo—silicone, a little soft, and not too big—and tease myself with it for before lubing it up and inserting it. (If I'm feeling decadent, I'll add a small butt plug at this stage too, for a really full feeling. I have one that looks like a little red pacifier.) Then I take my 'Betty Dodson Special,' the Hitachi Magic Wand vibrator, and place it not on my clit, but just above it. I spend some time building up and then backing away. I go at it this way, on/off, build up and back off, for as long as I can stand it. Then I turn it on high and clench the head of the vibrator between my legs, squeeze, and hold on tight!" —Trish

"Raised a Catholic schoolgirl, I didn't start masturbating until late, around 11 or so. My favorite toy has always been my hand, well, really my finger. Usually I stroke my clit, occasionally fingering myself simultaneously. Now I know a lot of girls like to use 'the wand' or a favorite dildo, but I fear the time when I will be stuck without modern technology and only a vague memory of how to get myself off otherwise." —Gina

"I lie facedown on the bed, my chin or the side of my face resting against a pillow. I put my hands on the sides of my labia, often through my clothes, and put pressure there as I swing my hips from side to side like a dog wagging its tail. As I reach climax, I speed up my hip swinging and press harder against my labia." —Rachel

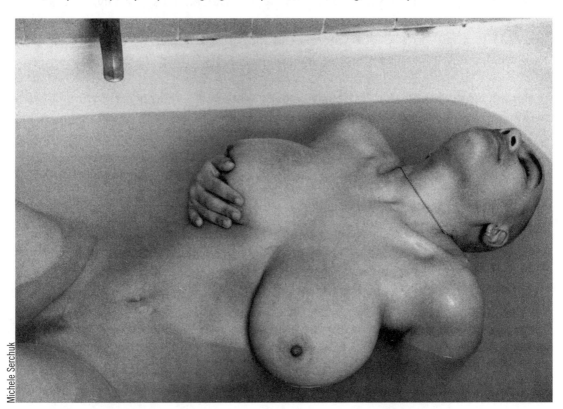

22

Michele Serchuk

Give a Great Erotic Massage

by Deborah Addington

A lover of mine once broke the ice in bed by playing a little game with me. She had me close my eyes. She took my hand and held it palm up, exposing my inner wrist, forearm, and elbow. She said, "OK, I'm gonna run my fingers up your arm. Tell me when I get to the very middle of the inside of your elbow."

Stop reading—right now—and try that on yourself. OK, so how close did you get? Within an inch? Dead on? And did it feel, well, kind of exciting?

If touching yourself can be that hot, just think what a light hands-on could do to incite your baby. Something like "Aw, hard day at work, love? Here, let me help you relax with a nice back rub" could be all it takes to lead you closer to her heart (and elsewhere).

Know Thyself

If you don't know what those magnificent nerve endings of yours can do, how can you expect to incite hers? So run a tub—yes, for yourself. Make aquatic love to yourself. Observe what feels best—from the toes up, or wrists first? After you towel off and lie down, touch yourself all over again. Check out every crevice, crack, and crease. Smell your cunt juice. Taste your fingers. Explore. Use your body and its responses as a template for what you might do for her.

Be Prepared

The hour of her massage, put your tools within reach: fresh towels, a sheet, and a bowl of warm water to keep your lotion or oil warm. My favorite massage medium is actually a personal lubricant called Eros; it doesn't taste bad, it doesn't get tacky or lose its viscosity, and it feels amazing. As for where the massage happens, location isn't as important as being able to get at her from all sides. If you're using the bed, lay down a protective cover. You can also use a kitchen table; just make sure to pad it with something soft. Make the room warm enough for her to be comfortable naked— you might break a sweat, but that's better than having her all tensed up and shivery from a chill. Turn the answering machine volume down and the phone ringer off.

Get Environmentally Sensitive

Experiment with lighting—try candles or lamps with scarves. Ask if incense or aromatherapy is OK with her, and don't forget music: Try the instrumental version of the soundtrack to *The Crow* (you'll want the version by Graeme Revell).

Clean Up Your Act

Apply the info you gleaned about yourself to her bath. Wash her hair, condition it with something expensive, and wash her face. Wow, huh? When she's squeaky-clean, maybe slide into the tub with her for a quick rinse. Try leaving your clothes on; it's a taboo sort of thing, and defying taboos is hot. When you're done, dry her off with a warm, fluffy towel.

Patience Is a Virtue

And a good masseuse is always virtuous. If you just met Ms. Right (or even Ms. Right Now) you wouldn't throw her down on the bar and fuck her without at least

24

Michele Serchuk

a handshake, right? Same principle applies here. An erotic massage should be a massage first, foreplay second.

Start at Her Feet, Proceed to Her Brain
Our feet carry us. Those two relatively small appendages bear our bodies' burdens, and it's thankless work. Start at the toes and work your way up. At the same time tell her a story that will lead her mind down a path to a safe, cozy place while you smooth the tension from her toes. Run your fingers through her hand and tell her you're running your hands through summer grass; get between her thighs and tell her you're stopping to smell the roses.

Find Out Where Not to Touch
Getting acquainted with her sweet spots means also getting acquainted with her "NO" zones. Say she moves away from your hand. If you were to make the same motion while being massaged, what would it mean? If you're still not sure, you can ask.

Be Firm
Whether you're rolling your knuckles up the line of her calf, or rolling the pads of your fingers down her spine as if those muscles were dough, make each motion deliberate, appropriate, and thorough. Go with the grain when you rub muscle tissue. If you're doing her leg, rub the entire leg before moving on to the next part.

Apply the Finishing Touches
With the same gentle touch you began with, firmly run your hands once more over her flesh. She might enjoy a light scratching of not-too-ticklish areas; scratching helps bring the blood back up to the surface of her skin and heightens its sensitivity. Encourage her to sip a glass of cool water; it will help her body flush toxins released by muscular manipulation, and she'll feel invigorated instead of achy tomorrow.

Save the Breast for Last
If you've left your love in a state of luscious lethargy, let her drift for 15 or 20 minutes so that her blood pressure and heart rate don't drop into the rhythm of true sleep. When you wake your snoozing beauty, she'll feel deliciously refreshed and ready to romp.

DON'TS:

•Don't forget the most neglected parts. The face, fingers, legs, scalp, and torso are least accustomed to touch and are often the most grateful and responsive.

•Don't *ever* break contact. Always leave one hand in contact with her—if you break contact, you interrupt the circuit of energy you're exchanging. That kind of a jolt can ruin the yummy effect all of your efforts.

•Don't be insensitive. If she's shy, use a sheet or light blanket to cover the areas you're not working on. She won't relax if she's worried about having her boundaries trespassed.

•Don't undercommit. Rule of thumb: at least two hours for a full-body massage, and one-half hour for each body part that needs special, additional attention.

Tribadism: Rub Your Way to Orgasm

by JoAnn Loulan

There are ancient rites of rubbing on stones for good luck, and there are ancient rites of rubbing for muscle relaxation and healing. It is high time we gave due love and attention to the ancient rite of rubbing thigh unto thigh. It's called "tribadism" when you actually rub so that there is contact of the clitoris, labia, and general yoniville and another woman's leg, thigh, arm, hip—in general, any body part that isn't a tongue, mouth, or finger (those delicious art forms have their own terms).

So the deal is that women-loving women used to be called "tribades" in honor of this way of making love. In fact, Sappho wrote about rubbing clits in some of the fragmented poetry left from those ancient Greek times. Could rubbing clitties be the oldest form of lesbian love? Who knows, but it sure feels good.

Could rubbing clitties be the oldest form of lesbian love? Who knows, but it sure feels good.

Let the Play Begin
Rubbing is a wonderful way to start sexual play. It's good for women who are afraid of having something inside their vagina. It's a sweet treat for those looking for new things to do. It's also a great way to reintroduce sex for women who have been away from it for a while. It's nonthreatening and feels good too. Wow: two-two-two treats in one!

Spread 'Em
Spread those two sets of legs and do the scissors with them—move them far enough apart so your girl can get her spread legs intertwined with yours. OK, now move your 'gina in close to her leg/thigh/kneecap/whatever and get some clitoral contact.

Sliding

Get some lubrication on the legs doing the rubbing—vegetable oil, massage oil, or vaginal juices, just so the friction is at your clit, not your leg skin. Advantage here is that you can spread your juices in a way that feels good to both and won't spread any negative germ vibes.

Pull Your Clitty Out

For more intense feeling, reach down, spread your pussy lips and pull your fur up, so your clit is closer to slickness. There—that feels good, huh? Tilt your hips forward so you can keep contact with her. Sometimes our clits need to be free!

Touching for Fun

Now start doing the hump; you'll feel the friction start to build in a way that feels good. Keep rubbing back and forth between the two of you—one of the ways to deal with lesbian merging in a positive way.

Get the Lips Moving

Make sure you and your partner are talking during all of this so that your positioning—which is key—is right. Sometimes stomachs get in the way, sometimes thighs are rubbing, not yonis. Pay attention and let each other know what is going on.

Rub and Learn

You get to see what kind of stimulation feels good to your partner and vice versa. You can actually see it and feel it. Talk about positive reinforcement!

Cooking With Vaginal Drippings

Rub those visible and smellable juices on the thigh, leg, knee, etc. This is especially wonderful for women who have a hard time with the smell or taste of vaginal juices. Get used to the smell by spreading it on another body part. Put your finger in the juice and taste it; this is a less threatening way to get used to the flavor so you'll be more prepared to lick her vaginal lips, clit, or the vagina itself. I love the way menstrual blood spreads as well. You can really make an art project on someone's thigh, stomach, leg, or wherever.

28

Get to the Clit

Put your finger in between your tangle of legs so that the clit gets more direct action. Get your vibrator in on the act if you want to. Adjust the pressure on the clit so it suits your partner. Be sure to tell each other how to make that happen.

Spasm Into Orgasm

You can keep that motion going until the clitoris feels so good it wants to spasm in a way that says "orgasm." Rubbing each other is such animal energy—are you inspired to try something else now?

DON'TS

•Don't always expect orgasm. Direct connection isn't always possible with different kinds of bodies or flexibilities. Rubbing can be a way of simply getting things going.

•Don't give up after one time. Coming from this kind of friction takes practice, just like any new way of orgasming.

• Don't forget about STDs. You can catch genital warts and also herpes II with this kind of touch. Get tested, and talk with her about her body too. It's not a crime to have a sexually transmitted disease, but they are zero fun, and some have serious consequences.

Lesbian Breast Worship

by Heather Findlay

More so than any lesbian body part, goddess-given or store-bought, breasts and nipples are an ideological battleground.

True, they haven't triggered as much heated language in feminist circles as their sister in silicone, the dildo. But that's the point, so to speak. For lesbians, there's an untapped reservoir of fear, anxiety, and desire beneath the notion of breast worship.

When I solicited help for this article from a carload of dykes last weekend, all I got was a tired, saggy "Ugh." Why is it that fisting, butt-fucking, and Daddy play are the stuff of café conversations, while breasts and nipples seem almost taboo? One would think that with an average of four boobs in every act of lesbian lovemaking, these mammalian wonders would be identified pure and simple with all-girl action.

After all, in straight male sexuality they are. I believe this is part of the problem. From Renaissance Madonnas to *Juggs* magazine, straight men have blithely claimed a monopoly on breast worship. Those of you who know something about 15th-century painting and modern censorship know there's nothing natural about these genres'—or their het male readers'—predilection for titties both pert and ponderous. Michelangelo and DaVinci, for example, were fags. And moreover, if corporate advertisers wouldn't pull the plug on *Playboy* if it were, that bosom-burdened bastion of "men's entertainment" might be more invested in clit and pussy.

Nevertheless, there's still something uncomfortably "male" about breast worship. A quick perusal of feminist erotica—including *On Our Backs*—will turn up very few of the classic breast-oriented poses (shirt pulled up slightly over the nipples, etc.). It's almost as if we lesbians are afraid to tread on such well-trod—and often exploited—ground.

Another difficulty some lesbians have with breast worship is what I call the "tomboy factor." Many dykes mark their fall from grace at the pubescent moment when the evil agent of estrogen caused them to grow tits. It's not a question of whether you identify as butch, even though a number of butches I've slept with do not appreciate having their breasts touched. Some of them go so far as to demand that their undershirts remain on during sex. In any case, breasts are a painful

reminder to many of us that we no longer have the privilege (and fun) of being boys.

Butches do, however, have a thing for their lover's breasts. Nothing makes my sweetie more content than to plant her nose at the top of my cleavage. She then gently lifts my breasts to her cheeks. Last week this simple gesture caused her to say "Mama" ("That's Mama sir to you!" I replied, thinking Freud might have something to say about this little interaction.)

Of course there are exceptions to the rule against public lesbian breast worship. Annie Sprinkle's bosom ballet comes to mind (my dear friend Claire proudly displays a photo of herself, crowned by Annie's gigantic knockers, on her fridge). And when it comes to breast and nipple decoration, lesbians, fags, and other sexual outlaws rule the field. There's hardly a lesbian left in San Francisco without a nipple piercing or breast tattoo. All those Los Angeleno femme-femme couples should, with the help of lacy underwires and push-ups, raise lesbian culture to new highs in lingerie. Lesbians have proven to be experts too when it comes to eroticizing differently abled breasts; the ubiquitous Hella Hammid photo of a modern Amazon, arms reaching toward the sky, mastectomy proudly displayed, is evidence of that.

There's room for improvement, though. Few lesbians realize there's no physiological reason that nipples shouldn't be considered sex organs. Like your clitoris and vagina, your stimulated nipple fills with blood, gets swollen, and becomes very responsive. A stiff tit is, in fact, a natural lesbian erection.

I've never witnessed it, but a few women reported to Masters and Johnson in the '60s that breast-rubbing alone could bring them to orgasm. One of the breast-orgasmic lesbians I know actually prefers her lover to stimulate her breasts more than her pussy. When she's being fucked or sucked, added attention to her breasts can produce, in her words, "incredibly intense" climaxes.

The one time a breast-orgasm almost happened to me was after a good half-hour of sucking, pinching, rolling, and biting. I learned from this experience that, for breasts to be truly worshiped, one must immediately discard the notion of getting to "second base." If you're going to treat your lover's breasts as sex organs, then don't bestow them with only a few caresses on your way down to her bush.

Some lesbians are also guilty of reducing the breast to its nipple. The truth is that the entire breast can be an erogenous zone. Chesty women report to me that the flesh beneath their breasts is a particularly voluptuous—and vastly underrated—area. Inserting one's tongue, hands, head, or whatever else will fit in there can lead to untold ecstasies. And the possibility for fantasy in these cases are endless. Think about it: With that warm, damp fold between the boob and the upper abdomen, it's as if full-figured gals have three cunts, one between their legs and two beneath their breasts.

This kind of fantasy, I'm sure, lies behind the wonderfully perverse act of tit-fucking. *Plenty* of lesbians tit-fuck. To place a dildo in the hot, sweaty crevasse between two huge boobs and then to pump—right there where everyone can see it—only makes explicit our universal, if unconscious, association between cleavage and crotch.

Some informal research has confirmed my suspicions that bra busters are generally more sensitive than blips on the pectoral horizon. The roots of this are probably as much psychological as they are physiological, and I'm sure there are many exceptions. Alas, I am not one. On a good day my teenager melons will fill a mere B-cup, and they are medium sensitive, so I like my lovers to pinch, nibble, and clamp so I can feel what they're doing.

Implements always help sensitize nipples. A trip to your local sex store will reveal a wealth of tit clamps—some of them very elaborate—that have the added advantage of freeing hands for other activities. A trip to your local hardware store can produce electrical clamps, chains, and even string that (with a pair of pliers or a slipknot) can be transformed into a delightful torture device. Some lesbians like to connect to their lovers via tit clamps and chains. Others wrap the chains or cords around their bodies so that any movement will cause a painful little tug.

Tit torture does, however, require some safety precautions. Because it stops the flow of blood, the longer a tit clamp remains attached, the more painful it will be to remove. Removing a tit clamp should produce a slightly intensified version of the tingling you feel when a sleeping limb "wakes up." But not more. If a bound nipple turns blue, you've left that device on too long. Warn your partner (or yourself, depending) and support her when you slip it off.

Pain, of course, isn't everyone's cup of tea. Especially if you're working with sensitive breasts, smearing food on them, brushing them with fur, or just rubbing clothes against them can be plenty pleasurable. But when it comes to my Iron Lady equipment, well, if I have to tell a lover more than twice that she needs to bite my nipples, it's out the door with her.

If you're lucky enough to be sleeping with a woman who's lactating, you should know that some studies say that breast milk can carry HIV, the virus that causes AIDS. Ask Mama to come on you, not in you. For that matter, if you're really into mother/child fantasies, you can just *imagine* that she's lactating. That's totally safe, and my friend Judith points out that it gives a whole new meaning to the term "baby butch."

Most of all, take care of your titties. The breast cancer epidemic is particularly threatening to lesbians—apparently because we don't nurse babies as often as other women—so don't neglect your exams. And if you are tempted by implants, educate yourself about the side effects, which can be very scary indeed.

Breast worship and nipple play have a long, sometimes glorious, sometimes sordid, history. *On Our Backs*'s well-endowed associate editor tells me that at Mardi Gras in New Orleans there's a century-old tradition of calling out to women, "Show us your tits!" Observers of all genders throw costume jewelry to their favorite exhibitionists ("I got a great string of gold beads!" reports Diane). According to legend, Japanese geisha girls used to attach bells to their nipples so they could make music, literally, during lovemaking. But my favorite episode from hooter history occurred in 1597, when Queen Elizabeth I shocked a French ambassador by wearing a gown that completely exposed her bosom (so much for leading Parisian fashion!). So keep these queens, prostitutes, and party girls in mind the next time you're faced, hopefully up close, with one or more of those lickable, suckable, squeezable buds.

How to Play With Her Tits

by Diana Cage

The prevalence of big-titted bimbos in mainstream porn has led many a lesbian to believe that breast obsession is the sole territory of het men. But I'm here to tell you that's not true. Lesbians like tits too! I'm not ashamed to admit I've got a thing for big boobs. The fact is, boobs are part of the whole womanly package. Big or small or in-between, they're a supercharged erogenous zone (as well as wonderful to gaze upon). Nipples can be extremely sensitive, and in many women there's a direct, almost electrical, connection between the nipples and the clit. I know women who can orgasm from nipple play alone, and if that isn't a reason to explore serious breast play, I can't imagine what is.

Warm Her Up
Want her to shudder at your every touch? Start lightly. Gently stroke the sides of her breasts with your fingertips and palms. Touch her softly, tease her, until she starts to ache for more. Wait until she's actually pressing herself against your hands before you give her the stronger sensation she's craving. For the strokee: Entice her. Find out what she likes to look at. Wear revealing tops. Busty? Push-up bras are good. Corsets are even better. Small breasts look great braless, especially beneath tight, white T-shirts.

Nipples Are for Sucking
Nipples feel fantastic between your lips and under your tongue. Wet her erect nipples with your mouth before blowing cool air on them. Nibble and suck them, but first gauge her pain tolerance. If she says "harder, harder" you can bet you're doing it right. If her breasts are large she might be able to suck her own nipples. Ask her to perform for you. Is she lactating? If you both are fluid-bonded (meaning you both have agreed to only exchange bodily fluids with each other), taste her milk.

Different Strokes
Try out different types of sensation on her until you find something that drives her wild. Rub an erect nipple with ice, then wrap your warm lips around it. Different temperatures will elicit different responses. You can bite them hard or nuzzle them softly.

The Butch Body

Some butches feel ambivalent toward their breasts. Perhaps they never learned to eroticize them or they feel uncomfortable with the idea of tit play because breasts are seen as girly parts. Breasts can be an outward indication of a femininity that butch dykes don't feel inwardly in touch with. If this is the case, remind her that boys have nipples, too. Gay men know all about the pleasures of serious tit play. If she's still reticent, try referring to her breasts as "pecs." Talk dirty and call her a fag. You could open up a whole new erogenous zone for her.

Squeeze her breasts firmly with your hands. Pinch her nipples, gradually increasing the intensity. Try brushing them with different textures. Hard, scratchy things are exquisite torture. Soft, fuzzy things will make her purr. Here, kitty!

Clamp Down
Nipple clamps, clothespins, barrettes, and other pinchy things can be used to keep the nipple stimulation going while your hands and mouth are busy elsewhere. If the clamps have a chain connecting them, pull it while you lick her pussy. Or have her keep it in her mouth like a bridle while you fuck her. Keep in mind that clamps restrict blood flow to the tissue. Once the initial shock of pain subsides, she'll feel a dull ache—but the pain comes back when you remove the clamps and blood flows rapidly back into the area. Don't leave them on for too long. You can damage tissue. Twenty to 30 minutes maximum is a good rule to go by.

Piercings Are Fun
Piercings are more than just decoration. Many people find that nipple piercings make their nips more sensitive. Try tugging the rings or barbells with your teeth or rolling them around in your mouth. Always make sure a piercing is completely healed before you play with it.

Titty-Fucking
Seeing your cock buried between a woman's soft breasts is a visual thrill that can't be beat. Lube up your dildo and her chest with something nonsticky. Hand lotion or silicone lube works well. (Water-based lube will dry too quickly.) Have her kneel in front of you and push her breasts together. Then slide your cock between them, back and forth. Build up a good rhythm—really let yourself go. For the fuckee: That big rod sliding back and forth between your boobs feels pretty good, doesn't it? I bet you've never felt so objectified before. Isn't it hot?

Worship Her Feet

Rachel Venning

All day long we tromp and stomp doing errands, getting to and from work, maybe even jogging or hiking. Poor little tootsies. With every step they collide with the ground with a force greater than the weight of the body above them. How faithfully they serve us, and how little love they receive in return. While a few devotees are so enamored of feet that they become fetishists who require a foot or a shoe to have sexual satisfaction, most of us are more traditional tits-and-ass girls. You may not need 6-inch stilettos to get you aroused, but cultivating an appreciation of toes and feet will make you a preferred lover.

Pamper Her Feet

A pedicure makes feet feel so much better. If you're more of a stomp-around-in-steel-toes type, trimmed toenails and well-cared-for cuticles will make your feet happy and your lovers more likely to ogle your arches. For those of you just getting started, set yourself up with one of those kits available at any drugstore—it has clippers, a nail file, cuticle pushers, and fun foam toe separators. Soak the feet first to soften them up.

Paint Her Nails

If you're a femme (or a nail polish fan), the best person to maintain your feet is your lover. If she doesn't suggest it herself, show her your new nail polish and ask her to do it for you. There is no end of fun painting possibilities.

Rub Them the Right Way

When her dogs are barking, a foot massage will help release the tensions of the day, bring a smile to her face, and perhaps soften her up for further adventures. Having your shoes and socks lovingly removed, the little lint balls whisked away from in between your toes, and the tired foot muscles tenderly rubbed is an ideal way to transition from the hectic demands of being out in the world to the intimacies of time with your sweetie. Spoil her feet with a peppermint foot balm. Reflexology, shiatsu, and other massage traditions use special points in the feet that are especially good for

37

Fancy Footwear

Whether it's stilettos, thigh-high latex, or a well-loved pair of work boots, shoes can add a lot to a foot encounter. If you want your feet to be worshiped, dress them like goddesses. At one sexy extreme are see-through plastic pumps, but your daily footwear can be plenty hot. In the dog days of summer, think toe cleavage. Any sandals in which your toes are squeezed gently together and exposed are sure to entice admirers. For a more authoritarian look, go with boots—the shinier, the better. Whether or not you have a date to appreciate your efforts, sexy shoes are a self-care ritual that will have you walking taller and feeling good.

releasing energy. For starters, try the side of the big toe and the sensuous valley between the toes and the ball of the feet.

Use Your Tongue
Let your tongue do the walking. Take that traditional foot massage and sex it up. Use that soft mouth to stimulate the tender spots. Pay attention to how she's responding, and if she gets the giggles push harder with your tongue, or back off for a moment till the tickles subside. Licking, kissing, burying your face in her feet will all feel wonderful. Take as much of her foot in your mouth as you can, and suck with abandon. It's hard to deep-throat a foot, but it's fun to try.

Shine Her Shoes
Let her know you've got her feet in mind by buffing her boots or shining her stilettos. Shoe care is a sure flag that you're a foot-worshiping acolyte preparing the temple.

Boot-Licking
If your lover is a top, lick her boots. This will give her (and you) a psychological and sensory thrill. As you devotedly tongue your way along her arch and across her toes, press hard with your tongue so she can feel it through the leather. Give her a show—let her see your tongue slide across her shoes, arch your back so your ass is in the air, and if you're very, very lucky you may get a spanking.

Toe-Fucking
Toes don't always have to be passive recipients of devotion—they can fuck too. Five sexy fat little piggies sliding against your clit can feel divine. And with a nice smooth pedicure, they needn't stop there! Penetrating with toes is sexy and fun. For a power surge, do it to a girl lying naked on the floor. Or try getting off against a bound bottom's willing feet. Explore a variation 69 with toes instead of mouths.

THREE

ORAL FIXATION:
KISSING, LICKING, TALKING

Kiss Like a Pro

by Tracy Bartlett

Kissing is a fundamental erotic art, but it seems to get neglected as such, even though kissing is often where the whole game starts. Like all erotic arts, it is a skill that can be improved upon, and your best teachers are your lovers and friends. Kissing is a entire erotic world unto itself as well as a form of sexual communication. How you kiss telegraphs information about what kind of lover you will be. Being a good kisser will make her want more. Bon appetit!

Let Anticipation Build
Rushing it is the single most common mistake (meaning, erotic-energy reducer) lovers make. Flirt until she's moving closer to you. Stay close until she's aching for you to kiss her (if you're not sure, ask: "I'd very much like to kiss you right now, may I?"). Kiss her softly until you feel the urgency build to kiss deeper. You get the idea.

Make kissing a staple of lovemaking, not just a warm-up act. Kissing is appropriate anytime. After oral sex, it's a fabulous taste treat.

Vary Techniques
Avoid the mindset where you can't "go back" to something you've done earlier. Soft kisses complement deep, hard kisses. A particularly fabulous hand job may inspire you to kiss all her fingers in appreciation. Punctuate mouth kisses with kissing/sucking her neck, inside bend of the elbow, behind the knees, armpit, and so on.

Surprise Her
Keep her on her toes by varying the types of kisses you deliver. For example, most people expect a peck when parting company in public. Every so often, plant a big,

41

wet, sloppy one on her at the bus stop. Likewise, remember to occasionally press her up against the wall, tangle your fist tightly in her hair, growl "You look good enough to eat" in her ear, then kiss her softly and dash off to work.

Remember Make-Out Sessions?
They're still hot! So take your date, friend, or wife to the drive-in and make out through the whole movie. Invite friends over to play spin the bottle. Hey, we're big kids now—we can do whatever we want!

Try Sensory Deprivation
While kissing, try sliding your hands up over her ears so your palms form a seal to block out sound. With eyes closed, this added sensory deprivation serves to heighten the tactile sense and focus her attention so that your mouth becomes her whole world.

Use Mouth Toys
Try kissing and passing various objects between you. Grapes and cherries work particularly well. Ice can certainly add a thrilling sensation while kissing (not to mention the places that might enjoy the caress of an icy tongue). Wine or sparkling water can be passed from one mouth to another, introducing the sensation of "drinking her in." Gravity can help with that last maneuver—position yourself slightly higher and let the wine spill from your mouth into hers.

Talk Sexy
Of course I am not suggesting interspersing kisses with excerpts from a lecture on federally supported municipal bonds. But sweet compliments whispered into her mouth are very likely to be welcome. It's flattering to be observed in detail, so describe to her (in your sexiest voice) the smell of her hair, what you thought when you first saw her that night, how hot you are for her, how you've been watching her for an hour, what you hope to be doing with her later.

Weave Kissing Throughout Sex
Make kissing a staple of lovemaking, not just a warm-up act. Kissing is appropriate anytime. After oral sex, it's a fabulous taste treat. There's a powerful intimacy involved in joining mouths and breath. Try keeping your mouths together and breathing as you get close to orgasm. Don't try to navigate tongues; just let your open mouths touch so that you're hot, panting, and your mutters of "yes...yes..." go right into each other's mouths.

Observe Her

We tend to give what we want to get, so pay attention to her style and technique. Does she push her tongue deep into your throat? Does she nibble your lips? Does she kiss with her lips for a long time before using her tongue? How much pressure does she use pressing her mouth to yours?

Communicate

This is, of course, as with any sexual activity, the most important skill. There's such a huge variety of desires that it is impossible to "just know" everything she likes and doesn't like. There also needs to be room to discover new desires. Try setting aside time for kissing play that isn't in the heat of passion (but could lead to that). Use that time to educate and explore. Kiss for a while, then talk playfully, but in detail, about what you like and what you would change. Take time to tell stories that reveal erotic patterns (e.g., your first lover kissed you in the woods at summer camp, so the smell of pine is a turn-on for you). The more you practice (as with any skill), the more comfortable it will get. The more you get to know each other in this type of setting, the more knowledge you'll have when you're in the sweet thick of it.

DON'TS

•Don't assume she likes what you like. Ask. Experiment.

•Don't ask sweeping questions such as "What do you like?" If talking in detail is difficult for someone (which is true for most of us), this is too overwhelming a question. Instead, ask for responses to specific actions. ("Do you like it when I suck on your lower lip?" "I'll start soft and get harder; tell me when it's too hard." "Do you want me to push my tongue farther into your mouth when you are more turned on?")

•Don't kiss with cold sores. Keep the gift that keeps on giving to yourself, gals. Those unfortunate irritating outbreaks can challenge us to be erotically creative! Good thing we can't get them on our hands, eh?

• Don't rush into using your tongue. Kissing with just lips with a soft open mouth is a delicious sensation and a strong anticipation builder. Be a tease.

43

How to Express Yourself Sexually

by Rachel Venning

Expressing yourself sexually is the key to mindblowing orgasms, incredibly hot sex, and a deep soul connection with your partner. We've each got a deep well of creative erotic energy inside; tapping into that source will enable you to thrive sexually. The circumstances of your life may change, lovers can come and go, you may be single, but if that connection is strong and vital, you'll have erotic joy throughout your life.

Know Thyself

If you don't know what turns your crank, there's no way you'll be able to masturbate yourself into bliss, much less ask your partner for what pleases you or lead her into a shared sexual adventure. If you aspire to be one of those older women who radiate sexual charisma and satisfaction, start practicing now on really tuning into your erotic self.

Dial "O" on the Pink Telephone

Masturbation is much maligned as the last recourse of those who can't get a date, but that Neanderthal view will only leave you dependent on skilled partners for sexual satisfaction. Take your love life into your own hands; masturbation is, as Betty Dodson says, "the love affair with yourself that lasts a lifetime." Make a self-love date and treat yourself as you would a cherished lover—prepare for your jill-off session by pampering yourself and creating a sensuous environment for your date. Give yourself time and space to really explore yourself. Don't rush into getting off the quickest way you can. The more energy you put into getting aroused, the bigger and better your orgasm is going to be.

Cultivate Your Fantasy Life

44

If you don't have a full tank of sexy scenarios bubbling up and ready to rev your engine, it can be helpful to fuel the flames with pornography and erotica. One-handed reading, in the form of skin mags or steamy literature, or sexy videos and DVDs, can help you figure out what makes you hot, if you're in a more exploratory phase, or provide ideas for scenarios if you're thinking about getting into role-playing with your lover.

Smut Mouth

Use dirty talk to communicate with your lover: "Stuff it in harder, you nasty pig!" sounds better than "Um, would you mind just pushing a little more?" Explicit language and four-letter words can also be turn-ons in and of themselves. It's important to be able to talk about your genitals. "Cunt" and "pussy" are two words that'll get you far in life. If you don't know what to say, try saying out loud what is happening: "I'm fucking you so good, I feel your pussy grabbing onto me, I'm going to give it to you so good…" It doesn't have to be poetry. Everything you do to express yourself—making noise, moving your hips, grinding, clenching, and touching—works to make a deeper erotic connection.

Don't rush into getting off the quickest way you can. The more energy you put into getting aroused, the bigger and better your orgasm is going to be.

Dress to Impress

A hot outfit can help you feel stronger and more centered in your erotic self. What's hot to each person varies. To me, 501s that are about one day away from disintegrating into lint are the sexiest attire around. Others might find PVC hot pants he best way to strut their sexual stuff. Or maybe you cream for scarves and chenille. It's also fun to take on another persona. Instead of dressing up as yourself, pick a sexy character or archetype and dress up as her or him. Ask your lover to play along, and use the costumes to inspire the dialogue: "Those sailor pants make me want to fuck you, cabin boy! Drop trou!"

Keeping the Love Alive

Novelty is one of the big factors that make sex exciting, but how do you keep novelty at the center of your sex life when you're in a monogamous relationship? Trying new things is the only way. That could be new positions, locations, toys, dynamics, exhibitionism, or role-plays. If you create scenes with your sweetie in which you take on other personas, it's almost like you're not monogamous after all. And remember that law of physics, "A body in motion tends to stay in motion." The same thing holds true for eroticism: The more you put do it, the more you'll keep that fire burning.

Go Back to School!

As with almost any skill, to be a maestra of sexual communication, it helps to get some instruction. Check out some of the following resources for adult sex education. The Body Electric School offers weekend-long workshops for women on self-defined eroticism. You'll also learn how to give (and receive) a full-body erotic massage. At women-run sex-toy stores, educational programs (including workshops on talking dirty) are regular evening fare. Independent sex educators such as Annie Sprinkle regularly tour, giving workshops and performances.

Have Great Oral Sex

by JoAnn Loulan

Clean Up

I know it sounds unfeminist and all, but sometimes we need to sweeten ourselves up for someone else's tastes. Lots of women stop going down on their partners because of the simple issue of smell. Want to be right, or get laid?

Touch Her

If she's going first, take mental notes—go down on her like she went down on you. If you're going first, spread her legs and stroke her slowly with whatever you want: your hand, your lips, your hips, silk, velvet, feathers. Get her flesh ready for you. Lick slowly up her thighs until you get close to her vagina. Put your fingers to her lips, and spread them open. I always think women's genitals look like some beautiful, primitive chiton that's soft and furry. And there's nothing like the wonderful slipperiness of a woman's vagina. It's the moment right before your second date and a U-Haul, so make this moment conscious and powerful and fun.

Yep, You'll Need Your Tongue

Work her with your tongue like a beautiful lizard drinking water off a flower. Stroke every inch of her labia, clitoris, and vagina. Put that tongue up in her vagina. Forget the orgasm, forget the kids, forget your chores. Oh, sweet mystery of woman! Nothing is like the intimate act of supplication. Oh, and spend a lot more time licking her cunt than you spend looking for a parking space or waiting for a bus. This is the elixir of the goddesses. Don't miss a drop.

Hit the G Spot

The best way to find her G spot is to look at her clit, put your fingers in her vagina, start stroking once you are at the middle knuckle on your finger, and keep moving up slowly. A lot of women can't feel it, so you need to move slow and soft to get the right sensation for her. Stroke toward your face and the back of her clit.

Check Out the Cool Spray

Because you're grooving on her G, she may spray some of that elixir from her parau-rethral sponge (the technical name for the G spot) out through her urethra. Don't be grossed out—it's not pee. It may smell like pee somewhat, but only because it's coming out of the same tube. Take that spray and rub it all over her, all over your mouth, and lick it up onto her clit.

Pull Out Your Dildo

Make sure it's warm! Keep the stimulation going on her clit—she needs to keep that vagina oiled and ready. See if you can keep your tongue on her clit, and grease up that dildo for her. Now slide it in. Move in and out, back and forth, slowly and then at whatever speed feels good to her. But you knew that.

Ask Her

Some girls like it rammed, some like it s-l-o-w. Raise your tongue for the second it takes to ask " Do you like this? Shall I go faster? Slower? Stop? I want to do just what you want me to do." Of course, she may be the kind of girl who wants you to take advan-tage of her and not ask. You need to find this out now, OK?

Stick Your Finger in Her Ass

Wow, this could be heaven. (Although for some this could be hell—careful.) Go slow, use lots of lubrication, and don't put anything that was in her ass in her cunt. Make sure there's enough room for all you're trying to do. Only stretch if it feels good. And keep the tongue moving, girlfriend.

Pull Out the Plug-In

Vibrator, that is. Move it against her skin—her vagina or ass, her breasts, anywhere you can think of. Don't kill her with overstimulation, though—just do what's good for her and feels fun for you.

DON'TS

48

•Don't forget to use a barrier. If you or your partner has a sexually transmitted disease or infection such as a yeast infection, venereal warts, or herpes, place a dental dam (avail-able at sex-supply stores) or plastic wrap over her vagina. Be careful with the plastic wrap: if the licker has had drugs or alcohol, she could asphyxiate. You may also want to use a barrier if you're unsure of your partner's HIV or AIDS status. No data supports the trans-mission of AIDS from vagina to mouth, but err on the side of caution.

•Don't engage in oral sex when either of you has a cold sore. Cold sores are the same thing as herpes. Lots of people have 'em. Don't stress, just don't go down or let your partner go down on you during an outbreak unless you use a barrier. One herpes sore could spread from lip to lip, vagina to vagina, and one or both of you could end up with vaginal herpes.

•Don't have oral sex after you lubricate. That stuff can taste really crummy.

•Don't lick around the anus before you lick around the vagina. Bacteria that lives around your anus will wreak havoc on a vagina. If you want to rim, cover the anus with a dental dam, then lick away.

•Don't force your partner to have oral sex. If your partner is phobic about oral sex, don't make her go through with it—heck, 30% of lesbians don't like going down. Find something she does like.

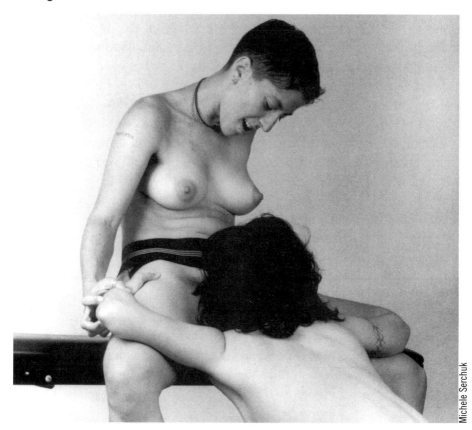

49

Michele Serchuk

Talking Dirty to Your Lover

by Marylayna Dawson

"Say something dirty to me," my lover whispered into the phone. "Get me hot."
Even though I'd had experience as a professional phone-sex operator, I was struck dumb. I didn't want to mouth the same clichés I used on strangers who paid for my words. I felt as awkward as I had when a long-ago lover had made the same request, before I'd acquired expertise in the field. In fact, the pressure was intensified now, because I was supposed to know how to perform. There's a big difference, I learned, between talking dirty in a professional capacity and getting your lover off. After all, as a pro I'm anonymous, but in my role as a lover, the words I whisper will affect, for better or worse, my relationship.

"Please," Cindy pleaded. "I'm so horny and I miss you so much."

We'd only been seeing each other a few months; between our busy lives and the eight miles that separated us, we didn't see each other nearly often enough to stoke our smoldering newborn passion. She needed more. She needed, if not my body, then my words—and after all, most orgasms do take place between the ears.

Besides, I fully understood this particular form of horniness, a hunger for words. As a writer and phone-sex operator, I thrive on language. A lover can fuck me silly for hours, but it's only when she whispers something dirty to me that I sail over the top.

So I decided to get over my feelings of awkwardness, ceremoniously cleared my throat, and cooed, "You're real hot and wet tonight, aren't you, honey?"

"Yes," she whispered.

"Too bad I'm not there to help you out. But I bet you know how to do yourself just fine, don't you? Come on, doll baby, put your fingers in your pussy. Go ahead, stir up those juices."

She moaned.

"Go on, put 'em there. I want you to stick two fingers in and work up to a froth, then rub the juices on your clit. Is your clit hard for me, baby?"

"Yes," she panted.

"Good. You know how I like a nice hard clit. While you're doing that I want you to imagine me in front of you—standing over you—my cunt in front of your face. Do you want it, baby? Huh? Wanna lick my pussy?"

Her moans increased in intensity.

50

Hallelujah, it was working! The techniques I used with my customers—and those that they sometimes used with me—were proving just as effective with my beloved. Heady with power, I proceeded, describing scenes from our short but rich past, as well as a few choice fantasies I'd been harboring. Not only did Cindy come—so did I! After that, we continued to talk dirty to each other, an aspect of our sex lives that is not only satisfying in and of itself but also feeds our fleshy encounters, since we've learned through our phone conversations the best ways to get each other off.

Phone sex between lovers can be another variation in a rich sex life, or it can be a vital necessity when circumstances force lovers geographically apart. Most people are understandably phone-sex-shy, for many reasons. Some people don't like the phone in the first place, perceiving it as a barrier rather than a connecting agent between two people. Others are uncomfortable uttering sexual words and their fantasies and desires. Still others can engage in nonsexual phone conversations for hours and scream wild obscenities in bed, but can't seem to combine the two models of communication.

And that's all we're really talking about here: communication. The telephone is an instrument of communication, like the pen, the body, or the computer. The voice is also an instrument of communication. And I'm quite sure that I don't have to remind *On Our Backs* readers how important communication is in a sexual relationship.

So, assuming I've convinced you and you've gotten through your inhibitions, at least in your mind, here are Marlayna's tips for quality phone sex:

Know Your Audience

You have a distinct advantage over the phone-sex operator, who has to intuit her customer's sexual tastes from very little information within minutes. You know what your lover likes. Does she melt whenever you suck her tits? Then talk about doing it! Does she like it when you're dominant? Then dominate her! Slaps? Clap your hands once or twice—I guarantee she'll cream. (By the way, while the sound of a smack comes through the wires quite nicely, the same does not hold true for sucking or licking noises—these tend to sound sloppy, if not fake. On the other hand, holding the mouthpiece of the phone next to your wet pussy while you finger it can be quite effective.)

Get Her to Do Herself

51

I don't care how silver your tongue is, if she doesn't touch herself she's not gonna come. She might get wet, but without self-stimulation she won't get off. Whether or not she's inhibited about masturbating, alone or with you, the best way to accomplish this is to tell her what to do.

You know when you're about to go over the top and your lover says something like "Yeah, baby, grind it" or "Come on, do it for me" in a commanding tone? That's exactly how to talk dirty on the phone. "Go on, girl, rub that clit. I know how you like it. Suck that dildo up into your sweet pussy. Think about me on the other end of it, fuckin' you good." This dovetails right into my next tip, which is…

Create Strong Visual Images
Whether your lover likes elaborate psychodrama or straight-on sensuality, you should verbally paint a picture to accompany her masturbation. Your storytelling in this situation serves the same purpose as *On Our Backs* or *Bathroom Sluts.* You're a pornographer, baby—an artist, writer, director, psychiatrist, actress, and whore all wrapped up in one sexy voice. So do it! If you two are dominant/submissive, with you as the top, tell the bitch to shut up and open her mouth for your dick. Bring in a third (or fourth or fifth) woman and force your lover to service cunt. If you're usually submissive, tell her all the things you'll do for her, then beg and plead for her to come in your mouth. If you've never explored this aspect of sexuality, the phone might be a less threatening milieu in which to do so.

Or maybe your girl has elaborate fantasies, like being kept in a harem with hundreds of women. Tell her the story, paying close attention to detail: clothing, behavior, activities. As with all good porn, the plot should titillate by slowly building to a rich and raunchy full-blown climax—and I do mean climax.

Another possibility is to use a past scene from your relationship that got her off. Maybe she watched your reflection in the mirror while you sat in front of her, teasing her clit with your strap-on. Or maybe she sat on top of you while you tickled her nipples. Whatever got her off then will probably do the trick again—all you have to do is re-create the scene with well-chosen words.

Talk DIRTY
While creating a vivid image is of paramount importance, almost as important is your choice of language—the dirtier the better. Forget *vagina, breast,* and *dildo*; it's *cunt* (or *pussy*), *tit,* and *dick* (or *cock*). It's *fuck* and *suck* and *bite* and *rub*. It's *Eat me baby grind your pussy bite my tit lick my ass squeeze those tits and get down dirty you fucking slut!*

52

Repeat
After you've been talking dirty for a while, you'll know which stories and/or images work best. Don't be afraid to repeat them. I know it's hard to get past the feeling that you're being unoriginal and boring, but the truth is that sexual fantasies are to adults

what fairy tales are to children; we're comforted and reassured by the repetition, and it gives us a secure framework in which we can let loose and come. (This lesson was brought home to me by one of my customers, who loved to hear me talk about my lingerie, particularly panties. When I inadvertently called them underwear she said petulantly, "You have to say panties!")

Listen for Cues and Respond to Them
If she moans and breathes heavier, follow the line that produced the response. She might not talk much, but will occasionally toss out a word or phrase that tells you where she wants to go. You may have been about to put her in a hot tub when she mentions the shower—so switch your locale. In other words, be flexible.

She Comes First
If you're the one talking dirty to get her off, then that's your purpose. You're gonna get hot, no doubt about it, but it would be selfish and cruel of you to subordinate her needs to yours. By all means, play with yourself as you talk dirty, using hand or vibrator or dildo—your mounting excitement will be transmitted through the wires. But wait for her to come first, then ask for whatever you need to finish off. If you can manage a simultaneous orgasm, you have my undying admiration—I've yet to achieve synchronicity on the phone (and only rarely in the flesh).

Integrate Talking Dirty Into Your Relationship
This is the big bonus. Exploring fantasies on the phone will ultimately enhance what you do in person. You'll loosen up, and you'll become more apt to find yourself talking dirty during sex. You might even break through barriers because you've approached previously forbidden or sensitive areas behind partial anonymity—after all, she never saw you blush when you confessed a desire to try nipple clamps.

Practice Your Lessons
Lie down in bed. Hold your vibrator to your clit. Pick up the phone. Dial her number. And let it rip. Ah, I can just hear those hot wires sizzling all across America—music to Marlayna's horny ears.

Perfect Your Pussy-Licking

by Rachel Venning

Cunnilingus is the Holy Grail of lesbian sex. Given that, it's no surprise that some of the performance anxiety that straights experience around intercourse we dykes might also suffer when it's time to put our mouths to the test. Cultural myths about nasty vaginas just add to the pressure. Pussy-munching is best when both people are into it. Doing it should feel really good and exciting to the giver. As good as it is for her cunt, it hopefully will also be for your mouth. Whether you're a natural muff-diver who started eating out your best friend in ninth grade, before you even knew what a lesbian was, or a late-blooming lady coming out in her 50s, here are a few tips to try on your next labial loll.

Mix It Up
If all you do is lick up and down, up and down (a.k.a. "fence-painting"), chances are your partner will get bored after a while. Try some variations in movement and pressure—use your lips, breath, and teeth in addition to your tongue. Change positions. Use your hands. Get your whole creative body involved.

If It Ain't Broke, Don't Fix It
Most women orgasm in response to rhythmic stimulation, so if you're in a groove that's building her up, don't suddenly change what you're doing. Finding the balance between variety and consistency is the key to being an oral expert.

Lick Her Like an Ice Cream Cone
54

Big soft licks from stem to stern with a full wide flat tongue stimulate all the nerves in her genital area. Go deliciously slow to make her feel like a yummy dessert being savored, or speed it up a bit and focus more on the clitoral area to push her toward orgasm.

How Do You Know if She Likes It?

With your face buried in her cunt and your ears straddled by her creamy thighs, it can be hard to talk about how things are going. So look for more subtle signs of her enjoyment. If she raises her hips to meet your mouth, that's a very good sign. A lubricating vagina and swelling vulva and labia that spread open as they become engorged are also a sure sign that she's responding favorably. So is a growing clitoris. An all-over skin flush, rapid breathing, and writhing are also clues. Clutching the sheets is excellent, and so are hands on the back of your head pushing you in for more!

Circles and Eights

While direct clit-licking can be too intense a touch for many, the swirl of a tongue ooping around the top, along the sides, and under the clit can be exquisite. Dress it up with another loop around the vagina.

Scratch Your Nose

While licking her clit, insert two fingers into her vagina. Curl those fingers up toward your tongue, capturing her clit and G spot between your mouth and fingers. As your tongue licks up, pull down with your fingers; get a rhythm going. Or try licking her G spot. Shove your tongue in there as far as it'll go. Some women can stick their G spots out or almost out if they bear down.

Dive In

It's good to build up the intensity level of sensation gradually, but once you're into it, use your whole face. Bury yourself in her pussy, get your tongue in as far as it will go, use your nose for more pressure. Not only does this feel good physically, but it also lets her know you're really into it and that her cunt is not gross or dirty to you. Hint: If your eyelids aren't sticky, you're not doing it right.

Straddle Your Lover's Face

If lying back to be licked is too passive for you, hop on top. From up there you can control the pressure and area of contact. To make this position even more fun, tie your lover down to the bed before you mount her, and couple your mustache ride with firm directives: "Stick your tongue out!" "Open your mouth!" "Suck it, bitch (or boy)!" And so on. Bottomy munchers will, well, lick it up.

Suck Her Into Your Mouth

Gentle suction is a nice variation on the licks and downward pressure of most oral-sex acts. Try sucking harder and see if she likes that. While you've got a nice piece of clit and cunt sucked in your mouth, lick it while maintaining the suction.

Lick Her Asshole

Use a barrier for hygiene, or if she's very clean and you don't penetrate, you may choose bare tongue on skin. The asshole area is rich in nerve endings, so all the varieties of oral stimulation—licking, sucking, nibbling—can feel wonderful.

Plug Her Holes

While going down on your lover, stick one (or more) fingers into her vagina and asshole simultaneously. This complete stimulation of her genital region may be accomplished most easily if the receiver's cunt is at the edge of the bed and the doer is kneeling on the floor.

56

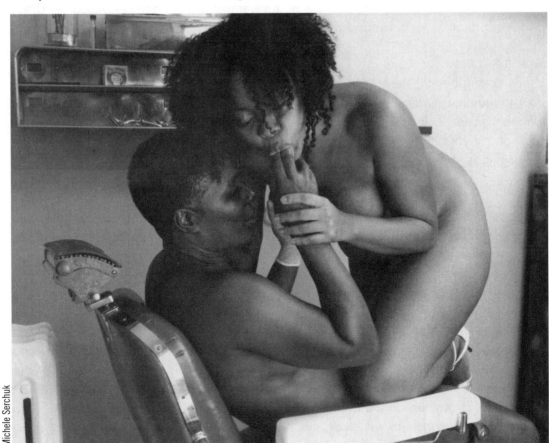

FOUR

PUSSY PLAY:
MAKE IT PURR

How to Shave for Sex

by Diana Cage

Nothing says ready-for-sex like a bare vulva. Picture a woman's shaved, glistening wet cunt—the lips are bare and parted, her swollen clit exposed. Hot, isn't it? Of course it is. And that's exactly why you would want to get rid of all that stubborn pubic hair, so you can see it. Shaving your pubic area allows a higher tongue-to-skin ratio, and nothing feels softer and more velvety to your fingertips than a newly shorn pussy. As an added bonus, you'll get to see more of the action while fucking because it won't be hidden behind a lot of curly dark hair. Removing the hair from your vulva is like undressing it. Take your kitty (or your lover's) from schoolgirl to call girl in a few easy steps.

Gather Your Tools

You'll need a razor, hair conditioner, shaving cream, and a hand mirror. I personally swear by Gillette's Mach 3 razor for this particular purpose and won't go near my crotch with anything else. Many women I know, however, tell me that disposable razors also work very well and actually help to prevent ingrown hairs from occurring because they don't cut the hair as close to the skin as a triple-blade razor. Ultimately, go with what feels right to you. Whatever kind of razor you choose, though, use a brand-new blade each time you shave to avoid irritation.

Trim

If your pubes are long you'll need to trim the hair down to a manageable length before you shave it off. Beard clippers work well for this, but small scissors are easier to maneuver. Trim as close to the skin as you can safely manage. Be careful down there—and go slowly! I know someone who has a notched labia from being a little clumsy with the scissors.

Take a Bath

A nice hot bath will prep you for a comfortable shaving experience. You want the hair to be as soft as possible before you try to remove it. This is an important step. Women who've shaved once without heeding this advice remain forever convinced that there's no way to go bare without a lot of itching and irritation. But they are wrong. And they're forever doomed to miss out on the pleasure of naked pussy lips against a nice wet tongue. Make it erotic. If you'll be shaving your lover, join her in the bath. Wash her cunt gently and apply conditioner to her pubic hair. Let it soak in while you gently wash and fondle the rest of her. Get her in the mood. If this is your bush's first introduction to a razor, soak in the bath for at least 20 minutes.

Wash and Go
So, you've soaked for a sufficient amount of time. You've applied conditioner to your pubes and let it sit for a minute or two. You're rinsed and ready to go. Now comes the tricky part. Prop your butt on the edge of the tub and grab your razor. Lather up with shaving cream or gel and decide what you'll be taking off and what you'll be leaving behind. A fully bare mons might look too prepubescent for you. You have the option of shaving the lips and leaving a bit of a beard on top. Perhaps you want a landing strip, or maybe you want the whole thing naked. Make up your mind about where to begin and make a few strokes in the direction of the hair growth. Rinse the razor in warm water after each swipe. The idea is to do this in as few strokes as possible to help avoid irritation. Try not to go over the same area repeatedly.

The Nitty Gritty
Your cunt has a lot of nooks and crannies and crevices that can be difficult to reach. To smoothly shave the inner bits of your outer labia, stretch them taut with your hand. For your perineum (the space between your vagina and anus) you'll want to squat in the tub and check out the area with a hand mirror. Make sure to carefully shave around your asshole for a totally smooth experience.

The Grand Finale
When you've finished, rinse off the shaving cream and pat dry with a towel. Apply a lotion to soothe the skin, but be careful of those with scents or other additives that may irritate your skin. Baby oil can also be used, but avoid baby powder, which 60 may irritate the vulva and vagina. You might want to opt for a product called Bikini Zone, which also helps relieve irritation caused by shaving. Some women suggest using a loofah sponge on the days you don't shave, when you take bath or shower. Gently rub the loofah with and against the hair growth to remove dead skin and keep the hair follicles open, reducing the likelihood of ingrown hairs.

Dare to Be Bare

Find something suitably crotchless or see-through to show off your new do. Or simply flaunt it naked for your lover. Make sure to enjoy all the new sensations you'll experience. Notice how soft and smooth your skin is. Notice how nice lube feels against your naked skin. Your lover's tongue now has a whole new terrain to cover.

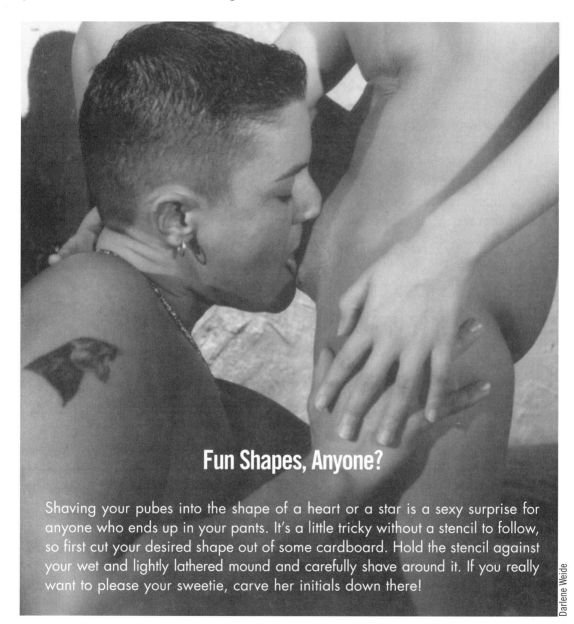

Fun Shapes, Anyone?

Shaving your pubes into the shape of a heart or a star is a sexy surprise for anyone who ends up in your pants. It's a little tricky without a stencil to follow, so first cut your desired shape out of some cardboard. Hold the stencil against your wet and lightly lathered mound and carefully shave around it. If you really want to please your sweetie, carve her initials down there!

Darlene Weide

61

Annie Sprinkle's Models of Orgasm

by Dr. Annie Sprinkle

Freud defined just two models of female orgasm: vaginal and clitoral. To me, that's like saying the world is flat! So I developed my own Models of Orgasm. I am a board-certified sexologist with a doctorate in human sexuality. But more important, my body, heart, and soul have been a laboratory for research on the female orgasm. Throughout my life I have personally experienced as many kinds of orgasms as I possibly can. I continue to discuss and explore this exciting topic with my friends, lovers, and other experts.

I am aware that my Models of Orgasm may be controversial. Some researchers believe clitoral orgasms are the real, true, and best orgasms, and to describe other types of orgasms gives women an excuse not to have clitoral orgasms or to consider

Energy (or "breath") orgasms can be created from rhythmic, deep breathing, or by generating energy in the body through intense physical activities.

them less important. Orgasm activists want to set the record straight after Freud misled us to believe that vaginal orgasms were real and clitoral orgasms were immature. Some are concerned that women will feel sexually inadequate if they aren't having many types of orgasms.

I want to make clear that one type of orgasm is not better than another. They are all simply different. We are all at the right place at the right time in our own sexual evolution, and whatever kind of orgasms a woman is having, or not having, is just perfect.

Dreamgasms: Alfred Kinsey found that by the age of 45, 37% of American females had dreams that led to nocturnal orgasm, what I call "dreamgasms." Sometimes we simply wake up and are in the midst of having this special kind of orgasm without any genital stimulation. Sometimes we dream that we are having an orgasm, and we do have one physically and the orgasm wakes us up. Based on my observations, dreamgasms may occur with strong vaginal and anal contractions, and sometimes not.

Microgasms: These are small, extremely subtle orgasms that can occur without physical stimulation. Similar to the idea that enlightenment is within us, orgasm is also within us. If we focus our minds on our erotic body and visualize orgasmic flow inside us, we can feel the tension and release of orgasm on a very subtle level. Ray Stubbs, author of *Sacred Orgasms*, calls these orgasms "spirit-body orgasms" and points out that they "could be easily missed if we are not looking for them." Sex researchers Beverly Whipple, Ph.D., and Gina Ogden, Ph.D., found during laboratory experiments that women could "think off" or have orgasms without genital stimulation. I know a number of people who can do this. This kind of orgasm can easily be taught. It's a great party trick!

Intervaginal Orgasms: In this category I lump together what are commonly called vaginal orgasms, G spot orgasms, and cervical orgasms—all types of orgasms that happen inside the vagina with internal stimulation by fingers, fists, dildos, penises, etc. I believe that many women are having intervaginal orgasms all the time, but don't acknowledge them as such. Women are looking for them to feel like clitoral orgasms, and they don't. If you think you're having vaginal orgasms, then you most probably are!

Energy Orgasms: Energy (or "breath") orgasms can be created from rhythmic, deep breathing, or by generating energy in the body through intense physical activities such as swimming, running, risk-taking, or listening to a piece of music. Physiologically, breath and energy orgasms share similar traits with clitoral and vaginal orgasms—e.g., elevated breathing and heart rates, sweating, and flushing. In the tantric version, "the Wave," one undulates erotically, thus "activating the cerebral spinal fluid and orgasmic reflex." In the Native American "Firebreath Orgasm," one lies down and breathes up through the chakras. Barbara Carrellas and Kate Bornstein teach a version which they call "Gender-Free Orgasm." Sunyata Saraswati, author of *Jewel in the Lotus: The Tantric Path to Higher Consciousness*, teaches a version called the "Cobra Breath Orgasm."

Some yogic practitioners are able to generate what is perhaps the most intense kind of energy orgasm, the kundalini orgasm. Experts warn of the dangers of these

63

extremely strong orgasms. A friend of mine had one, flew off his chair, fell, and became paralyzed. A woman I know had a nervous breakdown that lasted more than a year. A kundalini orgasm can also be extremely healing, transformative, and enlightening.

Clitoral Orgasms: Perhaps the only thing we can all agree upon is that women have clitoral orgasms. The clitoris is stimulated, muscular tension builds, and vaginal contractions precede a release of the energy. These orgasms can be localized solely in the clitoris, or the feelings can spread up into the belly and groin and over the whole body. Clitoral orgasms can be extended into what is commonly called a multiple orgasm. Masters and Johnson found what they coined "status orgasmus," which is an orgasmic state that lasted "20 to more than 60 seconds." I've known women that could have multiple clitoral orgasms lasting several minutes.

Combination-gasms: Sometimes two or more types of orgasm alternate or occur in tandem. During a single sex session, a girl might experience all seven different kinds of orgasm, if she is very lucky.

Megagasms: These are the tsunamis of all orgasms! A megagasm is an intense, full-body experience, a deeply emotional experience, and for some, a deeply spiritual experience. A megagasm may last anywhere from 30 seconds up to, in some cases, an hour or more. In my instructional erotic video *Sluts and Goddesses,* I have a five-minute megagasm, with assistance from my two skilled dyke-orgasm midwives.
Megagasms are usually brought on by very intense physical stimulation such as very hard fucking combined with a really strong vibrator. Uncomfortable feelings or pain may also trigger them. There is often a huge release of emotions. It helps to have a partner—or two or three—who can handle the incredible intensity of such orgasms. Megagasms can come with past life recalls, or intense psychedelic-like imagery. They are primal. They are magical. They can create the sensation of being breathed-through by the universe, as if one is a channel for orgasmic energy and the force of life. Often when a person is in the presence of someone having a megagasm they will have empathetic orgasms, or what I call "contact orgasms."

65

Give an Awesome Hand Job

by Ana Lingus

The hand job may be the most maligned of all lesbian sex acts. Most of the sexually unsophisticated think of the hand job as an immature and cheap replacement for intercourse. Finger-fucking doesn't even rank as high on the sexual totem pole as a blow job. Why? Because the main perpetrator in the hand job is, of course, a hand—and not a penis. Even though the hand job is not just for dykes, like all lesbian sex in the eyes of the mainstream, the hand job has the misfortune of being considered "not the real thing."

Lesbians, as is evidenced throughout history from 16th-century gynecological tracts to Freud, have been notoriously handy with their goddess-given equipment—so much so that the hand has been nominated by some queer theorists as the "lesbian phallus," the primary lesbian sex organ, and *the* symbol of dyke desire.

Let us not forget that a well-delivered diddling can provide a mind-blowing orgasm just as well as anything else. One can actually practice and perfect techniques toward becoming an expert in the area of hand jobs. Here are some, er, pointers:

• *Find out about her solo sex practices.* How often does she masturbate? Does she like her digits to do the work or does she prefer a vibrator? If she's a frequent hands-on wanker when she's alone, chances are very good she'd like you to do the same when you're together.

• *Ask her to jill off for you.* You can learn a lot by watching her technique of getting herself off. Does she rub on top of the clitoral hood, to the side of it, or does she pull back the hood and rub directly on her clit? Does she stick her fingers in her pussy or up her ass while she's working her clit? Does she supplement with a dildo? If nothing else, you'll get a steamy show. Repeat as necessary.

• *Don't forget about her breasts—and yours.* Take time out to pinch and stroke her titties, or have nipple clamps do the work for you. If she's a breast woman, you can dangle yours in front of her while you do her, but you have your work cut out for you.

66

Hoist yourself up enough in bed to press your boobs into her face. Whisper dirty things like "Suck my tits, you animal!"

• *Be persistent. Don't despair if she takes a while.* Conserve hand muscles by alternating soft touches with hard ones. You'll avoid carpal tunnel syndrome and she'll appreciate the care and effort.

• *Rescue the art of copping a feel from the realm of "McSex."* Even if you'd rather be fucking but left your harness at home, perform due diligence with your digits. So you're skilled enough to make her come in 30 seconds—draw it out, tease her. Even if she's easy, take your time. Grope under her clothes. Unzip with your teeth. Stroke her naked thighs. Then slip your fingers in her hole. Take your time—unless the police are tapping on the car window.

• *Use lube. Don't give her a "dry fumbler."* Unless your partner gets superwet, using lube is a sure bet for everyone. Lube will transform you in her eyes from an insensitive jerk into a good jerk-off. Squeeze it into your hand and rub it around to warm it up; never apply lube directly to her pussy.

• *Make finger-play part of foreplay or the whole enchilada.* Don't assume she wants it and only it. Like intercourse, hand jobs don't do the job for all women. Or she may prefer it only as an appetizer, with licking as the final course.

• *Use mechanical assistance.* Especially if she uses a vibrator when you're not around (and especially if she's a really stubborn orgasmer) involve her favorite toy. Even if you massage for 20 minutes and Hitachi gets her off in two, it was still your hand job that did it. Tell her I said so.

• *If she likes penetration, put on a rubber glove, lube it up, and massage her butthole with your finger.* Stick it in. Use your other hand or your thumb to massage her clit. After she comes, press down firmly on her clit. Don't jiggle. You can extend her orgasm this way. If she's a multiple orgasmer, don't let her slip off the plateau: Let her rest for a few seconds, but keep her hard with persistent stroking.

• *Double the fun.* Exploit the practical advantages of the two-person whack-off. No bed needed, no undressing even.

The Ins and Outs of Fisting

by Carol Queen

I used to think of fisting as something gay men did, the word conjuring up images of leather daddies and steamy bathhouses. Don't get me wrong—I liked thinking of these things. Speculating about what my gay male friends did made for good masturbation fantasies—but it didn't seem very relevant to what my girlfriend and I did when we had sex.

It was the politically correct 1970s, and already I was in trouble with the lezzie thought police. Fantasizing about leathermen was only the tip of the iceberg. In real life I actually liked fucking—you know, penetration. I tried to give it up, but sex just wasn't as hot for me without the feeling of being slid into (or sliding into someone else). If I was-

Watching your wrist emerge from the body of your lover is a profound experience. Feeling it encircled by her very hot cunt is even more so.

n't being fingered while I was being licked, it took me a lot longer to come. My girlfriend was almost as bad as I was. We figured we might not get to lesbian heaven, but we'd have great sex on our way to hell. At least we didn't use dildos!

So it's somewhat surprising that my lover and I didn't spontaneously discover fisting, as delightfully preoccupied as we were with creative sexual heresy. We certainly discovered that two fingers were (for us) better than one; in fact, I could often be heard begging for a fourth. (She had slender fingers!) What's a girl to do when she gets all hot and crazy and her vagina's ballooning out because she's in high plateau?

Well, I know the answer to that now. That's a very good time to slip in the thumb.

Explain the pleasures of being fisted? Simple, my dear. There are times when four fingers just are not enough. Times when your cunt wants to be FULL, not just full. When your body begs for something more intense than the slippery in-and-out of a finger-fuck. There are times, for some of us, when only a hand will do.

69

For the fister the pleasures are more ineffable but no less intense. Watching your wrist emerge from the body of your lover is a profound experience. Feeling it encircled by her very hot cunt is even more so. Some women are turned on to fisting with dominant-submissive overtones, but others do it simply for the sensation—and the incredible intimacy and interconnectedness it provides.

So, want to get started? Here are some guidelines to ensure that your forays into fisting are hot and safe.

• Fister: Trim and file your nails smooth, please! And take off those rings. If you have any pointy hangnails, nip 'em off. Next, get out the latex gloves and water-based lubricant. Even if you don't ordinarily use latex and lube with finger penetration, use it now. This is not about who's at risk for what (well, it's about that too) but facilitating safety and comfort. Slippery latex and lube do just that.

• Fistee: Do you want it, darling? It's your responsibility to communicate your readiness—to start, to go on—to your partner. This is not a process that one person does to another; it's something two people do together. The woman who's being penetrated gets to decide how fast, how far, how much, and she tells her partner these things.

• Start doing whatever you usually do to create optimum turn-on. Make hot love, girls. Don't try this trick on a dry, sleepy pussy. Wake her up! Make her want it! And please, allow sufficient time. Slipping your hand into her 20 minutes before her parents arrive to take you out to dinner is a nice fantasy (downright nasty, in fact), but it's probably a bad idea. Being goal-oriented, either in terms of time or what you can "take," creates tension, and fisting logistics require an environment that fosters relaxation (at least until you both get good at it). Not every woman can accommodate a hand, and a woman who can accommodate one woman's hand might not be able to take another's. Some women will require many sessions before they feel relaxed enough and ready for more than four fingers. What to say about this state of affairs? Have a wonderful time trying! And never give yourself (or your partner) grief about the results. Fisting is not a performance, it's a process. If your forays into fisting don't feel like lovemaking, for Sappho's sake switch to something that does. You're not training for the Olympics.

70

• Now then, fistee, do you need to pee? Go do it. Fister, if she's taking four fingers deeply and wants more, coat your hand with lube—back as well as palm—then point fingers and thumb together (think of the shape you'd make to project a shadow puppet that looks like a goose). Introduce them into your partner's cunt, letting her guide the speed of entry. Some women prefer no movement at this point, but if the fistee likes it, you can rotate a little to further massage her cunt into relaxation. When you're up to the knuckles you might try separating the fingers a bit, stretching her cunt muscles even more. If this doesn't feel comfortable to her, stop. Some rotation is often necessary to get the knuckles past the ring of muscles that surround the vaginal opening. This is the time of most potential discomfort, so take it easy. The fistee can use deep breathing or other relaxation techniques if it hurts. Sharp pain is a signal to stop pushing and proceed more slowly (or wait for another day). Experienced fisters suggest keeping the back of the hand pointed toward the anus—the tissue of the perineum is stretchier than that at the top of the cunt, which is nestled into the pubic bone and doesn't give, and the feeling of knuckles against the pubic bone can be painful. So stretch assward instead of clitward. When she's sufficiently relaxed, your hand will likely slide right in, the fingers naturally curling into a fist.

• Now you can both enjoy the amazing sights and sensations. Lay your hands on her stomach, and feel the fist inside. (The bigger the hand, the more astonishing that sensation is.) If the fistee wants, stop right there. She may, however, want a little more action. Some women love the feeling of the fister's hand rotating inside them; some hate it. Knuckles can feel painful up against the sensitive urethral tissue, so keep communication going. Some women like as much fucking motion as the tight space allows, but again, stay in close communication to be sure you're not inflicting pain on the cervix. You may not be able to do the old in-and-out as intensely as you might with a dildo—knuckles are much harder than most dildos. Some women want very little movement on the inside, but lots of attention to the clit and other erogenous places. If the fistee orgasms, her cunt muscles will contract; the fit will get momentarily tighter, and, depending on the strength of her muscles, this can be alarming the first time you feel it. Rest assured—you're not likely to end up with broken finger bones.

• It seems hard to believe, but at some point you'll probably want to take your hand out of its new home. Do this *slowly*. Very. For one thing, coming out can feel very sexy. For another, it's a locus of possible discomfort; going slow minimizes it. This is again a time when a little rotation might be a good idea. When the fister begins to pull out she should straighten her fingers when she can. Notice the incredible texture and sensitivity of he fully opened cunt. Taking the fist out may not signal the end of your play!

• Factor in some coming-down time to hold and talk to each other. The fistee will probably not be striding boldly around the room right away; curl up together and come back to earth. One last hint: Kegel exercises, so good for increasing orgasmic potential and intensity, will also limber up an out-of-shape cunt. The greater the muscle tone the greater those muscles' elasticity. (Do the exercise by pretending to stop a stream of urine; the muscle that does that is the pubococcygeus. Contract and relax over and over. Do reps! Go, girl!)

My slim-fingered girlfriend is gone, and my current lover has big hands, so big that at first I worried we'd never get one into my limber and greedy—but nonetheless tight—pussy. Several marathons later, though, my cunt finally stretched the millimeters it took to engulf that large hand, and I felt the most intense sense of fullness I've ever experienced. I find that when my partner is fisting me I love to play with my clit and keep myself on the edge of my orgasm; unless I'm especially relaxed, the intense contractions of my come are too much when my cunt is so full. But when the hand comes out, I come like crazy—hear me howl! With smaller-handed partners I like getting (carefully) fist-fucked and coming, squeezing down on their wrists. As a fister, feeling those contractions in my partner is my favorite moment—that and when my hand first slips inside. It's a really incomparable sensation.

My most unusual fisting experience came at my birthday party two years ago. (I have birthday parties that could get me thrown into jail in many states of the union.) One of my lovers brought a new girlfriend along, an audacious redhead who proceeded, shortly after we were introduced, to determinedly work her little hand into my pussy. ("Uh...what did you say your name was?") Fortunately my lover was there to talk me through the relaxation that I had completely forgotten I ought to be doing, and we all lived happily ever after. I don't recommend that sort of behavior on first dates, but it certainly did endear the wild child in me.

I'm decidedly glad that penetration has been put into its proper perspective. It may be anathema to some women, whose preferences should be honored. I do worry that the pendulum has swung so far in the other direction that intense forms of penetration like fisting have become the new de rigueur girl sex, and a dyke who doesn't do it is considered hopelessly old-fashioned. It's OK not to favor penetration, and it's just as OK to like penetration so much that you leer at fire hydrants. Let a thousand sexual flowers bloom—like the steaming hothouse orchid, all purple and engorged, of the open, satiated, just-fisted cunt.

Fisting: How to Do It

by JoAnn Loulan

Get Your Minds Ready and Willing

Everybody involved has to be ready, willing, and able just for starters. Fisting takes lots of juice, lots of opening, and lots of trust. So talk it over, OK?

Get Out Your Wallet

Latex gloves for the fister will stop any viruses from passing from teensy tears in the fistee's vagina into invisible cuts and hangnails on that beautiful fist. You could skip the glove if you're not concerned about safe sex, but the hand slips in easier with a glove anyway, so what the heck!

You'll also need to stock up on some lube. This is essential! Store-bought is best, but vegetable oil will do if it's all you have. The problems with oil are that it's not viscous enough, it stains, and you'll need large amounts. The most important thing with the lube: Keep it warm and use a LOT of it. And I do mean a LOT.

Take Our Brief Vagina 101

In the normal sexual response cycle, there's a time when a girl's vagina is at its most flexible and ready to be open. This stage is named by different sex theorists as: plateau (Masters and Johnson), excitement (Kaplan), or excitement/engorgement (Loulan). The basic physical deal is that the vagina lubricates, the walls move somewhat apart from each other. The first third of the vagina narrows, and the back of it gets bigger and actually balloons out. How do you get to this magic state? Next step.

Warm It Up

Feel her all over her body, get her juices moving from wherever it is juices hang out when they aren't flowing out our vaginas. (Ever wonder where are they right now?)

Get Her Clitoris in on the Act

The clit is not just that nub between the lips—it has "legs" on either side of your girl's genitalia, on the inside, that contribute to the moving of the vagina gig. Stimulation of

the clit can be done in many ways—touch her anus, stimulate her entire genital area, talk dirty to her, tell her what you're about to do.

Chill Out

Throughout the entire process, use a slooooww hand. Fisting is an art of slow, gentle, forceful, determined movements that take concentration and cooperation. For the woman getting the hand job, make sure you're in charge of the pace. Don't think you have to make anything go fast, or that you need to make her happy. This is about making you happy (well, OK, both of you, but it's your body that's taking in the hand, after all!).

Prepare the Entryway!

Massage her perineum—that's the part at the bottom of her vagina that gets stretched to the max during childbirth. You have to get the same thing happening without the help of the special hormones that move her vagina apart during childbirth. You just have the elixir of love and lust. Don't be afraid to really move that skin. It needs to be able to stretch farther than you think, because once you get your hand inside her, you have to move in weird

74

ways so you don't have to amputate your arm, which requires her perineum to be quite flexible. Before the next step, her vagina should be wet, her perineum stretched, and you should have lube on your whole hand and your wrist and in her entryway—lots and lots.

Put in All Five Fingers
Your fingers should be pressed together, and your thumb needs to be snug in your palm in an aerodynamic-looking "duck" shape. (After your knuckles get in, you'll need to slowly, slowly curl those fingers.)

The hardest part is moving through the first part of her opening—it can hurt—so go sloooowwwwer than you think you need to. For the woman taking the hand, relax as much as you can and be ready for more relaxing and more directing. Your muscles are supposed to clamp down at this stage of the response cycle, which makes it a little weird to be trying to get in there at this point. The problem is, putting a fist in sooner is difficult because the vagina isn't opened up properly in the upper part. Ah, the yin and yang of life and physiology.

For the fister: Push down on her perineum as you move in, push and move, push and move, slowly slowly slowly, push down and move up, push down and move up. When you meet resistance, slow down, keep your hand where it is if she can take it, and hold it there until her muscles relax around your hand. If you are the one being entered, if you really want her to fist you, you are going to have to go through this bit of pain to get her hand in. Just think, beyond this barrier is freedom and a wonderful feeling!

Slip Past the Ring of Tightness
Once you get past the tight place, you'll feel some sucking and find a slippery, gushy wonderful tube that is her vagina stretched around your fist and eventually your wrist. Wow, what a feeling! For the one with the magical fist inside you—what a rush, huh? Fister: Make sure your fingers are tightly curled together, with the fingernails pointed toward the palm of the hand (no scratching the walls of the vagina!). Be careful, because as elastic as tissue is, you *can* rupture it. You may even be able to feel the balloon at the end of the vagina where the tightness is gone and you can actually move around a little. You'll both feel a suction. Don't worry, it's normal. You're pushing whatever air is there into a tighter and tighter space. You can continue to ask for lube if you are the receiver, and the giver can continue to put it in. Just keep putting more at the base of her vagina, and it will work its way up if you keep loading more and more.

Wow, you both made it! You can enjoy now. The fistee might want to touch her clit.

The fister may want to move her fist very, very gently. You both might want to have an orgasm, right now!

Sliding Back Out—Damn, I Hate That!
But you have to get to work, the kids woke up, whatever; all good things must come to an end, I guess. Slide out with the same respect and slowness with which you slid in. (As the recipient, make sure you're monitoring the situation. Tell your partner what feels good and what doesn't.) Keep moving your hand out slowly and when you get to the tight muscle, go even slower. If you feel sucking, just breathe with your own rhythm. Sometimes that sucking of vagina can be a little scary. It'll be OK; it's just trapped air. Keep the lube coming. You can also try to break the suction by placing a finger between her vagina and your wrist.

DON'TS
• Don't use a dirty fist. This includes a fist that has had any contact with the anus or has fingernails that aren't properly hidden from the vaginal tissue. If you have long nails, stuff cotton balls into the fingertips of latex gloves.

• Don't fist the unavailable. Don't fist someone who is passed out, asleep, or doesn't want it. Not only is it unethical, but fisting isn't a pain-free process, and you can tear muscles and tissue if you're too rough.

• Don't fist while inebriated. Don't fist if either of you is drunk or high. Make sure you're both sober enough to give and take direction.

SPECIAL CASES
Lucky Mama: Women whose vaginas are stretched from childbirth are a little looser down there, which makes fisting extra fun. If you haven't had a baby, no fear, it just might take a little more time.

Less Estrogen = Go Slower: Women whose bodies contain lesser amounts of estrogen changes (due to menopause, perimenopause, cancer, and other health conditions) may have thinner vaginal tissue. If you have low estrogen levels, it's even more crucial that the movement is slow, you use enough lube, and you both stay aware of what's happening so the fistee can slow her partner down if anything hurts at all, or if she starts to feel small pains that might be tiny tears in the tissue. This tearing is more likely to show up at your perineum and inner lips, but it could happen inside the vagina too.

How to Pump Your Clit

by Rachel Venning

For years our gay-male brethren have been using vacuum-pumping systems to increase the size of their dicks. Transgendered guys also pump their clits to get supersized genitalia. What most dykes don't know is that pumping your parts isn't just good for the gander. In addition to gender play, S/M, and medical scenes, clit-pumping lends itself to all sorts of visual satisfactions and sensory thrills. It's also fun for gearheads who love the latest sexual technologies.

The pump system consists of a small, clear cylinder that attaches via a flexible tube to a hand-operated vacuum pump. The pump creates a powerful suction that pulls blood into the clitoris and surrounding tissue. As the clit, its hood, and some of the labia become engorged with blood, you can see your tender button grow as it is sucked into the cylinder.

For some, the intense tugging sensation is enough to generate an orgasm. For others, the goal is to produce a clit big enough for penetration. Or the thrill may lie in playing with the swollen tissue after the cylinder is removed. Not everyone will like the intensity of the sensation. Here are the basics on how to do it:

The Right Tool

Purchase good equipment and familiarize yourself with it. Expect a high-quality pump and Pyrex cylinder to cost about $80. Cheaper options exist, but they don't work as well. Practice using the pump on your thigh and make sure you understand how it works. Test the quick-release valve.

Prepare for Landing

The pump works best if your tissue is already warm and your blood is flowing—ideally, you're already turned on. Alternately, take a bath or shower first. For a good seal between the flared opening of the cylinder and your skin, shave any pubic hair that would get in the way and use a thick water-based lube. (I recommend Maximus for this job.) Coat your clit and the inside of the tube to prevent chafing.

Pump It Up

Hold the cylinder snugly against your skin with one hand and use the other hand to pump.

Nipple Pumping

Originally, the cylinders that women use for clit pumping were designed for nipples. As is the case with your clit, pumping your nips delivers pleasurable sensation and enormous nipples. If you enjoy the feeling of hard sucking on your nipples, you may also enjoy the steady pull of a vacuum pump. The same basic guidelines apply: Go slowly, experiment, enjoy the visuals, and stop if it hurts.

Once the suction has created a seal, you can let go of the cylinder. Go slowly. Start with the valve open to feel just a slight sucking. When the valve is closed, each squeeze of the hand pump increases the vacuum pull on the clitoris and surrounding tissue, so pause after each pump to see how it feels. Experiencing pain? That's a good sign that it's time to stop. Although you might want it to, don't expect your new member to fill the entire cylinder. Experiment with releasing all the pressure and then pumping again.

Record It for Posterity

If you're with a partner, release the pump after a little pumping and enjoy the heightened sensations as she appreciates your fattened clit with her mouth. Don't overdo it; a little pumping goes a long way and overpumping can desensitize the tissue. If you find yourself numb rather than supersensitive, pump less next time. Where's the camera? She can document the amazing shape, color, and size of your engorged tissue swelling inside the clear cylinder.

Fuck Around With It

The pump and tube can be detached, leaving the engorged clit still vacuumed up into the cylinder, where it will stay until you break the seal by pressing the quick-release button. Play around with your new minidick. Gently tug the tube, hold a vibrator against it, ask her to suck on it. You can also fuck your partner while the cylinder is on. To make it more comfortable for her, swaddle the cylinder with a little padding to cover the valve end, and then cover it with a small condom. For more info on fucking with a pumped-up clit check out *The Ultimate Guide to Strap-On Sex* by Karlyn Lotney.

Enlarge It—Guaranteed!

78

For those who like to inflict sharp sensations on their lover's tender parts, pumping her clit will push her over the edge. And tops with butch bottoms find clit pumps menacing, technical, and well-suited to gender play. As some daily pumpers say, "This ain't no insta-penis!" Small, permanent increases over time can happen. But usually your clit returns to a swollen, but near normal, size as soon as you release the vacuum.

Find Your G Spot

Rachel Venning

You have a G spot. Every woman does. It is not a Holy Grail, a hidden treasure, or one of the lost tribes of Israel. It is simply a small spongy clump of tissue containing glands and nerve endings. It's wrapped around the urethra and gets firmer and filled with fluid when a woman is aroused. Some women ejaculate when the G spot is stimulated, but most don't. Here are some tips to help you hit the bull's-eye.

Imagine Your Vulva Is a Clock and Your Clit is High Noon
Recline in a comfortable position and dip a finger or two in your vagina. Curl them up toward 12 and feel a few inches up the vaginal wall for a coarse and bumpy texture. Voilá! Your G spot. The lengths of our cunts and our fingers vary so it may be too far up to reach yourself. Use a dildo or ask a friend to help. The nerves there are only sensitive to pressure so they respond more to a steady rhythmic fucking type motion than a stroking and gentle touch.

The Sensation of Before Ejaculation Feels Like Having to Pee
Before serious fucking or G spot exploration, make it a point to empty your bladder.

Work Out!
Well-toned pelvic muscles make your orgasms stronger. Clench and release those cunt muscles. Do a set, just like at the gym. You can do it anywhere—it makes waiting in line way more fun.

Masturbate Using a Curved Dildo to Get the G spot
The Crystal Wand is an S-shaped toy made just for this purpose. Or try the famous Hitachi Magic Wand with a G spotter attachment.

Come Often
As you devolve into that shrieking, wailing banshee of a sex pig that most of us love to be, and your self-control slips away, you're more likely to let that stream squirt.

80

What Is It? Why Is It?

Based on the small number of women studied, it seems that the G spot is physiologically analogous to the male prostate. The fluid we women ejaculate has been found to be chemically similar to male prostatic fluid. Many women report it to be clear and flavorless or even slightly sweet. Some say it varies considerably in both taste and quantity. A lot of research remains to be done. The G spot may be vestigial from another evolutionary moment. Or perhaps it's what we're evolving toward. (Heather has two biological mommies?) For now, its function is pleasure.

Read a Book
The Good Vibrations Guide to the G spot is a superbly informative and encouraging book on the subject. Or check out the time-honored classic video *How to Female Ejaculate*. Both are chock-full of inspiration.

Go Down on Your Lover
Then slide in a few fingers and curl them up as if to scratch your tongue from inside her. Press firmly with both tongue and fingers to squeeze that G spot. The moment of reckoning may soon be at hand. Will you spit or will you swallow?

Pull Out to Shoot
The bulk of a big dildo or even fingers can block off the urethra so that even though your body is ready to come, somehow it can't. So get out of the orgasm's way. This may take some practice if you have a strap-on in your lover's vagina. Hopefully she'll let you know. Remember, practice makes perfect.

Try the Back Door
The wall between the rectum and the vagina is thin, so if you angle your hand or dildo the right way you can stimulate her G spot through her asshole. This move wins bonus sexpert points.

Get a Plastic Sheet
Some girls don't just dribble out a teaspoonful or two, they produce major mattress-drenching quantities, so be prepared.

Fuck Hard
G spot stimulation and ejaculating orgasms happen a lot more with that pounding "I'm gonna give it to you so hard that your teeth will rattle, your will eyes roll, and you'll be begging Jesus for mercy" type sex than with anything else.

81

Use a Vibrator on the Clit at the Same Time
The steady hum combined with rhythmic penetration is just the ticket for a ride on the water-slide.

Have Fun!
Don't set female ejaculation up as a hurdle that you need to jump to establish yourself as a postmillennial dyke sex superstar. It ain't for everybody. And if you don't make a big wet mess, there'll be that much less laundry to do.

●FIVE

DYKE DICK:
STRAPPING, PACKING, SUCKING, FUCKING

Eating You by Inches

Butches and Bois Talk Dyke Cocksucking
by Dorian Key and Seth Custis

Cock sucking has become standard fare for many of us gender-bending dykes. But giving head to a rubber or silicone cock—strapped of course to one's favorite trick—may seem silly to some. "What's the point?" we've been asked. "It's not like she can feel anything." Ah…we disagree.

Many a packing dyke gets off from the pressure exerted on her cunt and the visual stimulation of having an eager dyke working between her legs. For many, getting or giving head is a favorite sexual activity. Indeed, quite a few of us, ourselves included, are obsessed with dyke cock sucking. We searched coffee houses, alleyways, and bookstores for light blue hankies stuck in back pockets and finally collected a gang of other boyish and butch cock sucking–interested dykes.

What gets you hard?

Alix: Seeing a bulge in a dyke's pants and when she has her hand on it. I love being forced to my knees in an alley, roughed up, abused, and having someone mercilessly fuck my face.

Meredith: A dick that's bigger than I can handle. A confident daddy, someone who's physically stronger than me, who'll tell me to suck cock whenever he feels like it, even in public. A daddy with steel-toed boots that I can service as a warm-up. I want that daddy to grab me and push me down to my knees and rub my face in the crotch of his jeans or leathers and grab the back of my head and force-feed me his cock.

NG: Someone kneeling in front of me, their hands behind their back, a butch or boy. Their height is important for a good angle. I want to stick my cock down toward their tonsils.

Sally: Most of my cocksucking fantasies are daddy-boy, where I'm teaching the boy how to do it.

Aussie Boy: One of my favorite fantasies is being a rough teenager and having my dick sucked off by another boy in the back room of a gay male leather bar, and then bending a faggot over and fucking him.

Cal: Femme girls, fag girls, boy girls—how they smell! I see two dykes, I'm one of them, we're hot for each other. In an alley that doesn't smell as bad as they really do, I cup a hand on my crotch, s/he notices and licks his lips. I see s/he's hungry and maybe packing too. I don't know which one of us will succumb first, who needs it worse. I start touching and pushing him up against a wall or metal grate door. We exchange rough kisses. S/he bites my neck and I grab his hair, pull his head back, sneer, "What do you think you're doing?" I check if he's hard and wet, make him taste his own pussy juice on my finger, get him weak, hungry for me. I put him on his knees and only let him rub his face against the cock straining against my jeans, but I won't pull it out yet!

What first gave you the idea to suck another dyke's cock? How does sucking another dyke's cock make you feel? What excites you most about it?

Meredith: It wasn't a thought, it was just a primal urge that I needed to have my mouth stuffed. It makes me feel like a fish biting a hook. I see myself as a pleasure hole, a fuck-face. The person I'm sucking off is a demigod, an authority of pleasure.

Alix: Serving someone, worshiping something, wetting it really turns me on.

Cal: I thought about sucking a dyke's cock as soon as I knew about girl-dicks. Sucking a femme's dick is *nasty.* I love the genderfuck.

Gretchen: I have some exhibitionist tendencies and that's what I like about cock sucking.

What size and type of dildo can you take in your mouth? How do you deal with your gag reflex?

Alix: I can take up to 6 inches in length. I'm not into whale or dolphin dildos. I prefer the cock-like ones, but no balls, not totally realistic. Black silicone is good. If I start to gag I back off and put my hand on the base of the dick.

Meredith: Seven inches—that's in the gagging realm. I like a realistic shape and color, silicon or rubber. When I gag I yawn in my throat, open my jaw really wide, and let my tongue fall forward as much as possible. Sometimes I get frustrated because I want nothing more than to feel someone's balls on my chin.

Cal: I can take the head of almost anything, and the full length of a 6-inch dick, more if I'm controlling my movements, less if I'm getting face-fucked. I pull back and swallow if I'm gagging. Someone I know practices on peeled bananas.

How do you like to give head? If you're into S/M, how do you relate cock sucking to it?

Alix: I start out teasing with my tongue, taking the head in, licking the underside, jacking off with my hand at the base. I like verbal abuse from the top. Cock sucking relates to S/M to me because I am having a hole opened by someone else. I'm an open channel, another sexual orifice.

Meredith: I tongue the head, showing the top how talented my tongue is, pop the head in and out of my lips. I take it a little deeper each time I go down. Sometimes I secretly use my teeth to get a good grip. The most exciting thing is having my throat violated and knowing when they're coming. My favorite position is being bent backward over a couch, with my head upside-down. I like having my face hit with a cock, when the top moans their pleasure, when I can smell their crotch. Cock sucking is a power exchange, with a dominant and a submissive, breath control, and a testing round for physical endurance as well.

Cal: I cup her balls and use pressure against her cunt. I like to make it visually appetizing. Maybe slide a finger under the dick onto her clit or in her pussy or ass. I jack myself off while giving head, if allowed. I like to have my master's boots firmly planted in my crotch or against my neck. Being choked or crying is also good. Face-fucking can be punishment and getting master's/Daddy's cock can be a reward.

Gretchen: I use lots of tongue work on the head, some hand pressure, sucking harder as I go on. Kneeling is my favorite position. I think about them watching me. I don't think of cock sucking as S/M really, unless I were being whipped or had my hands tied while giving head.

What first gave you the idea to have your cock sucked? How does having your cock sucked make you feel? What excites you most about getting head?

Alix: It seems to be a natural part of my sexuality, whether or not I'm wearing a dick. I feel like a teenage boy with a huge hard-on. When it's with an older woman, she's

like my mommy. It makes me feel like a virgin teenager. When I'm with another butch, we're both randy-ass teenagers. I love seeing a femme's lipstick smeared on my dick.

Sally: I feel paternal, like daddy's teaching his boy while being blown. I see myself as a daddy. It doesn't work as well for me when it's not daddy-boy.

Aussie Boy: Having my cock sucked makes me feel very powerful and male and at the same time vulnerable and gender-fucked. I like it when someone is really getting into what they are doing, getting lost in it, when they push themselves to take all of me in. If I am playing rough, I fuck their face. I like to look into their eyes while they submit to me.

NG: Fucking someone's face is a serious power trip. I like her to be extremely submissive or attempting to fight back, like in a rape scene.

Cal: Putting on my dick made me want to have it sucked. I've been a 5-year-old, an astounded teenage boy getting it for the first time, and an older daddy-leather type feeding his boy. I *love* when they're begging for it, so hungry they're shaking.

Gretchen: I like my cocksucker to be challenging, naughty. Sometimes I feel like a goober when I'm getting sucked off. I don't know why, but I usually feel silly, except when I'm focusing on watching them.

What about packing and favorite dicks?

Alix: Packing feels like an extension of my true identity. My favorite packing drag is leather pants or pin-striped suits. My favorite packing dick is 6 inches long and doesn't have balls. It's a gray, sort of realistic silicone one. I wear it in a custom-made harness. It's a codpiece originally made for a man, but customized to have a snap-off pouch with my dick underneath. I pack to the left and don't wear underwear.

Sally: When I pack and wear butch drag it totally gets me into my daddy role, protective, paternal, powerful, and cocky. I like to wear jeans, a T-shirt, flannel shirt, boots, leather jacket, jockey shorts or boxers, and a belt with my keys attached. My favorite packing dick is the 6-inch black rubber Ballsy SuperCock. It's pretty realistic, with veins, except it's not flesh-colored. I use a longer one if I'm going to be fucking. I'm always searching for more comfortable ones, that I can turn up while it's in my harness. I wear long jockey shorts under my harness so my hair doesn't get caught in it.

AB: I always dress male, and I pack often. Chaps are one of my favorite items of clothing. For daily packing I have a custom-made soft dick that's comfortable and realistic looking but not very functional. I wear it in a jockstrap. If I'm going out looking for a cocksucker, I wear my Jelly Boy. It's clear rubber, comfortable to pack, and a good size to wrap a mouth around.

Meredith: I pack usually when I have a sex or play date, or when I'm on the hunt. I like to wear leather pants or ripped jeans. My favorite packing dick is a homemade condom and hair-gel package with big balls. I wear a black or orange jockstrap, or sometimes tight Hanes underwear. My favorite cocksucking dick is a Peter North vibrating and squirting cock, 9 inches long.

NG: When I'm packing I don't feel any different than usual, except it's erotic because I only do it when I'm expecting to do something sexual. When I'm in butch or party drag I start to feel really intimidating. I wear black paratrooper pants, a big leather belt, and a black leather cap. I want people to know I'm a top. I use a two-headed flesh-colored dick because it's very flexible and can extend to whatever length I want. It doesn't shift around; I can tuck it in pretty securely in my harness.

Cal: I usually pack either in suit or in leathers. In a suit I'm more nervous, trying to be smooth. In leathers it's just sex.

Gretchen: Packing is fun! Someone told me they thought packing was empowering. I think it's campy. I feel playful when I pack. Sometimes I pull butch attitude and sometimes I go nelly and flame around. I wear jeans, boxers, sometimes suits. Packing in miniskirt could be cool but I hate skirts. I like to use my bright sparkly purple dick. I'm not really into penile dildos, although I think the goddess-shaped ones are ludicrous. I have a black leather harness that I wear over biker shorts, or just under boxers.

90 **How do you like to have your cock sucked? If you're into S/M, how do you relate cock sucking to it?**

Alix: I like to be worshiped by a skilled, competent cocksucker. I'm not into them being timid.

Sally: Whatever they do, they have to do it with vigor. The more they show me they like it, the hotter I get.

Meredith: I like it vigorous, having my cock pushed into my clit, deep-throating if they can.

NG: I like to fuck their throat. I like them to swallow the whole thing. Kneeling is a visual turn-on, but in terms of a good fuck I usually have the person's mouth and throat lined up for depth purposes. I lie someone down on the bed and tilt their head back. But no matter what I do, my cock has no feeling in it, so things that feel really good to boys don't do anything for me. I just want to grab their ears and ram. I don't want them to have too much control. A good way to do this is to have their hands cuffed. Fucking someone's mouth is definitely S/M because I'm doing it purely for my own gratification.

Cal: I like being sedate till they're getting me so hot I have to let go, even if it hurts them, even if they gag and choke and cry. I like being seated, with my boy between my legs. I like talking while they're sucking me, and getting fucked as I'm being sucked.

Coming while having your cock sucked: Tell us about it.

Alix: It's a total, whole-body ejaculation down someone's throat. I've had partners feel it. Pressure on my cunt certainly feels good, but I believe that good cock worship is cerebral. It's definitely different from coming while fucking.

Aussie Boy: A cocksucking orgasm is not unlike my other orgasms, but in a way it's better because it really blows my mind. I come as a direct result of having my dick sucked. When I wear a dick it becomes a part of my body.

NG: My orgasms usually come from between my ears. I usually have to have my hips moving at some time. The visual/mental image causes my orgasms while having my cock sucked, and from me moving. But getting my cock sucked is not the most intense kind of orgasm. I like to do it early on because it really turns me on. It's also not as debilitating as coming while fucking.

Cal: If my dick's being jacked off good while being sucked, I come from direct clit stimulation, but the feeling is real different. It builds differently and the come is external.

Hottest cocksucking experience?

Alix: Someone was 3 or 4 inches away from my crotch. I wasn't wearing a dick, but I could feel my cock, and the orgasm just blew our heads. It was exquisite, slow, pleasurable torture. We couldn't believe what had happened. I felt recognized. My dick was recognized.

Sally: We were both packing, this fag-dyke-boy I had a date with, and he had a very big dick. I wanted to show him off in the Castro, so we cruised the video stores, looking at the boy pornos. All of the gay boys really didn't know what to think. Everyone did double takes, triple takes. It was really fun. I kept warning her not to go off with any of them and then I took her home and punished her because she did want to go off with all of those boys. Of course she had to suck me off, before, during, and after I punished her.

NG: I was at a play party. The bottom was in a sling with another woman fisting her, possibly both in her cunt and ass, something very dramatic. I had the bottom's head tilted way back, and we both slammed into her at the same time.

Cal: On my first date with two femme tops and a daddy, after being stripped, beaten, and teased, this woman took me downstairs and the daddy ordered me to fuck her. After that I was lying back, she got on top of me, touched me everywhere, took my dick, stroked it, and started sucking it. I was so hard and horny from fucking her and being topped all night. She slipped her fingers inside me and fucked me and sucked me, and I came hard again and again, shooting come down her entire fucking arm.

To those of you who managed to make it through this article in one sitting without a little assistance from someone's hand or mouth, congratulations, you deserve a gold star, or perhaps a Gold Coin condom, slicked down your dick by the cocksucking trick of your dreams. For those of you who didn't, shame on you, you little perverts! But remember, that's how we like you best.

How to Suck Dyke Cock

by Rachel Venning

Sucking dyke dick is a psychological and physical art. As dykes, we're somewhat lacking in the nerve-ending department, as far as our plastic penises go. But what we lack neurologically, we make up for in imagination and enthusiasm. Here are some tips from both sides of the harness to make your next blow job a mind-blowing experience.

Use a Realistic Cock

Blow jobs are no time to surprise your sweetie with one of those lavender dolphin dildos from the '80s, cute as they are. For decent dick sucking you need a sexy number with a clearly defined shaft and head (maybe with a piss slit), and veins and balls if possible.

Connect With Your Cock

When you strap on the dick, take a few moments of private time to really connect with it. Touch, it rub it, and if you're packing, enjoy the feel of it pressing against your pants.

Think Psychic Dick

Although you don't have a flesh-and-blood penis, your mind can have a hard-on that's as raging as anyone's. The dildo is the physical expression of a psychic reality, and that dick can feel fantastic, rubber or not.

Do It Somewhere Nasty

Something about cock sucking calls for dark alleys, bathroom stalls, and parked cars. Let the staging add to the sexiness.

Put on a Good Visual Show

When you're sucking, remember that your playmate is getting off largely on imagination and the look of your hands, mouth, tongue and head. So make sure there are good sight lines and keep your actions visible.

How Queer Is That?

If I had a quarter for every time a dyke looking for her first strap-on (often at her girl-friend's urging) asked me "What's in it for me?" I'd have enough for a hand-me-down Harley. The dyke blow job is the ultimate in gender-bending sex theater, because really, what's in it for anyone? The answer is the old truism that our biggest sex organ is between our ears. The point is desire. The idea, the visual thrills, the feeling of power, the unique physical sensations all combine to make our motors rev. A woman on either side of a dyke blow job is as queer as can be—so don't be surprised if self-consciousness sets in. If you haven't done it before you may find yourself thinking something along the lines of *This is weird*. Let the thought come up and, like a master of meditation, let it go. You're doing this because it feels good to you, that thick cock in your mouth, or watching your lover's head bob diligently up and down your shaft. Get into the perverse thrill, and when you've both come your guts out, give yourselves a pat on the back for being brave. It ain't easy being a dirty-minded sex freak (but at least it's not lonely).

Add a Hand Job
Use your hand to push the base of the dick into his/her cunt. The most physical sensation for the receiver will come from that one point of contact, so make it work. Rhythmically thrusting with your hand along the shaft into the base while working the head in and out of your mouth gives both a visual and a physical thrill. Another good reason to hang on to the base of the dildo is to control the depth of the thrusts.

Go Deep
If you can deep-throat, do it. That's always impressive and exciting—no matter the gender of those involved.

Get Real
Treat the dildo like a real penis—focus on the things that feel good to bio-men: Stroke the vein along the bottom, tongue the slit, gently tickle the balls.

Be Safe, Be Sexy
If you like using condoms to keep the dildo clean—perhaps because it might go from your mouth to your cunt, to your partner's cunt to someone else's ass, and back again—it's a great opportunity to show off that Safe Sex 101 trick in which you roll the condom on with your mouth. Practice first.

94

Add Some Buzz (Or More)

If you want more genital stimulation than the psychic thrill or the base of the dildo pushing into your vulva can provide, consider tucking a small bullet-shaped vibrator between your harness and your clit; several harnesses have a built-in pouch for just this purpose. Some girls won't mind if you slip some fingers in their pussy while you're blowing them. Others might find that upsets their psychic gender-bending state. So check in. A finger in the ass, however, is a perfect complement to any blow job.

95

Michele Serchuk

Why Does Cock Sucking Get You Off?

Readers Tell Us Why They Love Getting and Giving Blowjobs
compiled by Gina de Vries

Happy Hooker

"For me, being penetrated feels inherently submissive. It's especially hot to be penetrated orally. I'm a hooker, and it's always hot to take those work skills home to my FTM lover." —*Lydia*

Virtual Reality

"Strap-on sex is really hot for me in general, and cock sucking is my absolute favorite part of that. Strap-ons become an extension of my lover's body and my own body. At a certain point I'm not just sucking a silicone dildo; I'm sucking my partner's actual cock, and I'm not just fucking someone with a strap-on—it's my actual dick inside them. Regardless of the gender of the person I'm with or what our physical anatomy is like, this otherwise inanimate object becomes part of the body and becomes this incredibly hot, sexy thing." —*Star*

Aural Pleasure

I love getting my cock sucked. I really enjoy the way my girl's mouth looks stretched around a dildo. She gets very into it. It excites her to be fucked that way and she makes these little moans and sighs that get me hotter and hotter as I near orgasm. I can come from receiving a really good blow job. The pressure from the base of the dildo on my clit and the erotic visual of a hot femme on her knees gets me off." —*Randy*

Fag Porn

96 "When my lover sucks me off she looks and feels like a hot fag boy. It's one of the most exciting things we do together. It gives me days of fantasy material afterwards. I like to jack off thinking about my dirty girl-boy on her knees with her mouth wrapped around my tool." —*Nan*

Rise to the Challenge

"It's a challenge to give a good blow job. I love the reaction I get from my boy, the soft little moans he makes that let me know whether I should be going fast or slow. I am a sexual submissive, and I really enjoy being dominated and being on my knees and being told what to do." —*Cortney*

Power Exchange

"I love to feel the pressure of her throat against my pubic bone while my hand is tangled in her hair. On the other hand, there are times when I love to hide under her short skirt and take her femme cock as deep into my throat as it'll go. It's one of my favorite ways to twist the butch/femme dynamic—it's an exchange of control. Power and vulnerability are hot when they're offered up like this." —*Silverhand*

Transforming Top

"I love taking something that's usually associated with bottoming—things like cock sucking and taking it up the ass—and transforming it into something I do as a top. It's like, 'Hold still so I can suck your cock, boy.' I love it." —*Wendell*

Taboo

"One of the reasons I find cock sucking so hot is because of the taboo surrounding it. Women aren't supposed to have cocks, especially not ones that are black or purple or green. It's very erotic doing something that you're not supposed to do. My lover sees her cock as an extension of herself, and loves to be serviced and have it sucked. My number 1 reason that cock sucking is so hot is that it drives her crazy!" —*Danielle*

The Many Joys

"There was a time when the very idea of cock sucking turned my stomach. Now I think it's hot because it's part of the dominant/submissive activities I enjoy with my submissive girlfriend. The idea of a warm, wet mouth wrapped around my strap-on is exciting and enticing. It's taboo—which makes it attractive in a naughty way—and now it's legal in Texas! Visually, it's incredibly sexy, and with the right tools it can be physically fulfilling too. My favorite Chris Cooper illustration depicts two devil chicks, one on her knees sucking the phallic barb of the other's tail." —*Torrid Darkwolfe*

How to Strap It On

by Rachel Venning

Certain things go together: peanut butter and chocolate, raindrops and roses, dykes and dicks. There's something about a hole. Once you get over the fear that wanting to strap a dick on means you want to be a man—or that wanting to receive the plunge and thrust of a hip-driven love stick means you're straight—the wide world of dildos and harnesses is yours to explore. Here are some tips to guide you on your strap-on adventure.

Foreplay Isn't Just for High School

Kissing, petting, licking—all that hot, sweet action will get you juicy and primed for the main event.

It's All About Attitude

Not that snotty stud attitude, but the vibe that you're doing it to have fun, to sweat, and to get off.

Cinch Your Harness Up Tight

The more securely the dildo is attached to your body, the more control you will have and the more sensation will travel through the dick and harness to you.

Use Your Hands

You're not just a piston with a mission—you're a multitalented, multilimbed sex machine. Don't get so caught up in the technicalities of steering your pocket rocket that you forget the pleasures of squeezing. Pay attention to her nipples, kiss her throat, reach down to her clit (or yours), and turn up the intensity.

It's Not the Size of the Boat, It's the Motion of the Ocean

Put some surge and roll in your action and your lover will want to cruise with you time and time again. If you're pushing it in, go for the soft parts. Angle your dick up toward her G spot; don't bang into her spine.

Get the Most Out of a Lesbian Blow Job

The visual excitement generated by your bobbing head, stretched mouth, and lasciviously lapping tongue are important stimulation. Wrap your hand around the base of her cock and pump vigorously. As you slide your hand down, make sure the pressure pushes into her clit. The combination of seeing you; feeling the energy of your queer, queer love; and that push into her pelvis may make her come.

If You're Knockin' on the Back Door, Take It a Little Slower

Many women prefer a smaller dildo for anal penetration than they do for vaginal sex. Use plenty of lube, start out with fingers to ease into it, and make sure the penetration is angled toward her G spot, not straight up along her spine.

Explore Different Positions

The missionary position allows for salt-licking, tongue-kissing, face-to-face intimacy, but other positions have their charms as well. For cervix-bangingly deep penetration, rear entry lets the dildo in about an inch farther. If the receptive partner scoots her kitty to the edge of the mattress while the dildo-wearer stands by the side of the bed, that feet-on-the-floor stability can make for long sessions that are easier on the knees, back, and shoulders of the fucker.

How to Pick a Dick

If you've got a steady girlfriend, the two of you should do the shopping together. The best strap-ons are the ones in which the harnesses and the dildo are sold separately. Check the width of the fingers you like for penetration to get an idea of what diameter dildo to choose. Silicone is the best material for dildos because it retains body heat, has a gently resilient texture, and cleans up in a snap. If you're not sure of the size—or even whether you'll like it at all—go for a less expensive rubber one. For harnesses, the most important features are comfort and fit. Leather is very comfortable, while denim and nylon are lower-cost options and rubber can make for fetish fun. Some harnesses are G-string-style with a single strap, others have two straps that come around the sides of the ass like a jock strap. Choose whichever suits your taste. If you like to use thick or thin dildos, a harness with an O-ring that snaps out allows one to pop in the ring that best fits the dildo (standard O-rings fit average-size dildos just fine).

Keep It Realistic

A bulge is hot, but a tent pole is a turn-off. For the most realistic, manlike package, try a soft, squishy dildo made just for that purpose. If you want to pack with the toy you're going to fuck with, try wearing snug briefs (boys', of course) or a jock strap to keep that woody in the shed until it's time to get choppin'.

Ham It Up!

You've got a dick, so maybe you wanna be a guy—not all the time maybe, but at least for one night. Don't be afraid of your erotic imagination. Play Daddy and his princess, Mommy and her best boy, or leather fags in a Folsom Street alley. Or you can be a chick with a dick, a cocksure femme... Whatever your fantasy, live it out.

100

Pack Like You Mean It

by Rachel Venning

Packing isn't just what you do for a trip; it's also something you can do for a date. Packing is the fine art of wearing a dildo under your clothes. It signifies your sexual readiness. It tells your potential partner that you were thinking about sex before you even left the house. Packing can also be a way of conveying a masculinity—whether you're a drag king, FTM, butch dyke, or just a gal who wants to fuck her gender. Sometimes packing is just about creating a good-looking package to catch the girls' eyes. To help you look and feel your best while dressed for success, here are some tips to get you started.

Ready for Action

If your objective is getting laid, you'll want to pack a dick stiff enough to fuck with. For maximum realism, get one with balls. The most realistic features, such as subtle flesh tones and a skin-like feel, can be had with a cyber-skin model. But for a toy that can stand up to the rigors of both sex and packing, silicone is a better material. Look for a dick that's pliable enough to bend while still firm enough to feel good. Vixen Creations's Johnny is a good one, but there are lots of sizes and shapes out there, so pick one that suits you.

The Package

Some dykes pack in order to express a more masculine identity. If actual fucking isn't in your plans, consider building your bulge with more pliable material than a typical dildo. Softpacks are mushy cyber-skin dicks designed to cut a very realistic and comfortable silhouette. They aren't designed for sex, but arranged just so, in your tighty whiteys, they feel good pressing on your pubis and will pass a crotch cruise. If you don't have a softpack, try rolled-up socks. They will need more adjusting but will do in a pinch. Check out Karlyn Lotney's *The Ultimate Guide to Strap-on Sex* for tips on how to build a soft packing device.

Strapped

A dildo that's curved is often easier to bend in your pants (or panties). Keep in mind that the stiffer the toy, the more difficult it will be to pack in an unobtrusive way. If

Use the Urinal

Peeing standing up, especially at a urinal in the men's room, is the sine qua non of passing. It really helps with that all-over manly feeling. While some dykes have mastered the art of the standing piss sans equipment, there are several items on the market designed especially for this purpose. One is called the Magic Cone. It's a disposable paper cone that folds flat until you're ready to use it. Pop it open and one end fits close to your crotch, allowing you to urinate from a standing position. Another good device is the Freshette—a soft plastic form about the size of half a mango cups under the urethra and sluices fluid out a short plastic tube. Shake it out and off you go. You'll never need to squat to pee again.

you're going to be wearing it for long stretches, choose a harness that's made of softer material with minimal hardware. Wear the harness loose under your clothes for maximum comfort, and quickly cinch it up when it's time to play. If you'll be going through any metal detectors (meeting your sweetie at the airport?) get one with plastic fasteners, or one that's all elastic.

How's It Hanging?
Batten your woody down with a jockstrap or two pairs of tight briefs to keep from pitching a tent in your trousers. Very tight pants can also help secure the schwing. Packing your dick with the tip bent down provides maximum sexiness while grinding on the dance floor. A big one makes a statement—you'll risk being called "tripod." If you don't want that much attention, try bending it up and tucking the tip under the elastic waistband of your underwear or the waist strap of the harness. It will be less obvious but still apparent to anyone with a discerning eye.

Dress to Impress
Packing a dick adds a lot to an outfit. A sailor suit is always cute, but with a torpedo tucked in the trousers it's got a lot more sizzle. The same goes for businessman, cowboy, and even Boy Scout. Not that bois and butches get all the fun. A femme with a surprise packed into her panties can flip her date faster than a fry chef at a cook-off.

102

SIX

BACK-DOOR WOMAN:
BUTT PLAY

Explore Your Back Door

by Rachel Venning

There's a popular but erroneous belief held by many lesbians that anal sex is 1) painful; 2) dirty; and 3) something only gay men would want to do. None of this is true, and anal sex can be a source of deeply pleasurable and exciting sexual fun. For back-door beginners, the best place to start is with a little self-exploration. Then you'll be ready to share the love with that special someone. Here are some tips to get you going.

Warm Up
Don't rush to penetrate. Just let yourself feel the different textures. Try clenching your anal sphincter really tight and then relax. Feel the change with your fingers. If it feels good so far, go ahead and slide in a well-lubed fingertip. The resistance you feel is your anal sphincter, which maintains a state of tightness to keep the rectum closed.

Relax
Notice how much tension you carry in your ass and try to lessen it. We live in an anal-retentive culture, and most of us walk around with our butts clenched so tight you'd think we were holding the Hope Diamond in there. If you relax that tension, you'll feel lighter, less stressed out, and more able to notice the good feelings the butt can provide.

Keep It Clean
Warm water and soap are all you need to keep clean and ready to go. If it's more than a surface scrub you're after, try a gentle warm-water enema. Simple bulb-style enemas are available at most drugstores and are easy and painless to use.

Don't Forget the Lube
Unlike the vagina, the asshole is not self-lubricating, so if you're going to be doing any penetration, you'll need lube. For anal sex, the best lubes are thick ones that have some staying power. Try Slippery Stuff or Probe Thick, two water-based lubes that go the distance.

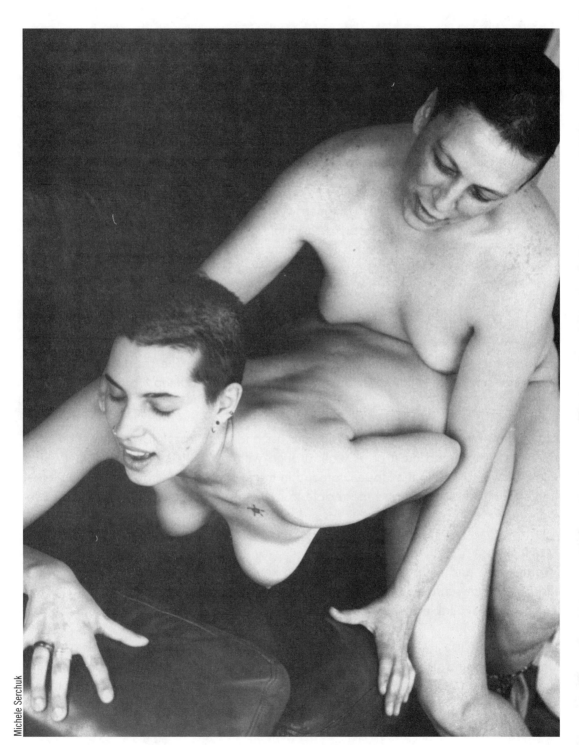

106

Rim It

To be sure to avoid any creepy crawlies, use a dental dam or a sheet of Saran Wrap between mouth and asshole—a dollop of lube on the skin side will help make it feel mm-mmm good. The soft, squishy, yet firm feeling of a tongue on a nerve-rich asshole just can't be beat. While you're mixing it up with tongues, or doing some traditional clit-licking, try sliding your little finger in her back door.

Aim for the Spot

If you're the one who's doing the penetrating, make sure you can picture where your fingers, dildo, or other toys are going. Angle toward her G spot. The anus and the vagina are very close—only a thin wall separates the two spaces—so many of the same pleasurable sensations (like G spot stimulation) that come from vaginal penetration can come from anal penetration too.

Pick a Dick

One of the nice things about being a dyke is getting to choose the size of your dick. For anal play you may want to start with a smaller toy than usual. Also, a lot of women prefer toys that are smooth and consistent in diameter down the length of the shaft. Because the sphincter naturally closes around anything that enters, toys with lots of bumps and ripples may produce more sensation than they would vaginally.

Plug It

In addition to strap-on dildos, there are other toys made especially for anal pleasure. Butt plugs can be popped into place and then left in while other activities are under-

Anatomy

Butt sex feels so good because of the many nerve endings and the concentration of vascular tissue in that area. The proximity of the anus to the structures of the clitoris also makes it possible to reach orgasm through anal stimulation. The G spot—which is the urethral sponge wrapped around the urethra, physiologically analogous to the male prostate—is just behind the front wall of the vagina. Pressure through the ass toward the G spot can lead to powerful G spot orgasms. If you're going to do deep anal penetration, keep in mind that as the rectum is curved, it's not the best place to stick a hard, straight object. Something bendable and with a little give to it is best.

taken. Most plugs are shaped like elongated diamonds, cinching to a narrow waist before a wide base that anchors the plug outside.

Try the Beads
Picture a row of beads (usually about marble-size) attached to one another by a string, with a ring at one end that one can pull to remove them. As the beads go in, the sphincter deliciously opens and closes over each one. Try pulling them all out at once right at the moment of orgasm.

Fuck Your Gender
Ass play and gender-fucking make for a great couple. Fucking like fags is doubly homoerotically hot when you're really queer girls, and sex in an alley is twice as good when she pulls down your Levi's and plows your ass.

108

Michele Serchuk

Handballing: It's Not Just for Fags Anymore!

by Tristan Taormino

Although gay leathermen pioneered the practice of anal fisting, they no longer have the market cornered. Plenty of dykes already know the pleasures of vaginal fisting, and many of us have gone knocking on the back door in search of anal ecstasy. Rectal fisting fans describe it as an intense, intimate, even spiritual experience. So dust off those red hankies, and get ready for my guide to the new school of butt-balling.

Clean Out

Although it's optional for most anal play, an enema is a must for anal fisting. A clean rectum makes penetration safer and more comfortable for everyone. Have an enema at least two hours beforehand to give your body time to recover. Plus, the thin layer of mucus that coats the rectum needs to regenerate, because it helps protect sensitive tissue. Use plain warm water and rinse until it comes out clear.

Relax

In our stressful world, chilling out can be a tall order, but your body has to be relaxed so that those all-important sphincter muscles will be open to the task. Take a warm bath, have a massage, or for you multiorgasmic chicks, get off, since having an orgasm is a great way to relax all over!

Be Present

Anal fisting can be a powerful, even a little scary experience, so both the fister and the fistee should be 100% present. My preference is for all parties involved to be sober, because drugs and alcohol impair your judgment, dull your senses, and could result in pushing your body further than you should. So take a pass on the poppers.

Play Safe

Whether or not you regularly use them for penetration, latex gloves (or nonlatex for those with a allergic reactions) make your hand into a smooth, seamless tool for pleasure. They protect the bottom's bottom from jagged nails and any other rough edges that might irritate her ass.

Lube, Lube, Lube!

Leave that Crisco in the kitchen! While it may be OK for leatherboys, if Crisco makes its way into your pussy—and inevitably some will—it will hang around and give you an infection. Use a water-based or silicone lubricant that's the consistency of hair gel. Thicker lubes (AstroGel, Maximus, and Eros Gel, for example) dry up less quickly and have a cushioning effect inside the delicate rectum. Reapply lube to your hand as often as needed. Once you get up to four fingers, you can pour lube onto the palm of your hand, and let it slide down onto your fingers inside.

Work up to It

Using fingers and toys, you'll want to stimulate the ass as you gradually get it to open up. The trick with anal fisting is to do enough play to get it open but not too much to make it tired and sore. Figure out what works best for the fistee, whether it's finger thrusting, dildo fucking, or butt-plug training.

Plug It In

Using a butt plug is a great way to warm up someone's ass for anal penetration, and using several plugs in increasing sizes is even better. Put a plug in her ass, then lick her pussy, finger-fuck her, spank her, do whatever it takes to get her aroused. Take that plug out and replace it with a bigger one. I especially like to work my way up to a big butt plug with a wide neck, which not only relaxes the ass but also opens the sphincter muscles.

To Clit or Not to Clit

Some women say that if you're working their clits, you can put whatever you want in their asses. That's because clitoral stimulation gets their bodies aroused and their entire genital regions engorged. Others say that if you touch their clits, they clench down, which makes anal penetration less comfortable. You have to figure out which method works for you. Won't it be fun figuring it out?

110

On Our Backs

Once you have worked your way up to three or four fingers or a sizable toy, find a comfortable position, because eventually you'll be far enough into the process that you won't want to stop to reposition. Some people prefer to be on their backs, face to face with their partners with access to nipples, pussy, and clit. Some people prefer doggie style for fisting because it allows deeper penetration.

Communicate

Talk to your partner as you play with her ass. The fister should check in regularly, and the fistee should call the shots: when to back off, when to move to something bigger, whether she wants more in-and-out or a higher speed on the vibrator. Likewise, talk to each other afterward. Find out what worked and what you can do better. Then you'll be sure there's a next time.

Michele Serchuk

111

Rim Like a Gay Boy

by Rachel Venning

Rimming, also known as analingus, is the fine art of licking ass. Done right, rimming is pure devotion expressed through the tongue in worship of that sensitive, nerve-filled enigma: the asshole. Devotees of rimming laud the subtle pleasures and star-rocket thrills that it can offer. Gay men have long known and loved the act of rimming, and with these quick tips you too can be fast on your way to exquisite pleasure.

Waiting to Exhale

Anal tension is epidemic among Americans. It may sound like a joke, but most of us walk around with a clenched asshole at all times. Most of the time we aren't even aware of our anal tension. If you let that tension go and relax your anus into a soft little puddle of flesh, your partner's velvety tongue will feel a whole lot better against it. Get your butt in the mood by breathing in deeply and squeezing your PC muscles. As you exhale, let your clenched little pucker relax. Try it a few times and notice the difference.

Deal With Your Shit

The biggest obstacle to deeply satisfying oral-anal pleasure is the fear, for both parties, of encountering shit. Rather than trying to repress your concerns, a little preparation can alleviate them entirely. A thorough cleaning will leave the anus as clean as your garden-variety vagina—and we lick that all the time! Even though tongues can not actually probe very deep, you should shower as if they can. Hot water and a soapy finger will relax your sphincter and leave you ready to party. While you're freshening up, take time to notice how your ass is feeling. Get relaxed. Anticipate the pleasure you'll feel as a slippery warm tongue glides across all your nice clean folds. A sheet of Saran Wrap or a Glyde dam slipped between mouth and pucker will guarantee a cootie-free experience.

Get Cheeky

Your tongue, lips, breath, and teeth, as well as your hands and body, can all work together to turn you into a butt-loving machine. Nibble her ass cheeks and rub her

Enemas

An enema will go a long way toward making you feel confident about that eager tongue that's begging to lick your ass, and a simple squeeze-bulb enema is not hard on the body or the psyche. Just fill it up with warm water and empty it into the rectum for a quick rinse. Release the water into the toilet, and you're all set. If possible, wait an hour or so before penetration to give your ass a chance to refresh its natural lining and to make sure all the water is gone.

thighs, butt, torso, breasts—whatever you can reach. The asshole itself is dense with nerve endings and incredibly sensitive. Don't bite too hard, but don't treat her like a porcelain doll, either. Let her feel your desire, and she'll feel more desire herself.

Find Your Spirit Animal

For its size, the tongue is the strongest muscle in the body. Think of all the ways it can move. Though soft, steady licks will probably become the centerpiece of your technique, don't be afraid to mix it up a bit. Tight, darting licks, circles, and sinuous tongue twists will all spice things up. If your sweetie is a pig for feather-light touches behind her knees and on her feet, encourage her to wallow with a similarly light touch on her rosebud. Lap her up like a kitty with a saucer of milk, or ravish her like a dog with a bone.

A Path to Ecstasy

Rimming is a more subtle pleasure than cunnilingus. While it's possible to have an orgasm from any kind of touch, rimming is not usually the fastest route to climax. Set aside goal orientation and become one with the rim job. The slow, sensuous act of rimming is like a massage and can transport both people to another plane. Be one with the tongue, be one with the ass, let go of your hold on time and space and let rimming be your magic carpet ride.

Make It Routine

Rimming is easily incorporated into cunnilingus. The space between the ass and the cunt, the perineum, loves to be licked. Rimming also makes a good warm-up for anal penetration. If you want to fuck your lover in the ass, rimming can soften her up so that the penetration is more pleasurable. Generally, rimming is best done before anal fucking, because no matter how well you shower, fucking can drag bacteria to the outside world.

113

Great Anal Sex Porn

Videos for the Back-door Woman in All of Us
by Laura Weide

Plenty of dykes view anal sex as an activity on the periphery of sapphic sexual expression. If you are one of those cunnilingus snobs, these videos just might help you get past the perineum and into a new world of sensual delights. The butt-fucking porn in this column offers not only some of the hottest on-screen scenes between anal aficionados but also instruction for satisfying anal sex, to try alone or with a partner. Whether you're a full-fledged ass-fucker, a bona fide rimming nut, or simply eager to progress past tentative rosebud massage, you'll enjoy these erotic and educational videos. Don't forget the lube!

Uranus: Self Anal Massage for Men
[Joseph Kramer, 1996]
There is much to learn from our gay brothers about anal pleasure, and especially from masturbation guru Joseph Kramer. With his gentle voice, this adept anal educator talks his audience through a range of exercises aimed at helping viewers become more embodied in their anal sensations. A lithe, well-muscled model demonstrates on himself as Kramer offers tips and techniques designed to relax the sphincter muscles and increase body awareness. The mind-blowing anal breathing segment offers a simple yet revolutionary method for relaxing the anus. The segment also includes a range of external massage and penetration techniques you can use on yourself or your lover. Keep in mind that the G spot is analogous to the prostate gland, so Kramer's techniques can bring women the same pleasure.

Captured
[Passion Fruit Productions, 2001]

A smoky voice narrates this porn noir sexcapade. A high femme and her girl gang (another femme and a cute butch) abduct a smug cop and drag him over the fiery coals of their dominating desires. Independently made, it's a breath of fresh air from the mainstream porn aesthetic. It goes without saying that you'd never see a stud-belted butchie, looking like she just stumbled out of a dyke dive for a smoke, in your standard porn fare. Well-made, well-paced, this flick reaches a high point when the bound cop becomes exuberantly receptive to butch dick. Rough energy all around.

Ultimate Guide to Anal Sex for Women
dir. John Stagliano
[Evil Angel Productions]

Ultimate Guide to Anal Sex for Women 2
dir. Tristan Taormino and Ernest Green
[Wicked Productions, 2001]

Tristan Taormino not only penned the buttsex bible for women, *The Ultimate Guide to Anal Sex for Women*—she turned it into a two-volume, mainstream porn movie offering something for practically every taste. The first follows a Taormino-led workshop for porn stars interspersed with scene after gleaming hot anal scene, featuring stellar performers like Chloe and Sydney Steel. *Ultimate Guide 2* offers a more cohesive structure, more explicit sex tips, and some virtuoso performances that will leave you wiggling your hindquarters. In the second film the talented Taormino provides hands-on coaching to porn star couples and helps them problem-solve as they strive to accommodate a beefy-size penis and achieve satisfying orgasms from anal penetration. Gorgeous sex toys, vibrators, threesomes, strap-ons, and dungeon accoutrements punctuate the action. Teaching by example, Taormino straps it on and delivers a flaming femme-on-femme scene.

Bend Over Boyfriend
dir. Shar Rednour and Jackie Strano
[Fatale Productions, 1999]

Bend Over Boyfriend 2
[directed and produced by S.I.R. Productions,1999]

Dyke pornographers Jackie Strano and Shar Rednour burst onto the porn scene, directing a flick for straight and bi women with male lovers—a primer for chicks with dicks with wanna-be anally receptive boyfriends. This follow-up sequel, *BOB 2*, offers "more rockin' and less talkin'"—though it certainly delivers plenty of applied information. The directors elicit some truly inspired performances and scalding dirty talk from the real-life couples in the four vignettes. Standout scenes include a cross-dressing cop who gets dressed down and properly penetrated by a working girl packing her own kind of heat. And a sweaty pony boy bucks ecstatically under the gentle hand of his sexually loquacious "trainer."

Bottom line: When will we see *Bend Over Girlfriend*?

San Francisco Lesbians #7
[Pleasure Productions, 1999]

This garage-porn compilation of dyke-sex vignettes includes the hottest dyke anal scene I've come across. Two real-life lovers don gay-boy drag and play out a searing role-play that culminates in a truly inspired anal scene. The scene is arousingly authentic and the chemistry between the women palpable. Their incendiary dirty talk keeps them in a lather and serves as a model for good communication during anal play.

Nina Hartley's Guide to Anal Sex
[Adam and Eve Productions, 1996]

Nina Hartley's bright-eyed and down-to-earth exposition of anal pleasure for women and men (and her exquisite heart-shaped ass!) make this a classic anal sex instructional. Nina—whom you'll recognize from the pages of *On Our Backs*—is a registered nurse, porn star, and advice-column writer. She's the teacher you never had in school. The convivial demonstrations with her two male and one female models teach tips for communication and a range of techniques to try.

SEVEN

LOVE HURTS:
BDSM AND LEATHER SEX

Opening the Doors to Divine Pleasure

by Cléo Dubois with Neo

It all started when a sweet boy named Barry called me from his sling. "Hey, lady, come over here and fist me. You have small hands…"

I fell in love with leathermen's sex rituals at the Catacombs, the now infamous gay men's S/M club that thrived in San Francisco during the '80s. I remember the first time I fisted someone. I stopped in the middle, feeling squeamish at the intensity of the act, then went back for more. The next Saturday night I got fisted for the first time. Surrounded by a family of queer men having intense leather sex, I came, cried, laughed, and screamed, "I am home!"

I used to be quite happy with my straight, vanilla sexuality. If you had asked me about my fantasies, I would have said I didn't have any—I simply followed my bliss. But one fateful Saturday night that bliss led me to a private play party, where spread-eagle on the pool table and bound with scarlet rope, a young blond woman was dis-

> **During my first bottoming date with a powerful butch top, I was able to reclaim my inner little girl. Oh, how scared and excited that little girl was, kneeling blindfolded in front of *her*, a top in chaps!**

played as an appetizing centerpiece. She wore a big smile on one set of lips and green grapes spilling profusely out of the other. Dared by my friend to taste them, right there I had a juicy introduction to playing with women in bondage.

BDSM and fisting changed my erotic landscape. I finally understood I could take charge, and get what I wanted, without being manipulative. And because I knew my boundaries would be respected, I could also give up control. Now I realize that during these early cathartic experiences my consciousness expanded. I got in touch with my archetypes. Everything about me connected, sexually and spiritually. I filled in the dots between explosive orgasms and being in goddess space. I understood that slut and goddess are not opposite, but on the same continuum. I am Kali's servant and feel her fire in my sadistic pursuits. When I am in sync with my bottom, as I am whipping, caning, or piercing, I feel a shift of energy. My skin and the air in the room become electric. As I hold the space and step aside of my ego space, I let my Kali archetype guide me to provide the grandest possible experience for my bottom. And I'm taken along on the ride, because that's how energy works.

During my first bottoming date with a powerful butch top, I was able to reclaim my inner little girl. Oh, how scared and excited that little girl was, kneeling blindfolded in front of *her,* a top in chaps! Her face was covered with a leather mask. Only her eyes and short, cropped hair were visible. I was intimidated and excited and wondered what she would do to me.

My fear and my excitement became one. The more turned-on I was, the more embarrassed I became. Her hands knew just exactly how to caress my breasts and my cunt. I begged for her whipping and spanking and truly melted in her hands.

That top opened a door that to this day hasn't closed. Over the years there have been countless hot times with other women, butch and femme, lesbian and bi. The enduring friendships I made with some of the women I played with carried me through the plague of AIDS that was just around the corner.

We need pleasure so big that it connects us to the divine. That pleasure I have found in the erotic rituals we call S/M play. Intense sensations experienced in trust and respect can open the door to our inner spaces. There our spirit soars.

Perhaps, like me in 1980, you don't have fantasies. But if you dare to venture on the dark side of eros you may find insights, healing, and joy you never expected. Transcendent sexuality is about exploring our fantasies, opening up to more energy, more love, deeper knowledge of ourselves, our lovers, our truths. My boi is a whole generation younger than I am. And she too has experienced transformation through sex. I asked her to share her experiences for this essay.

I wasn't attracted to femmes when I became Cléo's boi, which made it less intimidat-ing to play with her, because I felt impenetrable. But as we played, I had Oedipal fan-tasies. I felt like a young boy wanting sex with his mother, as a symbolic way of crawl-ing back into the womb. I found it disturbing and tried to ignore it. I didn't know how to accept or explain my attraction to her. Then one night she was paddling me, and

121

the intensity was making me high, and I started rhythmically thrusting forward. I was sweating, muscles rigid, strength surging through me—and without even being touched sexually, I was fully aroused. I wanted to roar. I felt entirely male, in a way I never had before.

Being a boi is something I wasn't allowed to do growing up. Boys were allowed to play rough, get dirty, make noise, step outside the rules. They weren't expected to behave all the time. Girls were expected to be clean, pretty, quiet, calm, obedient. I didn't fit any of the norms, and I didn't know I could be anything else.

Before Cléo, I believed femmes could only be aesthetic tops, not "real" ones. Bound in corsets, precarious heels, and long fingernails, makeup running worse than my sweat—they might look scary, but that was all. It seemed to me that femmes merely exaggerated the traits I had refused to adopt. I might be a small butch, but at least I'm a butch. I thought that in the real world, butches were on top. That changed for me the first time Cléo bound me to a cross, whipped me until it rocked in its moorings, and dug her long fingernails into my back. I wasn't laughing. I was high, fast and hard, and knocked down off my pedestal. I learned respect.

My flavor had always been a butch top giving me a hard but simple beating, making me feel powerful. Cléo used her femininity to tease, torment, and manipulate me. She found my ticklish spots, she made me blush, she built up my ego, she knocked it down again until I screamed and begged. Her appearance cloaked how controlling and focused she really was. I felt like a clumsy, foolish little boy who had only been allowed to feel big and tough. And I enjoyed the lesson. Everyone has boundaries, but I have found that when I think I'll never do something, I have some exploring to do.

I was drawn to S/M and body ritual because I could play whatever roles felt right, pushing past socially imposed limits to the other side of my nature: externally sexual, acutely focused like a beam of light, fire to complement the water of my female internal sexuality. I found completion by facing duality. Being able to express both masculine and feminine energy made me comfortable with my body.

In a world where so many things are taboo, desires are nurtured and fears are confronted in cohesive safety. Facing fear and winning definitely changes me, every time. I'm able to explore my desires without being so afraid of emotional repercussions.

One hot summer day in a grassy meadow, I looped ropes through steel hooks in my chest and over the branch of a tree. I rocked back on my heels, skin stretched taut, and swung like a bird. Warmth and calm flooded me. I threw my head back, laughing, weightless, liquefying, dissolving into the earth. I felt deep inside myself and yet as if I had no body at all. Wind caressed my face, drumbeats throbbed like my heartbeat. I glanced at Cléo, flying beside me, and wondered if she was in the same place. It felt like everyone there that day had become part of the same big orb of energy and light. The truth is, it doesn't hurt, but you think it will, and unless you get over the fear, you never know. There is freedom in taking that leap.

Tie Her Up

by Rachel Venning

Ah, the taut pull of arms stretched just to their limit, the soft bite of a rope harness holding the vulva spread, the inescapable hug of coils wrapped securely around one's ankles. Rope bondage offers all the security of the more quotidian cuffs and shackles, plus a sensuous thrill that surpasses any other type of bondage. Whether you employ rope simply for binding wrists, or elaborately for decoration, rope has a unique feel. Bottoms will appreciate it and tops get an unparalleled chance to strut their stuff. Rope bondage divas make bondage as much an art as a kinky pleasure, but with a little practice even a beginner can easily make an elegant and secure knot.

> **Ah, the taut pull of arms stretched just to their limit, the soft bite of a rope harness holding the vulva spread, the inescapable hug of coils wrapped securely around one's ankles.**

Off to Homo Depot

A trip to the hardware store will provide you with a number of coil options. Solid nylon rope braid is good to start with. If it's bagged, flex it to confirm that it's soft and pliable. Get a 100-foot package of rope and cut it into smaller, more usable lengths. A good way to divide it is in into two 10-foot lengths, two 25-foot lengths, and one 30-foot length. To stop the ends from unraveling, wrap the tips with electrical tape. Color-code the tape to the length of rope and you'll always know which one to reach for. While you're at the hardware store, pick up some eyebolts. They can be very handy in converting your boudoir into a dungeon.

Boy Scouts, Anyone?

The Wrap is a clever and secure way to tie someone's wrists or ankles together with

124

a short spreader bar-type space in between the limbs. Have the bottom hold her fists about 8 inches apart. Drape the rope over the wrists so an equal amount hangs on either side. Bring the ends up and around the top of the wrists again, looping the rope on either side of the original loop. One end will be closer to the hands, the other closer to the elbows, five to six loops total. On the last loop, bring the ends up from the bottom at the middle of the looped rope. Bring them over the top and wrap them around the loops in opposite directions toward the wrists. It should be a smooth series of smaller loops, no crossing over. Stop about 1 inch from the wrist, and tuck the ends under the last loop to cinch the knot. The knot can be tightened or loosened by grabbing the center loops with both hands and twisting them in opposite directions.

Make a Plan

Bondage scenes are more fun if the top can move smoothly between activities without a lot of untying and rearranging. If you want to have penetrative sex, tying your bottom to a chair won't work, nor will tying her up with her clothes on—unless you are prepared to slice the clothes off as part of the fun. A relatively easy way to tie someone up for a variety of activities is to have her spread-eagle on the bed. The bed will support her weight, so there's less strain on the bottom, and in that position a lot of the body is exposed. All you need is a feather, an ice cube, some clothespins, and you're set for the evening.

Stay Safe and Sound

Talk to your partner and agree on desired activities and a safe word. The top should always be able to slip one finger (it's called the "pinkie test") between the ropes and

Learning the Ropes

For detailed knot how-to's, including diagrams, there are many good books. *Japanese Rope Bondage* by Midori is my favorite. Other useful titles include *SM101*, *The Erotic Bondage Handbook*, and *The Klutz Book of Knots*. Perhaps even better are the many Web sites devoted to knot-tying. They have animated graphics that make it easy to follow along as the knots are demonstrated. Start at www.knottyboys.com, make sure to check the macramé sites, and surf away. Bondage can be done with simple knots, so start from where you are (you can tie your shoes, right?) and have fun as you learn.

the skin of the bottom. It's important to avoid pressure on the joints, particularly on the wrists and ankles. Have safety scissors or a knife to cut the rope quickly for immediate release in the event of an emergency. A bottom can topple a chair if her feet are secured to it and she leans forward, so think before you tie. Broken noses are nasty scene-enders. If you are bound and you start to feel numbness or pain, tell your partner. Bottoms may become too high on endorphins or too tripped out on pleasing their partners to adequately monitor themselves, so tops should look for changes in skin color and feel for loss of warmth, not just ask if everything is OK. And rope bondage should never be used on necks.

Erotic Spanking

by Lolita Wolf

Spanking has always had a strong association with punishment. It was a way to instill basic "family values": Tanning a child's hide would teach him or her a lesson. But some of us get spanked just because it feels good. Do it the right way and it can give you and your partner much pleasure. The goal is not to hurt your partner but rather to give her an erotic and sensual experience.

Get Comfortable

You don't need any accessories or physical preparation for this activity, but it is a good idea to find a position that works for both of you. You will want to stay in this position for a while. Try sitting on the couch with your lover across your lap. Or I love what I call the "princess position," in which I pile all the pillows behind me on the bed and relax, propped up like royalty with my lover under my hand.

Pause during the spanking to caress her very softly or to use your fingernails to lightly scratch her. You'll be surprised at how sensitive her butt is after she's been spanked.

Enjoy the Intimacy

This is a different kind of closeness, and it's especially sensuous if you're both naked. Feel the weight of your partner's body, her skin texture, the way she breathes and moves. Hold her close to you with your nonspanking hand. This gives her a feeling of being protected and taken care of.

127

Start Slow With a Long Warm-Up

Rub her butt lightly. Take a lot of time and let her become accustomed to your touch.

Other Tips

• Try a little role-play scenario. Pretend to be a parent, baby-sitter, teacher, or nun, and act out a punishment spanking or a birthday spanking. Get into the fantasy of it and have fun.

• Control your environment. The room shouldn't be too cold. Set the lighting. Music can alter the whole scene: Madonna's "Hanky Panky" will set a very different mood than Gregorian chants. Add your own touches.

• Bruising. Sensuous spanking doesn't usually incur a lot of bruising, especially after a nice slow warm-up. But it can happen. Everybody's body responds differently. Apply ice or a cold pack after spanking to lessen the bruising. While cold is best in the first 24 hours, use heat after that. Keep her skin moisturized with some nice lotion. Arnica gel or ointment from the health food store also helps heal bruising.

• Never spank in anger. This is a fun activity for mutual pleasure. If you and your lover have a fight, spanking will not solve it. You need to sit down together and talk it out face to face as adults.

• Don't coerce you partner into doing this activity. Some people don't like it. It may not feel good physically, or it may push them to an emotionally dangerous space. Don't force it. Do something else instead. Or ask her to spank you! Some people like to spank, some like to get spanked, and others like it both ways.

Move to light pats and escalate slowly to slaps. If you take your time, your partner will adjust to the heavier sensations gradually. It's very important to build slowly so that your partner will interpret the spanking as pleasure, not pain.

Find Her Sweet spot
Everybody has an area that feels especially good. Mine is the lower half of my butt in the center. For me, spanking that spot vibrates straight through to jiggle my genitals. Some women like it higher or lower or even on the fronts or insides of their thighs. Explore and see what feels best to your partner. Spank around her sweet spot, and spank it directly.

Vary Your Spanks
Your hand is capable of imparting different sensations. A cupped hand feels completely different from a flat hand. Fingers apart gives a more stinging feeling than fingers together.

Striking with just the fingers gives more sting, whereas the whole hand gives more thud.

Vary the Stimulation
Pause during the spanking to caress her very softly or to use your fingernails to lightly scratch her. You'll be surprised at how sensitive her butt is after she's been spanked. Every feeling is now magnified. You might get a fun reaction: She may yelp or shudder or squirm.

Accessorize for Sensation!
Your hands are great, but try using some toys too. Drag some sensuous bunny fur or a pointy letter opener across her butt. Try spanking while wearing leather gloves or use a paddle. You may find that it's necessary, because your hand may get tired or your partner may want more than you can dish out with your bare hand. Everybody has different paddle preferences; see whether she likes leather, wood, rubber, or plastic. I like the fur-covered leather ones—they're very thuddy. You don't need to go to a fetish store and invest big money. See what you already have: a big wooden spoon, a spatula, a slipper, a hairbrush, or a Ping-Pong paddle! With my thuddy preference, I love those rubber flip-flops that are worn to the beach. Get creative!

Be Sensitive to Your Partner
Watch her body to see how she reacts. As you build up, her breathing is likely to change. She may wiggle or stiffen. She may moan. She may even break out into a sweat. Everybody reacts differently. If you aren't sure how to interpret her reactions, ask her what she's feeling. The same reaction from two different people may mean two different things, so don't assume.

Get a Rhythm Going
Once your partner is warmed up, get into a percussive groove. The beat (yes, that's a pun) should be determined by how your partners react. Many women can reach orgasm just from spanking. For others, it's good lovemaking all by itself.

Keep the Connection
Bask in the afterglow, both physical and emotional. Lots of cuddles and hugs. Or more sex! Spanking is a great foreplay to other activities like fucking, anal play, and fisting.

How to Play With Needles

by Lolita Wolf

When thinking of needles, most people remember going to the doctor and getting shots. Ick! The last thing that they want to do is play with needles. But once you get over that fear, playing with needles can be a lot of fun. Play piercing can give you a big endorphin rush. Just as long-distance runners experience a runner's high, using needles can leave you breathless!

Gather Your Tools
Most of these items are available at medical supply stores.

Sterile Needles: Any gauge between 21 and 26 is good (the higher the number, the thinner the needle). Thin needles like 23 or 25 are good for beginners. You don't want anything thinner because they'll bend or break. A good length is 1½ inches. In many states, needles aren't legal for purchase without a prescription; in that case, you can purchase them via mail order or from a local S/M product vendor.

Cleaning Supplies:
- providone-iodine (betadine) prep pads
- alcohol swabs
- benzalkonium chloride towelettes (individual packets of the above items are best to avoid cross-contamination)
- sharps container. This is for disposal of used needles. You can also use a plastic soda bottle with a cap. Always dispose of these containers properly. In most states, you can walk into any hospital and they'll take them from you with no questions asked. Never reuse needles and never try to recap them—that's how most needle sticks occur.
- a drop cloth or absorbent bed pad to protect the furniture. You probably won't have too much blood, but this protects any spills that may happen.
- latex gloves, paper towels, and a garbage can

Make Sure Your Environment Is Clean
Wipe down the surface of the play area and the table where you'll lay out your tools.

I like to lay out my needles, gloves, and cleaning supplies on a table covered with a layer of paper towels. While there are many positions for play piercing, I find it comfortable for my partner and me to sit in chairs facing each other so we can maintain eye contact.

Choose an Area to Pierce

Avoid the neck, face, hands, feet, joints, veins, and arteries. Pick a meaty area. A good place to start is the chest, so that you can face your partner. You can also pierce the back and the limbs.

Clean the Area You're Going to Pierce

Ask your partner if she's allergic to Betadine. Most people who are allergic to shellfish are allergic to it. If she is not, wipe the area with Betadine in the direction away from the area you wish to pierce and let the Betadine dry. Clean off the betadine with alcohol swabs, again wiping away from the piercing area. If your partner is allergic to betadine, then wipe the area clean with a benzalkonium chloride towelette. Throw away all used swabs and pads.

Now You're Ready to Pierce!

Unwrap the needles you've laid out on the paper towel. As you're ready to use each needle, separate it from the plastic sheath (which you can throw in the garbage). Hold the needle parallel to the skin. Do not stick them straight in! Make sure the beveled side is facing up toward you. Listen to your partner's breathing. I find it very spiritual to breathe along with her. While you both slowly exhale, slide the needle into the skin and back out. If you know anything about sewing, it's like basting. You don't want to go too deep—$\frac{1}{16}$ of an inch is enough. Most of the nerve endings are in the top layers of the skin.

Check In

As you continue along, check in with your partner to get feedback and to make sure that she is having a good time. Everyone feels things differently and has different needs. This kind of activity needs a lot of communication. Some people only need to take one or two needles to feel the endorphins. A set of eight needles is good for first-timers.

131

Make Pretty Patterns

Add more needles. You can make rows, circles, or just be creative. Just be careful that you don't stick yourself. Play with them. Try tapping the needles in the middle or at the hub (not the pointy end). Move the hub back and forth to twist the needles under the skin. These movements will create more sensations and produce more endorphins. You should still be wearing gloves.

Removing the Needles

The needles can stay in for 20 minutes or for a couple of hours. When you're ready, just slide out the needle and drop it into the sharps container. You can slide it out smoothly or twist it to create more sensation. Your partner may bleed a little. How much she bleeds will depend upon her body or if she has taken aspirin or drank a lot of caffeinated or alcoholic beverages, which thin the blood and promote more bleeding. Some people like to play with the blood or taste their own blood. You can too, if you both are fluid-bonded (meaning, you and your partner have agreed only to share bodily fluids with each other). Or just wipe up the blood with a benzalkonium chloride towelette.

After piercing, relax and enjoy the high. Drink some juice to replenish your energy.

Other Tips

• Use string. Lace some string or ribbon around the needles. This can look pretty. It can also act as bondage points. Gently pull on the string, which will tug the needles and create a different sensation. It's best to use lower-gauge (thicker needles) for these activities.

• It can be fun to pierce each other or to pierce two people and lace them together (not too close). Be very careful about cross-contamination of body fluids. Change gloves often.

• Another great way to learn how to pierce is to attend a workshop. Local S/M groups will often host an instructor, who'll give a demonstration. You may even get some hands-on practice with an experienced piercee before you try it out on your partner!

The Art of Cutting

by Rachel Venning

Are you a vampire fan? If the slash of rent flesh and the slow drip of blood make your cunt clench, add blood-play to your sexual repertoire. Whether it's the sensuous satisfaction of feeling your blade slice into the smooth flesh of your partner, or the tension and release of letting your lover penetrate you in this primal way, cutting can create intense energy and intimacy. If you're intrigued by blood and cutting, here are some tips to get you started.

Be Clean and Safe

Your first concern should be physical safety. Keep cuts shallow. Do not cut over any bones, joints, or tendons; avoid cutting on the neck or face. Stick to the back, upper arms, and chest or belly. If there is heavy bleeding or the flow does not slow down, call 911. To protect from infection, keep blades sterile; once you've opened the sterile blade, don't put it down or touch the blade to anything other than the skin. Lastly, the presence of blood increases the chances of transmitting blood-borne illnesses, so the cutter should take extra care to protect herself from exposure to blood—wear gloves and be careful not to nick yourself! Once gloves are donned, don't touch anything other than the blade.

Take Care of Each Other

Psychological safety is also important. Cutting is an intense experience, so negotiate. Any cutting, no matter how shallow, might scar. It's impossible to predict with certainty how permanently a cutting will scar. Given that the bottom may be living with the cutting for the rest of her life, it's important that she approve of the design. Have a safe word that will stop the action. If the cutting is a long one, the top should pay attention to the bottom's state of mind, because sometimes bottoms go into an unexpressive zone from which it becomes difficult for them to say that they need to stop. Check in with each other after the cutting; emotional repercussions can sometimes take a day or two. And if the experience was great, it'll be fun to congratulate each other on how hot you both are.

133

Choose the Right Tool for the Job

Knives make great props, but they're hard to sterilize, keep sharp, and control, so they aren't the best cutting implements. Razors and Exacto knives aren't sterile either. Scalpels are extremely sharp, come sterilized, and are your best choice. Moderate pressure can create a deep incision, so be careful.

Practice on Fruit

Cut soft plums or peaches, bananas, mangos, or very ripe tomatoes first to get a feel for your blade. Cut up as many as you want until you feel confident about how much pressure to use.

Disinfect

The person being cut should wash the area with antibacterial soap to remove sweat, dirt, perfume, etc. Before you cut, disinfect the skin with betadine or a similar surgical scrub. Clean skin outward in a spiral from the center of the area you're going to cut. No backtracking—that would just push the germs around without removing them. After disinfecting with betadine, tear open a fresh alcohol swab and wipe the entire area.

Cut Slow, Cut Shallow

Slowness gives control and allows both parties to savor the experience. It can take a moment for the blood to well up, so wait before assuming that your cut was too shallow. If the cut is shallower than you want it to be, you can cut again right away or at a later time. Never cut deeper than the bevel of the blade, which is about $\frac{1}{16}$ of an inch.

Fancy Designs

If you're ready for an elaborate cutting, draw it out first. It's hard to cut complicated designs freehand. You can draw directly on the skin with a surgical pen (available from a medical supply company) or draw with a nontoxic pen on transfer paper. Wet the skin, then press the drawing down to transfer it. Clean as usual. This may take a few tries before you get it to work. If you've never done a transfer before, practice before the big cutting. Ink that gets in the cut could cause a faint tattoo effect, so think it through first!

Straight Lines Are the Easiest to Cut

Visions of curlicues may be dancing in your head, but remember that the marks may be permanent, and no one wants a sloppy doodle as a perpetual adornment. Straight lines look dramatic and inspire fewer regrets.

Take Care of the Wound

Wash the cut and use antibacterial ointment and bandages to keep it clean. If you want a permanent scar, it may help to pick the scab, but do not fiddle with it so much that it gets infected. If you loved the cutting, you can do it again. Happily, skin is a renewable resource.

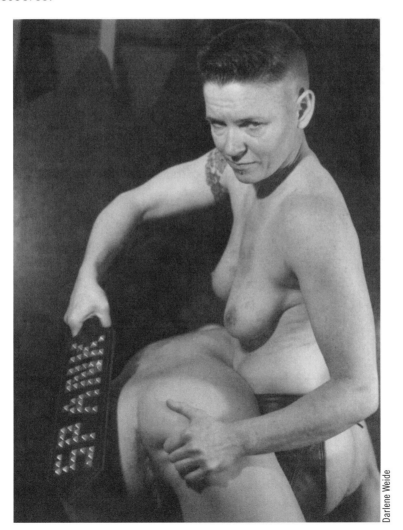

Darlene Weide

135

Playing With Fire

by Deborah Addington

Fags and drags don't have the monopoly on flaming. Females have long been labeled volatile—even combustible. Taboos are hot—and aren't we taught that playing with fire is dangerous and taboo? Fire is hot; it's the embodiment of passion and a thing of power with a life of its own. It must be treated with absolute respect.

What in blue blazes am I babbling about? Fire play, or flash-and-burn. Putting flammable liquid on skin, lighting it, and allowing it to burn—bright, blue, and briefly. We're not talkin' the human torch or anything—just people who have the hots for each other, some household items, common sense, and the following suggestions. As with any other intense activity, I recommend trying this on yourself before sharing your burning desire. Also, please read the instructions several times before starting, and practice on skinless chicken breasts before trying the real thing. You're playing with fire here!

Assemble Your Ingredients
You'll need:
- a fairly large bowl/bucket/pan of water
- isopropyl (rubbing) alcohol
- squirt bottles for alcohol and water (I prefer to use a squirt bottle for applying alcohol to cotton balls; you can also loosen the lid a little, using the bottle as a dispenser)
- cotton balls or pads
- an incendiary device that can be used with one hand (Note: Matches and candles should be avoided because they take two hands. Also, avoid refillable lighters of all types. They use naptha or butane—both extremely flammable—and make for potential minibombs in the presence of open flame. Bic types work well; the trigger-handled ones are nice and easier to control. They also keep the flamer's hand—which might just have some residual alcohol on it—away from the source of ignition.)
- clean towels and cloths, both wet and dry
- fire extinguisher (this isn't necessary, but you might as well)
- her

Prepare Your Tender Tinder

Burning hair smells...interesting. If you savor that scent, don't shave her. If your partner is too hirsute, shaving easily translates into foreplay. For some, just the sight of a straight razor elicits a cunt clench. Razor burn doesn't count as fire play, but it *does* count as open skin. Open skin means bodily fluids, which mandates protection. Besides, have you ever put alcohol in an open wound (on yourself and on purpose, anyway?). If she's prone to shaving reactions, use a depilatory cream to get her fur free. Make certain to remove all of the cream with soap and water. A nice warm shower or bath makes for thorough cleanliness and a soothing, intimate transition from the business of denuding your darling to getting down to business. While she's naked and wet, check for any open skin, cuts, scratches, abrasions, or bruises; those areas shouldn't be burned.

Prepare Fire Protection

Use rolled wet towels as firewalls, protecting hands, feet, face, and any other non-smoking area. Cunts and ass cheeks are fun to play with because they're soooo sensitive, but take extra care to extinguish *quickly*, especially where there are folds of skin. As long as you avoid open skin, it's OK to flame over tattoos. Avoid piercings; the metal may heat up and cause invisible but serious burns. Bellies, breasts, and backs? Sublime.

Think Fast

Get ready to act swiftly; alcohol evaporates *fast*. You have to follow all the steps outlined below—apply the alcohol, wipe any excess off of your hand, grab a lighter, torch your "pyromour," and extinguish her flaming flesh—all within a matter of seconds. Practice makes perfect; as mentioned above, hone your technique on some skinless chicken breasts. OK, here goes:

1. Put alcohol on a cotton ball. It should be saturated, not dripping.

2. Use it to draw a line, dot, your initials—whatever you feel competent with—on your flamee's body. Start small and work up. The more intricate the design, the harder it is to control the flame. You'll know when there's enough on her; it should look shiny-wet, not dripping. Use a damp cloth to erase any alcohol that went outside the lines and give your hand a quick wipe with a clean rag.

3. Light from the bottom of the design and watch the flame run, or light it toward the

center and watch her come alight. Either way, the flame should only be allowed to burn for an instant.

4. To cease the sizzle, follow the flame with your hand or damp cloth, putting the fire out well before it can do damage.

Cool Her Down

Ice cubes on freshly flame-kissed skin produce a delectably intense sensation. So will a mist of cool water, to a lesser degree. Try putting on some more alcohol, but don't light it. Anything that has an effect on skin—minty stuff, warming lotions, astringents, etc.—will produce fascinating results.

Safety Tips

- **Never, ever** use cigarettes, aerosol propellants, oils, or booze; they burn too hot and are hard to control.
- Repeated burns in the same area can result in serious injuries, from blisters to third-degree burns. Aloe vera gels and sprays are good for minor burns; for any serious injuries, see a physician.
- The effects of flash-and-burn are more spectacular in low light, but give yourself enough illumination to work by.
- Kid's flame-retardant pajamas are great for the flaming enthusiast; cut them into useful sizes.
- Eliminate fire hazards by immediately putting all waste in a trash can with some water in it.
- **DANGER SIGNS:** Redness or inflammation that doesn't fade or gets worse within 24 hours; blisters; skin that oozes fluid of any type. Severe burns require immediate medical attention.
- Seeing yourself ablaze can be frightening; risks run from the minor embarrassment of having the piss scared out of you to cardiopulmonary distress. I've *heard* of one heart attack as a result of a fire scene, and that was hearsay. I suppose a heart attack is possible, but it's way the hell unlikely.
- Going to have sex later? Remember that latex, rubber, and other petroleum-based materials are not only flammable, they burn hot. Be sure to only use those *after* your fire scene.

Afterglow

When the heat of passion is spent, wrap her in something warm and cozy. Despite recent flames, she may have a chill from the evaporated alcohol and/or endorphin crash. Keep her warm, and give her water. Flash-and-burn doesn't mean a flash in the pan; this may be the moment to draw her into your fire.

Cunt Torture Class

by Annie Leigh

The erotic possibilities of pain multiply exponentially when applied to the genitals. Flogging someone across their bare ass is hot—but the ass is well-padded and can take a lot of abuse. Bringing a woman to the brink of orgasm by continuously flogging her pussy lips or the hood of her clit requires much more skill and care.

Because the genitals are so sensitive, activities such as piercing and clamping take on a whole new level of intensity. I've been pierced before. I've had needles in my back, even my breasts. My pain tolerance is very high. But there are some spots on my body that seem too soft, too easily yielding to stand up to that type of treatment. The thought of those very same clamps and needles applied to my tender pussy lips terrifies me.

It began with the glamorous curvy girl. She was fitted with a rope body harness that gently spread apart her cunt lips, pulling them away from her clit and exposing her most tender parts.

Of course, because it terrifies me, it also fascinates me. And gets me extremely hot. So I decided to face my fears by attending a workshop on cunt torture. If you are going to be terrified and horny at the same time, might as well do it where there are lots of potential partners around.

The workshop was led by a gorgeous dom and her high-femme lesbian partner. They looked like pornographic bookends. The dom explained to us that women become excited when their genitals are stimulated—even if that stimulation is painful. And that was precisely why cunt torture was so erotic. When you are pierced and clamped, you become aroused despite yourself. Despite the pain—or because of the pain.

The bottoms she demonstrated on were lined up behind a table. One was a tall and lithe redhead with legs that went on forever, obviously a dancer at one time. The second one was curvy and glamorous with a beautiful face and full lips, and the third

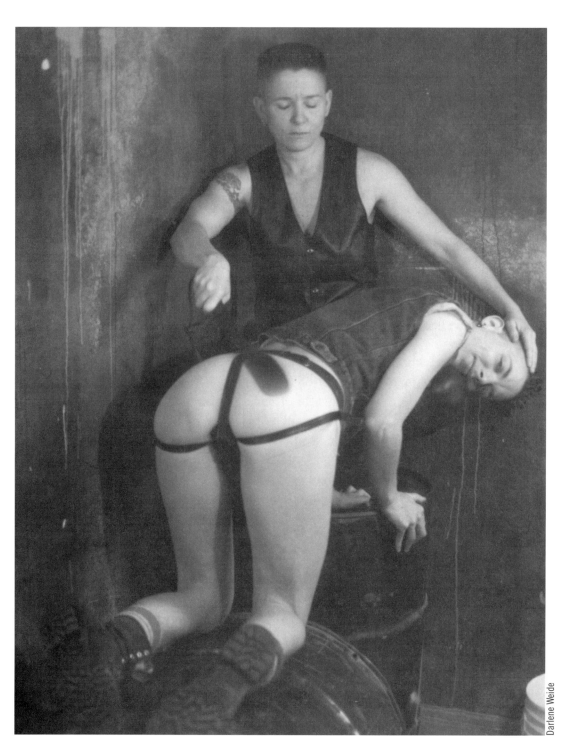

141

was tiny and vulnerable with small breasts and long blond hair. All three were naked.

It began with the glamorous curvy girl. She was fitted with a rope body harness that gently spread apart her cunt lips, pulling them away from her clit and exposing her most tender parts. After she pulled the harness tight, the dom poured Pop Rocks, that candy that pops and tingle when it hits your tongue, all over the girl's wet snatch. She was so juicy and aroused from being tied up that the rocks went off immediately, stinging and burning her in a delightful way. It was the cutest form of gyno torture I have ever seen.

The second willing victim was the former dancer. She had a naturally, delightfully submissive way about her. The top spread her legs and exposed her perfectly shaved pussy. The dancer winced prettily as the dom attached stainless steel medical clamps to her nipples and outer labia. Once she was sure the clamps were secure she threaded a length of bright pink nylon rope through the handles of the clamps and attached the ends to leather cuffs the girl wore on her wrists and ankles. Every time the girl moved any of her limbs it would pull on either her clamped pussy lips or her clamped nipples. And then, with a wicked gleam in her eye, the dom ordered her to get down from the table and crawl across the floor. The poor girl was led around the room on a leash, crawling slowly, each step pulling on her tender nipples and cunt lips. It was incredibly hot. My girlfriend, who up until this point had been bored, perked right up as she watched the pretty girl moan and gasp and slowly make her way around the room. The girl could only move very carefully. Tears welled up in the corners of her eyes, but her face looked radiant and sexy. She looked really turned on.

After her clamps were removed, a painful process in its own right, she was sent back to her spot behind the table and the thin blond girl was brought up.

According to the dom, the blond was a total pain slut. She could take all types of abuse and easily got off on it. First, the dom prepped her cunt lips by swabbing them with betadine. She then explained to us that she had designed a foam-core "butterfly board" to which she would be pinning the girl's tender inner labia, spreading them out like the wings of butterflies.

The board had a cunt-shaped hole in it and the dom pulled the girl's lips through the board and attached them to it with clamps. She then carefully pinned her labia to the board with 22-gauge needles. Three on each side. Every time a needle went through her flesh, the girl made a low guttural groaning sound. The whole audience was at attention. When all the needles were in place, as if they weren't painful enough, tiny thin candles were placed at the ends and lit so that the hot wax would drip onto her thighs and exposed cunt.

She was left there on display and the audience was invited to come up and study the technique and placement of the needles. The girl seemed happy to lie there, and she moaned nicely every time a drop of hot wax hit her skin.

When the last audience member had studied her perforated pussy lips, the needles were removed. She screeched as each one was pulled out and actually seemed very lightheaded after it was all over. Piercing is mind-altering, and I can only imagine how mind-altered she must have felt after having so many needles in such a delicate place.

I myself was pretty turned-on by the whole thing and quickly ran home for a little torture session of my own. But I'm not telling you what I did just yet. That's for a different column.

EIGHT

FUN AND GAMES:
FANTASY, FETISH, AND ROLES

Are You Into Role-Playing?

Readers Tell Us About Their Role-Playing Experiences
compiled by Diana Cage

Dressed to Kill
"When I dress up high-femme and go out, I feel like I am playing a role. I am performing, and I love it! I am very much into wearing corsets, garter belts, heels, feathers, and rhinestones, and playing the saucy, curvy, woman—to me this is a form of role-playing, but maybe not in the traditional BDSM sense." —*Carol*

Mile-High Club
"My partner and I are totally into role-playing. It makes sex so much fun. It started as a joke, but then we got so into it that we do it all the time now. She'll just look at me and say, 'Baby, let's pretend you're a flight attendant, and I'm a horny pilot,' and the next thing I know I'm ass up in the cockpit." —*Jo*

Licking Butch
"My wife and I have been together almost eight years, and when I want to spice things up, I put on my black lace teddy or corset and I become her 'mistress.' She is soft-butch and undeniably vanilla, yet when I kneel on the bed and demand a good 'boot licking' she becomes my whore. I love to shove my pussy in her face and tease her." —*Ann*

Body of Evidence
"I was photographed kissing a girl at a kissing booth, and it ended up being on the cover of the photographer's zine. About a week after it was published, my sweet butch daddy had a copy of the zine waiting for me to look at, so I could be sorry for what I'd done. She gave me a real good, bare-assed spanking for being such a whore and then a good fucking for being sorry about it!" —*Fifi*

147

Seriously Stiff
"My girlfriend would like me to role-play with her, but I can't take it seriously and I always laugh or break character at inappropriate times. I really would like to get into it to make her happy, but I inevitably end up feeling stupid." —*Samantha*

Office Romance

"The fun starts when the 'mistress' of the escort agency I work for calls me at home and informs me of my assignment. I'm told what role to play at that moment and what time my 'date' expects me. I've been everything from a business exec taking a client out for lunch to a doctor making a house call. My lady and I have made use of every piece of furniture in her office and a locked box of toys is kept in the bottom drawer of her desk. —*Dani*

Oh, Goddess, Fuck Me

"Do we like to role-play? Oh, goddess, yes! We have several different fantasies we play out. Sometimes I'm a big, bad, dyke cop, and she's the stripper I'm pumping for information. Or I'm a sacred whore in a Temple of the Goddess and she's a novice come to me for training in the arts of loving women." —*Delila*

148

Phyllis Christopher

Please, Daddy

Dyke Daddies Tell Us How to Get Them Off
by TJ Michels

Pleasing a daddy is hot, taboo-breaking fun made more deliciously perverse by its forbidden nature. Daddy play explicitly calls for trust, consent, and an erotically charged exchange of power.

Dyke daddies are often stereotyped as motorcycle-riding, chaps-and-boot-wearing butches (and that's certainly not a bad thing!), but we all know it takes more than image to make a bottom obey. Daddies must be convincing in their roles in order to be perceived and respected as such by their partners. Dyke daddies can be abusive, nurturing, or a little bit of both, but a good daddy must know a partner's limit…in order to push her just over the edge of it.

On Our Backs rounded up a group of hot daddies to find out what makes their dicks hard. And in exchange we learned to say "please" and "thank you, sir."

The scenes I do most often aren't structured fantasies; they're more intimate and fluid. They involve a lot of kissing, hitting, biting, slapping, spanking, fucking— cunt and ass—cocksucking, and various toys.

On Our Backs: **Tell us about your favorite plaything.**

Vick Germany: They can be submissives, masochists, high femmes, princesses, daddy's girls, etc., just as long as they are femmes. Hot, sexy, confident—they make my dick hard! "Sir" or "Master" are always lurking around and can become my main persona given the right set of circumstances.

150

angel: Mostly I play with bois, but I get the urge for special grrls now and again. I guess the truth is I will play with most anyone who knows what they want and is willing to work to get it.

Griffey: It's pretty broad—as long as you're queer. I've played with an FTM and I've had a crush on an MTF. I'm a top, but I've also explored sub space. To be a good daddy you have to know what it's like to bottom. And I've got my own masochist side too.

Jai Malaquaya: I play with boys, girls, and some who don't know who they are yet. Although I identify as a dyke, I still like to fuck, beat, and love on bio gay boys. (If they're smooth, hairless, and submissive as hell.) I'm uncomfortable with "butch," but it's applied to me more than any other term. I'm still very much a woman, but I'll never be a femme.

***OOB:* The first image I had of daddies was Tom of Finland's leathermen. What influenced your daddy style?**

JM: I learned what I know from Jeff Tucker, International Mr. Leather, 1994. And by flying by the seat of my pants: I watched a lot of scenes and relationships around me. I used all the top training I got as a "pup," I used my intuition, I used my gut instincts, I used my heart and my head.

Chase Pearce: I've been influenced by the screen daddies of the '50s and '60s like Hugh Beaumont, John Wayne in *The Quiet Man,* and James Dean in *Giant.* Also Jean-Luc Picard, "Daddy" of the Starship Enterprise.

angel: Mmm…Tom of Finland daddies. Also the ones in Pat Califia's *Doing It for Daddy*—every last one. Especially the priest. Yum. I'm mostly happy in my female body but definitely identified with my cock.

Griffey: I don't have an archetype. But if I ever spot someone that I want to be *my* daddy, that'd be it!

151

***OOB:* Do hunter-green hankies really work? How do you cruise or pick up potential play partners?**

VG: I've met most of my play partners either through the Exiles [a leather group] or through friends. That way I generally know that they're perverts and we probably have something in common!

CP: Leather is an excellent magnet. I flag as a daddy and add a red hanky to the left as well. My daddy attire is black button-fly Levi's, packing my favorite dick, black Doc Martens, a white button-down shirt, black tie, and leather vest. I also accessorize with a buck knife and leather wristbands.

OOB: And then what? To the dungeon? A rest room stall? The bedroom? Are there formal negotiations?

angel: Alleys, train tunnels, sex clubs, and a few times a year, the fancy dungeon. I don't have tea-party manners, so the fancier occasions tend to make me want to do something that borders on inappropriate. Some people need a lot of rules and protocol; I get off on being an outlaw. There's a mantra I like better: "risk-aware consensual kink." S/M is not safe, traditionally speaking, because people get hurt—that's the point. But consent is key. I don't have a formal process, but I do communicate. If I'm going to flog someone at a party, there's less negotiation needed than if I'm going to pierce someone multiple times and then set them on fire.

Kris L. Fetish: With a new person, it's essential to learn their boundaries. I love edge play but only if I know where that edge is. I prefer to play at home because I have access to all of my toys. But I'm certainly not above public sex—I like quick anonymous fucks in bathrooms and alleys, but they don't usually involve pain play. Just hot, dominant sex.

OOB: So what sorts of wicked scenes do you enjoy?

CP: I tend toward whimsy when I play. One of my favorite scenes was Daddy Mickey and Minnie Mouse, complete with ears and mouse hands. I made my girl sing the Mickey Mouse Club song while I was flogging her. She had to sing it correctly or face punishment. The punishment? Hot wax. For some reason she kept messing up the song.

152

KLF: I like to use different forms of torture: whips, floggers, belts, blades, etc. I also enjoy the dynamic in "rape" and "pedophile" scenes and the exchange of power they involve.

VG: The scenes I do most often aren't structured fantasies; they're more intimate and fluid. They involve a lot of kissing, hitting, biting, slapping, spanking, fucking—cunt and ass—cock sucking, and various toys, such as floggers, canes, paddles, zippers, nipple clamps—and coming.

OOB: Speaking of toys, what devious devices make Daddy the happiest?

CP: I have a dungeon in my home, with a St. Andrews Cross and a spanking bench. My personal favorite is my strap-on 8-inch dick. I have a small collection of knives that I love to use to cut skin.

JM: My mind. I use it more often than whips or restraints or paddles. It's fun to create that energy where my girl is scared and wet at the same time. I like it when I can create that in her without even touching her.

angel: My single tail, my violet wand, my blade, my teeth, my voice.

Griffey: Really sweet handcuffs with the red fur inside. But I also think mental restraints are more effective than physical restraints. It's the best way to discipline somebody.

OOB: And power? Is that the ultimate name of the game?

angel: Power may be part of it, but it feels more complex. I think I'm just wired this way. I can't explain why my hand wrapped around someone's throat always makes my dick hard.

Griffey: Power definitely gets me off. And knowing that a person is working really hard to please me.

OOB: Who's really in charge?

angel: Nobody. Everybody.

KLF: Top runs the scene; bottom controls how far it goes. "In charge" is a moot point. It's mutual.

VG: The bottom.

OOB: And do daddies need a little daddy-ing every now and then?

KLF: Not daddy-ing, per se, but a little affection and support feels good sometimes.

CP: Exploring a daddy-to-daddy connection would be hot.

Griffey: Yes!

About the Daddies

Vick Germany is a 45-year-old daddy, butch top, and San Francisco's Dyke Daddy 2002. "I've been a self-identified daddy for a couple of years," Vick says, "but in retrospect, I have been a daddy for far longer."

angel is a 29-year-old gender-freaked nelly faggot switch. angel adds, "I have been a top for nearly nine years, and playing with daddy stuff for about three and change."

Griffey is a 21-year-old trans man who primarily dates lesbians but has started dating gay men. "It's something I've wanted to do for a long time," Griffey explains. "In the last year and a half, I've been able to play that out."

Kris L. Fetish is a 26-year-old daddy. "I've identified as a daddy spiritually forever; in actual and mutual practice, about a year."

Jai Malaquaya is a 46-year-old fag in a woman's body. "Been a daddy for three years," Jai says. "Before that, I identified as a ma'am and a top."

Chase Pearce is a 50-year-old daddy. "I've been involved in the leather community for 16 years," says Chase. "The last six years I've identified as a daddy."

Role-Playing for Everyone

by JoAnn Loulan

Everyone has an idea of role-playing. It's passé, it's au courant, it's scary, it's weird, it's only for S/M players, it's…it's…it's… Well, as usual, not everyone agrees with, nor does everyone understand, this kind of sexual play. It's not for everybody, but it is between two consenting adults, and it's fun for lots of people.

What makes role-playing seem scary is the same thing that makes it so attractive: the power differential. Power difference is everyone's taboo and everyone's attraction. We're not supposed to have sex with people who don't match us, either by class, age, affiliation, or race. In real life there are lots of reasons why people who have a power difference between them can get in trouble with sex (e.g., Bill and Monica). The big reason is because no matter what, the person with less power has fewer choices. But we have fantasies *because* doing it isn't what we want to do in real life. Role-playing makes us wet because it's between two adults who agree to pretend they're someone they're not.

The roles are endless. The main thing is to pick ones that are fun for you both—so ask your baby what she'd like. Here are a few:

mistress/maid
president/intern
warden/prisoner
daddy/daddy's boy or girl
teacher/student
master or mistress/yard boy
baby-sitter/kids
neighbor/girl next door
prostitute/client
boss/subordinate
bikini salesperson/customer
doctor/patient
wife/husband

155

Pick a Role

OK, choose one from the list above or make one up. So who's going to be who? Choose or flip a coin. Let's try "mistress/maid."

Pick a Top

Who's going to be the top? There's always plenty of juice for the obvious top: The police officer tells the woman she's stopped for a traffic violation that she has to give her a blow job to avoid a ticket, for example. For our scenario, let's have the maid be the top.

Dress for the Occasion

Costumes are quite helpful. Some like to dress each other, some like to get dressed separately and move into the fantasy while they are getting dressed. The maid has no blouse,

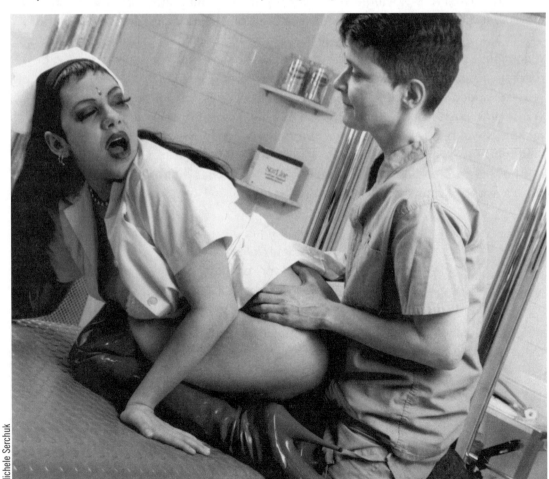

or a dress that's easy to remove; the mistress is in her nightgown or her fancy party dress.

Get the Scenario Straight
There needs to be a reason why the two are alone together. Here's an example: The mistress's husband has flown to Paris for the week, and the maid takes this opportunity to speak with her alone. Or the maid has waited for the mistress to come home while the rest of the household has gone to the ski lodge. The mistress wants someone to boss her around for a while, and it's not going to be her husband.

Start the Fun
Mistress begs the maid to forgive her for her class transgressions. The maid says it will cost her, so mistress pulls out her wallet. The maid says, "Not that way—you have to work for your redemption." Mistress says she'll do anything for the hot and exciting maid. "I see," says the maid.

Get Busy
Now the physical action begins, but don't forget: With role-playing, sex is just a part of the turn-on. Both parties must always be sucking energy from the power trip between them. The maid lays her mistress down on the bed and slowly strips her of all clothes. She also tells the mistress she'll tell the mistress's husband if she reveals any of this. The maid wants to continue to establish her control of the situation.

Stay in Character
The turn-on is heightened if neither person loses her role. If the phone rings, the mistress must ask to answer it. If the maid needs to pee, she tells the mistress to lie there and not move.

Improvise
The sex play continues to include whatever ideas and activities come to mind or body. The natural experience of these two characters is always part of the play, and they end the scene by going back to where they came from.

157

Plan the Next Time While in Character
Don't break character for the final scene. The maid has to pick up the children, the mistress's family returns, the maid has to go to her next job—it all keeps the sexual suspense going! The two plan to meet next Saturday night when the rest of the family is visiting their favorite aunt. The ideas are endless; the fun goes on and on.

Fuck Me, Jesus

by Michelle Tea

The whole idea came about because sometimes, when I'm being fucked really good, I start hollering "Jesus Jesus Jesus!" and my girl got the idea that perhaps she could actually be Jesus, so we set about preparing for the most elaborate role-play of our sexual careers: Jesus and Mary Magdalene. Sexy, perverted, and blasphemous—a thrill to top any of the run-of-the-mill power-imbalance sex-plays we're so fond of. Kassy, my partner in sacrilege, went to work cruising the Bible for info concerning Jesus' relationship with his famed consort. Incidentally, she didn't find anything in the scriptures that said what we were about to do was wrong. It does say not to take the guy's name in vain, but there is no prohibition against assuming his identity for sex games with your girlfriend.

"We whores know about you Christians," I murmured, sliding Christ's cock from his flares and slipping it inside. "You all touch each other when the women aren't around, don't you?"

I went to work attempting to transform my bedroom into the ancient temple where sacred harlot Magdalene pleasured her visitors. This was basically impossible. I'm sure the holy sex cathedrals of the Goddess were not littered with empty Budweiser bottles, dirty panties, and torn notebooks. I cleaned up as best I could, then lit a million sticks of incense, hoping to simply blot out the mess with clouds of spicy smoke. Next, I had to cook. Those ancient brothels weren't the wham-bam-thank-you-ma'am cathouses of today; the johns expected a meal on top of everything else. I cook about as often as I clean, so this whole scene was feeling ever more exotic, which I guess was appropriate. Should you like to try out this game with your own loved one, let me suggest the meal I prepared: grilled artichokes (buy them that way—don't actually grill them, silly!), dried olives, slabs of feta, dolmas from a can, and good, old-fashioned lesbian hummus. I added figs, some grapes, and a chocolate cake, all arranged on a tray decorated with tiny plastic fruits from the dollar store. I brought the food into my room, which was just billowing with smoke from the incense. There might have been an ancient temple under all that smog—who could tell?

Costumes were the next challenge. Kassy was locked in the bathroom, trying to dress like Jesus without looking like a dumb hippie. Caftans were unacceptable, we had agreed—same with the long, stringy hairdo and goat's beard. She'd stolen a pair of white bell-bottom pants from her dad and was applying sideburns to her face with spirit gum. We decided the scene would take place before Jesus had gotten so holy that he let his looks go—back when he was a young, strapping carpenter who maintained his facial hair. I found a long skirt and a weird, paisley halter top that used to be part of a psychedelic '70s bathing suit. I applied lots of eyeliner and a shawl for my head. I looked like a girl dressed like a gypsy for Halloween, kind of Stevie Nicks–ish.

Jesus knocked at my door and I let him into my den of smoke. "Wow," he choked. His benevolent eyes watered. "Welcome, Jesus," I breathed huskily, and we both cracked up laughing. It all felt really Dungeons & Dragons, or Renaissance Faire. Kassy looked good, like a foxy boy with cool sideburns in a pair of flares. We started chugging wine to loosen reality's grip. I started feeding Jesus—olives from my palm, bunches of grapes dipped into his mouth. I took his dirty feet in my hands and dunked them in a bowl of warm water, rubbed the grime away. It was kicking in—the wine, the asphyxiating smoke, our roles. I removed the shawl from my head and dried his feet with my hair, bent over in sweet servitude, meticulously wiping every drop with my long tangles. Probably the original Magdalene didn't leave streaks of blue hair dye on Christ's feet, but we live in different times. I anointed him there with frankincense oil I'd bought at the health-food store, climbed onto him, and began to undulate like a biblical lap-dancer.

Not surprisingly, Jesus tried to save me. He talked to me about salvation while gently groping my tits, the food I had prepared for him sitting in his belly. Being an ex–women's studies major, I explained to him the ways of the Goddess, how I was serving her divine decree of pleasure, and chastised him for trying to stomp out her rule with his newfangled ascetic religious movement. Never had I engaged in such a scholarly sex scene, and my defiant whore-brain sent pulses of excellent heat to where Jesus's rubber cock pushed against my panties. I teased him about his fisherman buddies—what did they do all alone together for weeks at a time in the desert, getting

159

high off sleep deprivation, no women in sight? "We whores know about you Christians," I murmured, sliding Christ's cock from his flares and slipping it inside. "You all touch each other when the women aren't around, don't you?" And so our Jesus scene slowly morphed into an excellent fag-porn dirty talk, and Mary Magdalene fucked Jesus into such a state of divine bliss he swore he'd end his killjoy religious movement and return his flock to festive paganism. Coughing delicately from the excess of incense, we fell into an ancient sleep.

When I awoke in the morning, I found I had a horrible case of food poisoning from those canned dolmas and was comforted by Jesus as I barfed into the grape bowl.

Beyond the Cucumber

Fun With Food
by Tasha Savage

So you've watched *9½ Weeks* a hundred times, each time salivating over the now-famous food-sex scene. You've fantasized that it was you—not Mickey Rourke—who used cherries jubilee to make Kim Basinger beg. But every time you suggest a food frolic to your own Bahama mama, she shoots another icky bottle of pseudo-pineapple body oil in your direction. What to do? Here are 10 hints that will help you and your lover learn how to properly play with your food.

Shower First
Any artist knows that a clean canvas is the best place to begin. Whether you have a long, hot bath or a quickie cold shower doesn't matter as long as it puts you both in the mood. Get her lathered up and—unless you're just a spectator—make sure you join her.

Use the food as your tongue.
Take a canned peach that's dripping
with syrup and rub the concave part along her clit.

Play Wih Your Food
It sounds obvious, but a lot of women don't think beyond the clichés. (How many times have you been propositioned with whipped cream and chocolate syrup?) Some of the best fuck foods are canned peaches, orange popsicles, and halved pears. But you can have plenty of fun with other foods too. Pomegranates are sexy simply because they leave a pink remnant of your lovemaking. Kiwis—with their juicy and malleable insides and fuzzy exteriors—will give any girl a thrill. Basically, any food you find sensual and arousing will do, but you'll get bonus points from the missus by paying attention to texture, consistency, and taste.

161

Imagine You're Blind

Learn how to rely on the tactile senses instead of your sight. A blind person doesn't care what an avocado looks like, only what it tastes, feels, and smells like. Blindfold yourself or, at least, close your eyes until you can use your fingertips, your tongue, your skin, and your nose—not your eyes—to navigate her body buffet.

Slow Down

No matter how fast you're going, you're going too fast. Food fun is always best when it happens very slowly in the beginning. Tease, tease, tease and, when she can stand it no more, then you can please. Don't worry about making her beg.

Don't Be Afraid to Penetrate

Women can't live by stimulation alone. Green bananas (or their cousin, the plantain) make great dildos. Peel first, then turn the banana so it curves up. Hold firmly in the middle (it can be done) and slowly push it inside her. When done properly, the banana penetrates her, rubs her clit, and hits her G spot in one fell swoop. One banana is good for at least 10 minutes (unless she's a real thrasher), and green bananas won't break off or mush into tiny pieces. You can have fun digging out any remains too, and you can rub the inside of the banana peel across her breasts and make her swoon like a jungle banshee.

Remember the Clitoris

Going down is great when she's dressed like a fruit salad. But don't limit yourself to that. Use the food as your tongue. Take a canned peach that's dripping with syrup and rub the concave part along her clit. If you flip the peach over, the rougher edge simulates a woman's tongue. She feels better than if you were toiling away with your tongue, and you have enough distance to watch her body change as she gets aroused.

Think Cheap, Easy, and Healthy

No meat, no protein. Vegetarian fits most dykes' politics and their budgets, since most fruits can be picked up for less than a dollar at any grocery store (though discerning dykes might prefer an organic outlet). Plus, if you've forgotten your sex toys, you can always find one near the register. (Butterfinger bars are fun for penetration, while chomped wintergreen lifesavers spice up oral sex.)

She's Not a Lollipop

Sensual licking is great, but too much in one spot and she'll feel like she's being

162

attacked by the cat. Avoid food that doesn't come off easily (though sensual, honey is a no-no for novices), unless your girlfriend has nerves of steel.

Remember She Has Knees
Smearing juice on the backs of her knees will get you further than any kiss. Don't forget to suck pomegranate seeds from her navel, nibble marshmallows between her toes, or write "I love you" in coconut milk on her back.

Clean Up Quickly
You *might* like to wake up with matted hair and sticky thighs, but whenever you have fun with your grub it's best to clean up afterward. Finish the night with a tub for two and, if you've penetrated, make sure to clean really well down there. (Experts are out on whether you should douche; unless you're really worried, don't.)

DON'TS
• Don't use anything hard. Pretzels make great bedside snacks, but during sex use soft, rounded foods (especially your first time) and avoid acidic fruits (such as lemons).
• Don't play with cukes. There are plenty of good "why cucumbers are better than men" jokes, but experienced dykes know cucumbers are too big, too hard, and too bumpy. Plus, they have a waxy coat that's laden with pesticides. Yuck.
• Don't start right after dinner: An empty stomach isn't necessary, but try to nibble after a six-course meal and you won't last through to her first orgasm.
• Don't go to extremes: Frozen popsicles and melted caramel might not be right for her first time out. Start with cool foods and experiment with more adventurous items later.

NINE

SO MANY DYKES, SO LITTLE TIME: POLYAMORY, SEX PARTIES, AND THREE-WAYS

Beyond Monogamy

Six Women Explore Polyamory
by Deborah Addington

Like polyamory itself, this discussion is a collage of people, terms, lovers, concepts and practices. Polyamory runs the gamut from fuck-buddy facilitation to multiple committed partnerships. To simply define polyamory in detail would be to limit its scope; instead, we discussed how polyamory functions as a framework in which to evolve and create loving, healthy relationships. Each woman on this panel does poly differently, which is as it should be. No two persons' needs are identical, nor are their practices in getting needs met. Sex is not an ingredient in polyamory: It's the cake you get to eat after slaving in a hot kitchen.

Polyamory means there's more than enough of me, others, and all the good stuff to go around. It means a bountiful world, filled with everything I could possibly want.

How do you define polyamory? What are other key terms essential to the discussion of this intricate issue?

Alesia: Polyamory is the willingness to engage in responsible romantic or intimate relationships with more than one person at a time. It is distinguished from "cheating" in that honesty and communication among partners is essential.

April: Polyamory is the desire and ability to form multiple intimate relationships which remain open to any desired expression. I have a diverse collection of amazing arrangements and non-arrangements with my most intimate friends.

Jackie: I don't really like the word *polyamory* when discussing my sex and love life. I am a very emotionally monogamous person, so the word's semantics hold no water for me when defining my lust and libido. My partner and I are in a very deeply committed relationship with each other, very much each other's primary. We call ourselves nonmonogamous or, more tongue-in-cheek, we reclaim the word *swingers*.

Deborah: Polyamory means there's more than enough of me, others, and all the good stuff to go around. I'm not afraid that I won't get my share, take someone else's, or lose the good stuff I already have. It means a bountiful world, filled with everything I could possibly want, accessible to me at all times. Poly is the ultimate combo rush of personal empowerment and pleasure.

Janet: I'm not all that enthralled with the word *polyamory* as it's currently used—often it's used to mean only multipartner ongoing committed romantic relationships, and to exclude other valid relationship patterns such as fuck-buddy circles, casual sex, swinging, etc. Still, *poly* is the closest term to my own pattern, which is to try to be open to whatever relationship possibilities present themselves, from a lifelong love to an absolutely transcendent one-night stand.

Shar: *Polyamory*? I like the term all right, but it doesn't ring strong for me. It's not sharp enough. I inevitably use created words like *polylustfun, multisex,* or *multilust.* Recently, we've been using *swinger* even though it used to be heterosexist and referred mostly to wife-swappers. We're reclaiming that word for the sexual excursions we share, because they tend to be orgies dripped in indulgence with decadent paraphernalia strewn about.

The definition of polyamory seems tied by the common thread of having more than one significant source of intimacy, whether that intimacy is physical, emotional, mental, or "other." Why choose a high-maintenance arrangement like polyamory? What makes it worth the communication and effort required?

Janet: I rarely choose a simple path when a complex one will do. I think I just have a very low threshold for boredom. Why be intimate with only one person when you can be intimate with several, when you can experience the cerebral and emotional massage of being inside the barriers of two or more wonderful, exciting people (and having them inside yours)? I've been monogamous; I didn't like it.

Jackie: Polyamory is not high-maintenance to me. Yes, you must be emotionally accountable, present, honest, and extremely reverential, but for me that's the only way to live.

Shar: Poly does require effort, but no more than any relationship. The big difference is that the language and sympathies for poly are few. With monogamists, if a spouse cheats or jealousy occurs, it can be discussed in the lunchroom cafeteria as loud as you want. If you're poly, then it's all hushed tones spoken to blank, astonished faces. Being honestly monogamous would be a lie of spirit, putting my passion and life in a cage for no damn good reason. How could I not be poly? It's natural. People getting to be their true selves and really shine is worth the work.

April: What I find to be of higher maintenance is keeping a healthy relationship in general. An interesting contrast I've seen between monogamists and polyamorists is that the polyamorists I know are much more inclined to maintain healthy relationships. I find that the only really tough part of polyamory is being interested in someone who has difficulty seeing poly as valid, or someone who sees it as a possibility but requires a lot of emotional growth in order to achieve a healthy practice.

Deborah: Everyone else seems to think that poly isn't "high" maintenance. Hell, yes, it's more demanding, if in no other aspect than the quantity of people with whom I interact. If I wasn't poly, I'd probably have a lot more free time on my hands. Fucking might be something that "just happens," but polyamory is not.

Some things are sacred, be they the bed one shares with one's partner, personal space, a middle name, the toy collection, the words "I love you," or some other item of intimacy. What is sacred to you, to your partner(s), and why?

Alesia: In my life, the divine is a very personal, very intimate force, and It is constantly expressing Itself everywhere. I am sacred, an expression of divine power and love, and as such I have taken a vow to treat myself reverently in all things, not just love relationships. Those with whom I have engaged in relationship are in holy communion with me, and I with them—not only when we're soaking mattresses, either.

Deborah: My body is mine, and mine alone; I share it with whom I will. Stuff I put in my body is sacred; I have my toys and share toys. Beds are sacred, but my bed—

169

like my body—is my business. Promises are sacred. That's why I almost never make them. My word is my bond, and I don't give my word unless I'm as certain as possible that I can keep it. Other than that, all bets are on.

Jackie: The vows my wife and I said to each other when we got married—total self-knowledge, honesty, and certain sexual fantasies, practices, and positions—are sacred. S/M-type role-playing, communication, and negotiation skills come in handy to keep things in a very clear perspective when it comes to others. Of course, we're intimate with others and can be lovey-dovey and sweet, but there are places that don't have to be shared with every single person that waltzes into your life.

Shar: The first sacred thing that comes to mind is time. Our individual time and our time with each other is sacred. We no longer fuck just anyone. People who don't have their shit together, those who are messy or energy vampires can be a fantastic fuck and I don't care. I'm already married to the best fuck in the world, so that's not what appeals to me.

Janet: Some of our "only for each other" stuff is BDSM-ish; neither of us wears anyone else's collar, neither of us calls anyone else "mistress" or "master." Also, I have strong feelings about the specialness of sleeping together—by which I don't mean the euphemism for "fucking"; I mean actually sleeping together in the same bed. We don't do sleepovers: If we're in the same city, we sleep in the same bed.

Is jealousy a given in poly situations? When do you first notice the symptoms of jealousy? How do you deal with it?

Janet: Jealousy is always a sign; it tells that there's something about myself I don't believe is lovable, or something I believe I'm losing that I don't feel I can afford to lose. Same goes if I'm feeling deprived of something I believe I should have. How do I deal with it? I live with it. Who says I get to feel happy all the time? I do my best not to let it shred me or cause unfair problems to my partners or their relationships. Then, I live with it, and it usually goes away after a while.

170

Alesia: Jealousy is a given in any relationship situation. It isn't just a poly problem! If someone tries to tell you they have never and don't ever experience jealousy, they are either the next incarnation of Jesus Christ or they're trying to pull the wool over your eyes. To deal with jealousy, I go within, call the jealous feelings out on the carpet, and subject them to the third degree. If the answers indicate to me that I've got some healing work to do on myself, then it becomes my priority to deal with that.

Shar: Jealousy is absolutely not a given in poly situations. People generally don't work on jealousy because it's socially sanctioned, so why should they? I learned to be firm, direct in communication yet unafraid, to listen to emotions without me having to do anything about them. I learned how to be very specific in my communication and not make assumptions. I learned that it feels really good for someone to trust you and change and grow because they feel so secure.

Jackie: When I feel jealous about something I try to speak up right away, but I am self-aware enough and honest enough to know the right words to use instead of just acting out. If I feel I need more attention, I'll ask and clarify what kind of attention I need. I absolutely trust my wife 100%, and I know truly in my heart that she only wants the best for me and that she's totally devoted to me. That is a beautiful, blessed thing I never take for granted. I know she'll respond kindly and consider my feelings.

April: I recognize jealousy as being based in fear, and I work to find the fear that is creating that reaction. If one of us is not willing to resolve the fear, then it's time to renegotiate whether we want to be in a relationship any longer.

Any advice for the beginning polyamorist?

Alesia: For anyone considering a poly relationship: Get inside your own head and your own heart and figure out what it is *you* are bringing to your relationship(s). Be aware that with each relationship you enter and begin to nurture, you are in the sacred process of creation. Be able and willing to recognize your own emotions, issues, and feelings.

Shar: To the beginning polyamorist, I say stick to your guns, but don't let your freedom become a cage. I preach this one in our poly classes—make love, respect, and honesty your new holy trinity. Practice being honest with yourself and practice with others; say what you know and say what you don't know. Have a sense of humor and adventure.

April: Read *The Ethical Slut* and/or anything that will help in expanding your consciousness concerning the important aspects of practicing healthy polyamory, healthy relationships in general. Look into finding a supportive and healthy community of polys in your area, or create one.

Jackie: Be 100% true to yourself. Trust yourself. The right people will respond. Don't lower your standards just to get laid—fuck with true reverence even if you just met the person. Be the best person you can be and share the love!

The Participants

April Cooper lives in beautiful Northern California with her two children. She is currently employed as a training specialist for an Internet and e-commerce technical support outsourcing firm. She is Jewish, bisexual, kinky, modern-primitive, a sensualist, and an artist/writer.

Reverend Alesia Matson, of the Church of the New Renaissance, is a bi/poly/stealth-kinky femme who has sustained up to five intimate relationships at one time but currently maintains her het marriage and female lovers. Actively poly for 16 years, she and her husband founded their church to support individual spirituality and alternative lifestyles.

Janet Hardy is a bi poly switch. As "Catherine A. Liszt" and "Lady Green," she has authored or coauthored seven books about sexuality and BDSM; her latest (with Dossie Easton) is *When Someone You Love Is Kinky*. She is the mother of two young adult sons and the president of Greenery Press.

Deborah Addington is the author of *A Hand in the Bush: The Fine Art of Vaginal Fisting*; she also teaches, freelances, and writes poetry. She is queer and poly; identifies as a hard, high femme; and is sometimes referred to as "tall, dark, and perforated."

Jackie Strano is a butch dyke living in San Francisco. She fronts the Hail Marys, an all-dyke hard rock band, and operates S.I.R. Video Productions with her wife, Shar Rednour. Together they created the best-selling *Bend Over Boyfriend* series and the dyke porn *Hard Love & How to Fuck in High Heels*.

Shar Rednour is a femme dyke living in San Francisco. She is the author of *The Femme's Guide to the Universe* from Alyson Books. With Strano, she runs S.I.R. Video Productions.

Make It a Three-Way

by JoAnn Loulan

We tried everything in the '60s: LSD, hitchhiking, sex with lots of strangers. One of the things we tried was three-ways: three-way casual sex (my first real lesbian encounter); having a partner and some known or secret lover on the side; or even three women living solidly together. Today many women still have threesomes as part of their lively lives—some bring a lover into the couple for a night of fun and frolic, while others all sleep together in the same bed for years. All of these can work if you stay conscious and respectful, and have lots of energy. For the sake of clarity, this how-to is about how you can bring a third lover into your relationship with your girlfriend. It ain't easy, but love never is!

Chain, Chain, Change
After being in a relationship for a while, switching the dynamic can be hard. Is one of you already turned on by someone else? Or are the two of you together inviting a third into your bed? The latter is easier, at least in theory, but it's not a slam-dunk. Now would be a good time to reassure your girlfriend that you want to be with her no matter what.

Any Hidden Agendas?
Do you want to break up with your lover, and this is a way to do that? Or are you doing this to save your marriage? OK, we don't have to tell you this, but these are not great reasons to go into a three-way. Just like babies, threesomes take more work than two-somes. You'll need more trust, love, and honesty between you, not less.

Make the Rules
Obviously, there are no rules, but you'll need to set some to preserve everyone's sanity. Talk to your partner: Are each of you ever going to be alone with the third person? Will you each actually have two relationships? What kind of sex is going to go on? Are lovers outside the three-way OK? If this ends up being a long-term gig, you'll want to be fair about holidays, birthdays, and other important dates.

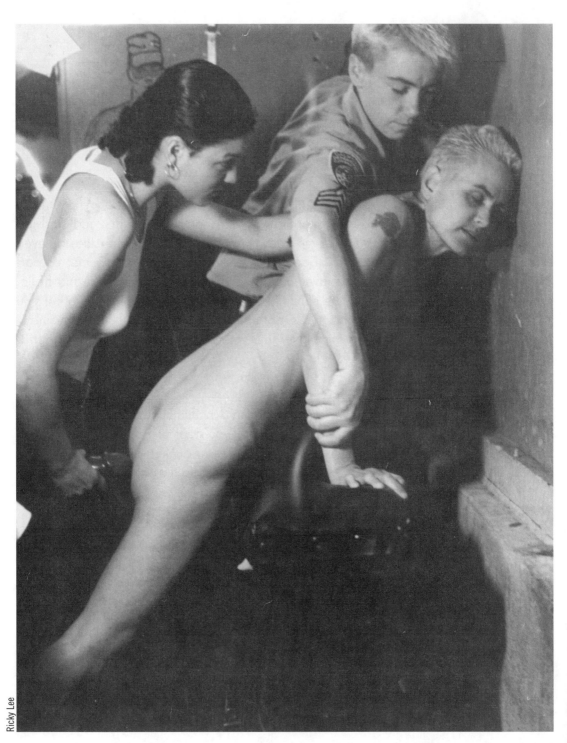

174

Pick a Third Woman
In the best-case scenario, you're both into the same woman. Whatever you do, don't say you're into someone you're not! That could be ugly, and it'll likely just get worse. If you haven't got a woman in mind, now is the time to go looking together.

Talk to Girl No. 3
Be absolutely clear and honest with the woman you're inviting into your relationship from the get-go. You need to tell her if she's going to have an equal part of the relationship, or if you want to keep your girlfriend as your "primary" relationship, with your threesome a "secondary" connection. If she has some hope of changing your mind, being jealous, or stealing you away from your girlfriend, it's best to find out now. If she's not into it, find someone who is.

How Do Ya Do It, Anyway?
Are two of you going to have sex while the other watches, or will there be lots of arms, fingers, and breasts moving and groping? You can watch while they do it, have both of them do you, or have someone watch while you get it done…it's really endless. Still, before you start, be clear about what's going to happen, at least for the first time, so there aren't as many hurt feelings. Try everything—who knows what you'll like!

Be Safe
Who knows who is doing who..is doing who…is doing who, and so forth. Invest in plenty of gloves and condoms. Change them often, and everyone needs to bring their sex toys, so you don't have to pass around one vibrator! Even if you're just spreading around a yeast infection, it can be a pain to get rid of.

Be Aware of Who's on Top
This isn't just about the sexual position, but the power difference between people involved. Does one have more power because she's the long-term lover, or because she's the new one, or because she has more money, or because she's a different class or race, or because there's a man involved, or because she has a child, or on and on? Discuss the possible power ideals, so when they come up everyone can say, "Uh…how do we fix it?"

No Means No
You can say no anytime—in the midst of sex; even though you said you would; even if your partner really wants to. You can even say no if you said yes and you meant

yes and you really want to...but it just doesn't feel right. And stopping—not necessarily for good, but at least to sort things out—is important, as feelings are crucial. A human heart is pretty special. Talk it out: Who needs what? Is it scary? What would make it work again? All of us just want to love and be loved—how can you make that work?

If You're the Third Woman

• Figure out your place in their lives. Ask questions, and ask for clarification. Don't assume until you hear it, and you still might want to check in periodically.

• Decide when and where you want to see them. Since they're the couple, they probably already have time they're both free; make sure it works for you. Do you want to see them more? Less? Speak up!

• Come out of the closet...or don't. When all your friends wonder who your secret lover is and you can't tell them, remember: You decided to do this, so be a grown-up—even though it's hard to do.

• Demand respect. If you're left out for the holidays, or you're at a public event and they don't acknowledge who you are, or you start to feel like a human sex toy, take some time out to think about what you need. Just because it's a three-way doesn't mean you can't get what you want!

How Was Your Threesome?

compiled by Yetta Howard

"I was playing Scrabble with a couple of friends, when we started to joke about the word 'fuck' as being on one of the triple-word scores. And then we weren't joking anymore. Two of us pulled off our third friend's clothes. One of us got her cunt, one of us got her ass. After we were finished with her, she fingered us both. Unfortunately, I ended up with a yeast infection because the same finger was used for both of us, not to mention that the Scrabble board was so badly dented afterward that we couldn't use it again. " —*Sabrina*

"In my first threesome, I was the proverbial third wheel. My two partners eventually ended up running off together and leaving me behind. And I still suspect they used to wait until they thought I was asleep, then have sex next to me, so that I wouldn't have to be involved! I'm almost relieved that we're no longer on speaking terms. " —*Jamie*

"Which one? There was the time I had done so much acid that I kept mistaking this guy's beard for a vagina and kept sticking my finger in it. Then there was the time when we were all drinking wine by a quarry. I thought it was going to be a threesome, and I began to kiss this girl's nipple. When I saw the look on my girlfriend's face, I realized that not only would there be no threesome, but I would also be traveling solo. Now I just photograph threesomes; it's much easier." —*Lee*

"My lover and I were both in the shower when we heard our third roommate come home. We jumped out of the shower and made her join us in a sordid sex game. We tied our roommate up to the toilet and made her watch us as we went back into the shower to fuck. This made her mad since she wanted to join us. We retied her to the base of the toilet and made her eat us both with her hands tied behind her back. " —*Vanda*

"It was our regular girlfriends' night: staying up late, watching movies, drinking wine. The conversation was sexy like it always was, but there was something slightly different.

At first I thought it was just the wine when my roommate Brianna's thigh pressed mine, but then Lynn's fingers were in my hair, pulling me toward her. It was perfect—the rest of the night was all sensation and soft flesh." —*Chris*

"I met this kinky married couple and started seeing them. At the time, I was recovering from a broken heart, so it worked really well—I could just step into a caring relationship. The sex was great, but my favorite part of being with them wasn't even about sex. I loved how we became a mini-family. I need a lot of attention, and with two people, I got it." —*Jenni*

"I was at an adult bookstore for the first time in my life when this girl asked me to go back to her place with her. When I got to the car, she said her lover was going to follow us. I freaked but thought, *Why not?* During the whole ride I was shaking to death, but when we got there the three of us sat down, talked, and then ravished one another. It was so good that I went back about 10 more times. I would still like to go back for more." —*Maria*

178

How to Throw a Sex Party

Rachel Venning

While many gay activists focus on the right to marry, let's not forget the right to forgo monogamy and madly pursue pleasure in all its forms. Forget about "It takes two to tango." Why dance with just one person when you can boogie with the entire ballroom? Why not take your sweetie and strut your stuff in a public playspace? Your sexy spark may inspire others, and their appreciation might be a turn-on you and your lover can share.

To experience group sex, threesomes, or the thrills of voyeurism and exhibitionism, a sex party is the place to go. As sex parties for lesbians can be hard to find, the easiest way to bring those scenes to life can be to throw the party yourself. Think about it as creating a sex-positive community, accepting one another's differences, and promoting safe sex. But also think about drenching the sheets, ogling the cuties, and taking that big bite of pussy pie.

Répondez S'il Vous Plaît

For the best party, invite everyone—especially the people you want to have sex with. Make some flyers and carry them around with you, and whenever you see someone interesting you can invite her. Give flyers to your friends to pass out too, and you'll have no trouble getting a crowd. And don't be caught sending invites the day before. Plan ahead.

Break the Ice

Get sexy greeters to welcome people at the door, give tours of the space, point out the equipment, and introduce them around. Having great food is important: Sex creates an appetite, and it's sexy to eat delicious stuff. A food area also gives people a place to congregate and something innocuous to talk about.

One possibility is to have some scheduled sex performances. If you do that, have breaks between the shows so people will have time to act on their inspiration. Set up a booth where a dom with a good arm will give spankings for a buck. If you create many opportunities for women to interact, you'll increase the chances of their finding someone new to play with.

Set the Scene

Make the space sensually appealing through dim lighting, sexy music, and good heating. Make sure there are good spots to have sex in. Folks throw sex parties in warehouses, basements, men's bathhouses—wherever they can find a space big enough that's willing to take the booking. Most of those places aren't designed for public sex, so you'll have to do some redecorating. Create horizontal spaces, because women like to lie down and roll around. Borrow dungeon equipment from local S/M clubs or enthusiasts you know. A few slings really set the mood.

It can help to create a room where no voyeurs are allowed and perhaps another where voyeurs are expressly welcomed. Ask local AIDS organizations for safe-sex supplies so there's plenty of latex and lube to go around. If there will be hot wax play, set up a space with floor coverings just for that purpose.

Have All the Supplies You'll Need

If you're charging for the party, you'll need a cash box with change as well as a reliable friend to be in charge of the door. Prepare some release forms and house rules. The release form is a release from liability and an acknowledgment that the house rules have been read. The rules should make clear your position on drugs and alcohol, safe sex, etc. (www.sexuality.org offers great suggestions on rules and releases). Other supplies you might need are plastic sheets, sharps containers, first-aid kits, and some good wall-to-wall porn if you've got a player available. Glow sticks for dungeon monitors are a nice touch; it makes them easy to identify.

It's My Party and I'll Fuck if I Want To

The hostess must have fun. Plan time to enjoy the party yourself. Get lots of friends and volunteers to share the work. If you have a door manager, a stage manager, a bunch of dungeon monitors, and an assistant to help with whatever comes up, you'll be prepared to enjoy yourself. Put a RESERVED sign on one of the slings and arrange a date.

House Party

If the party is at your home, you'll need to sex-proof your abode. Put away the pottery and hide the valuables. Remember that some women come in big gushing surges, so get plastic covers for the beds. Make sure the lighting is good (read: dim), and although you won't need an army of helpers for this party, get someone to DJ. A house party will be smaller, but it's also more likely to turn into an orgy.

Hotel California

by Michelle Tea

The Turquoise Desert Motel is located on a dusty side street in the worn heart of Hollywood, Calif. Its reputation gleefully precedes it: hustlers, whispers of crystal meth, mirrors on the ceiling, and muscle boys flexing on the walls. It wavers in the intense July heat, right across the street from a shitty little bar that, I'm told, the late Charles Bukowski used to get soused in. It looks right—this is the gritty landscape the writer's poems lived in: hetero alcoholica buttressed by a fagalicious fuck fortress. But tonight a different kind of action is going down at the Desert.

It's a big blur of rolling bodies and the silver flash of mirror everywhere. The boys are fingering me, so I lift Snowy's bedazzled half-slip and yank down her panties to give her the same treatment the boys are giving me.

The retro-raunch hotel has been invaded by hundreds of the freakiest, queerest artists the region can barf up. It's an 18-hour overnight party. Visual artists have been holed up in individual rooms and worked them into bizarre and enchanting environments. A stage erected by the murky swimming pool supports a steady stream of cabaret acts, with performances scheduled from dusk till dawn. Fabulous weirdos are everywhere—a couple of rowdy plushies, beers clutched in mittenous paws; a rouged and diapered adult baby, escaped from his playpen in the nursery room; a curvaceous knockout wearing nothing but pasties, sequined G-string, and orange feather-boa, walking carefully up the stairs in a pair of platforms, her eyes a-swirl.

I'm here with a tiny group of unbearably sexy kids. A tight quartet I've come to know intimately through some recent late-night spin-the-bottle parties. I know their mouths, and I know how far they'll go. Far. These kids are thrill-seekers. Chester's a rhinestone-eyed tranny with a handsome beard and a tight pair of pants. Snowy's a wild child, a chick out of *Go Ask Alice* who puts her eyeliner on in bed and makes you feel like hitchhiking in a pair of roller skates. The one with her hand on my ass is Kassy—she's mine. Shellacked pompadour shooting skyward like a klieg light, thrifted threads with labels like "Panhandle Slim" and "Rex Martin." We're hopped up on goofballs and looking for kicks. And it's happening all around us, right there on the stage as a glossed-up gang of hussies in vintage fringe and sparkle bump and grind their clothes away behind ostrich-feathered fans.

The vibe is sex, and the vibe is drugs. The 7-foot-tall drag queen presiding over the stage exhorts "Everybody have sex!" into the microphone, like these cats need any encouragement. The Jacuzzi is thick with faggots in sailor suits, jerking one another off beneath the bubbles. The rumor mill spit up an interesting morsel: A small cadre of drug dealers were invited, to keep spirits up and libidos raging till the sun cracks the sky. But that's a long time from now. My gang and I make the rounds, sleuthing out rooms with free hooch. We find one with a bunch of queens in caftans doling out freshly shaken martinis. They plop olives into our glasses with effusive smiles. There's more goodwill in this joint than the parking lot at a Dead show. Slurping our booze, we stalk past rooms holding amorphous disco ball creations that shoot Space Mountain trails onto the stucco ceiling. Toward the back of the courtyard we find a few rooms left undecorated and empty. A sign reading PLAY ROOM is hung above the door. We move inside and lock it up. I jam a chair under the doorknob just to be sure, and start laying out the drugs.

People on goofballs are real chatterboxes. In our talky haze, Kassy and Chester are actually brothers, Jimmy and Johnny. They're photographers with a lot of connections in Hollywood, they start talking like bigshots, like they can make Snowy and me stars. Snowy and I are seduced by their chatter: We wanna be stars. We tell them that we're underage, snuck out of our houses, and if the moms and dads found out we were shacked up at a hotel doing drugs with a bunch of fruits, it'd be off to boarding school for us. The brothers whip out cameras—cheap, disposable jobs, you'd think that would've tipped us off—and start snapping pictures of us, stretched out on the quilted motel bedcovers, rolling gooey, candy-flavored lip gloss onto our lips.

I don't remember which pervert suggested we start making out, but we do. Snowy's got the softest, most kissy girl-lips, and we both get carried away a little, eyes shut against the flash of the plastic cameras. Snowy's red lipstick is all over my face like cherry Kool-Aid. I feel hands coming at me, and they're not Snowy's. I mean—some are, exactly two of the hands are Snowy's—but then there's some more groping at me and

183

pushing my leather miniskirt with the safety-pinned hem up over my hip bones. It's a big blur of rolling bodies and the silver flash of mirror everywhere. The boys are fingering me, so I lift Snowy's bedazzled half-slip and yank down her panties to give her the same treatment the boys are giving me.

I don't know how long we were in that little room, but after we'd churned the air into a humid cloud, smudged up the mirrors, and mussed up the bed, the four of us clattered into the narrow porcelain bathroom, to zip flies and Kleenex our faces, rinse lube down the drain, and get our hairdos back together. We burst out of the powder room to find that a shady band of faggots had climbed through our window and were busy eating ass and sucking cock on our sex bed. Dizzy with one another and giggly from fucking, we dashed past them, back out into the circus.

How Was Your Sex Club Experience?

compiled by Diana Cage

Dickhead Dykes

"I went to a hippie sensuality party in Berkeley with my then-girlfriend. Both of us were bald, naked baby dykes—there may have been body paint involved. We were happily tribading when in comes this pack of hipster dykes and trannies who decide we need some help and start throwing sex toys at us! It was not a good introduction to strap-ons." —*Missy*

Floor-Show Fuckfest

"The first time I got fucked in public was at a play party in a mid-Ohio dungeon. I was most willingly tormented by a gorgeous red-haired top with cute glasses and a stunning red leather and chain-mail warrior maiden outfit. She set our scene by opening me up with a clear plastic speculum, so that she could inspect my warm, wet pussy. Then she blindfolded me and I heard the snap of a latex glove with delicious anticipation. I squeezed at her fingers and begged her for more. She slid her whole hand into me, finger by finger, slicking me up with lube while I moaned and babbled with joy. She rocked her hand into me until I rode it to an orgasm that made me scream, much to the delight of those watching." —*Jessica*

Dungeon Disappointment

"I went with my girlfriend to a local sex club to check out the scene. The theme rooms were awesome, and the fact that we only saw one other woman there didn't bother us at first. We decided to try out the sling in the prison room, but I hadn't been on it for more than a few seconds before at least 20 men surrounded the cell and started whacking off. We left the spot and kept exploring, but it seemed there were more people waiting to observe than there were people actually engaging in sex. It was really disappointing and not sexy at all." —*Carla*

Eager Ass-Slut

"I met my boi at a play party. We had met briefly before, perhaps exchanged a few

186

Ricky Lee

words, but never paid each other much mind until this particular evening. I wasn't there long before he approached me. And then it wasn't long before we had a room full of people mesmerized. We role-played a scene in which he was the bad school-boi, complete with smart-assed remarks. After administering some discipline and putting him in his place, I rewarded him by fucking his ass with my biggest sparkly dildo. He enjoyed every inch of it. Our audience actually applauded at one point. Only later did he tell me that that was a first for him. I was so proud, what else could I do but make him my boi?" —*kiki luv*

Champion Cocksucker
"I picked up a really hot dark-haired femme at women's night at a local dungeon. We spent about 20 minutes in a private room with her on her knees sucking my cock. We finally got so hot she begged me to fuck her. I took her out to a sling in the main room and rewarded her with my fist. She came so hard she screamed at the top of her lungs and sprayed ejaculate all over me. We had a pretty big audience and I know that turned her on. I've gone back to that same women's night many times but never gotten lucky like that again." —*Jamie*

TEN

LESBIAN GENDER:
BUTCH, FEMME, AND BEYOND

●

Nine-Inch Nails Meets Ken Doll

Secrets of a Racy Lacy Femme and a Rough Tough Butch
by Shar Rednour and Kris Kovick

Femme Secret No. 1
Cultivate two basic looks: Your prepared dolled-up look, and another that's equally prepared but doesn't appear so—your disheveled or windblown look.

Butch Secret No. 1
Butches have at least two distinct styles. With one you can close a deal or buy on a margin. It's confident and it's prepared. Your second look is premeditated. You're still street credible, but she can see through your image; your reflection turns her into a bowl of sweet cream.

Femme Secret No. 2
Indulge yourself in getting ready. *Always* get ready, but don't be above applying makeup in the car—which, of course, you know how to do.

Butch Secret No. 2
She calls them outfits. You call 'em clothes.

Femme Secret No. 3
You can wear pumps, so wear them. Should your feet start to hurt, sit. It is permissible to take off your shoes and accept a foot massage through your stockings. *Never* wobble or complain.

Butch Secret No. 3
Pumps...is that a noun or a verb?

Femme Secret No. 4
Tell her what you want.

191

Butch Secret No. 4
Take the toothpick out of your mouth when you're ready to kiss her. She'll tell you when you're ready.

Femme Secret No. 5
When talking to her, tilt your head and stare into her eyes. Periodically allow your gaze to fix on a part of her body while your mind wanders, which will make you cross your legs and lick your lips. When caught having dirty thoughts, blush.

Butch Secret No. 5
Do butches really have high-tech X-ray vision? Do we have night-sight? Can everybody see through her blouse or only you? There's no excuse for getting caught looking down her dress or up her skirt—unless, of course, she wants you to.

Femme Secret No. 6
Breathe into her ear.

Butch Secret No. 6
Keep breathing! (This can cost you at least $50 to learn in therapy.)

Femme Secret No. 7
Pout.

Butch Secret No. 7
Ignore her pouting. She'll ignore you ignoring her. Her lips will get thicker and thicker. It's cheaper than collagen.

Femme Secret No. 7 Addendum
Hey! Be pissed off and pout more!

Femme Secret No. 8
Don't cut your nails until after the third date.

Butch Secret No. 8
You are a finger acrobat, tongue dancer, stud bunny. Above all, you are the butler.

Femme Secret No. 9

The perfect femme would...well, gosh, any femme's perfect by the time she gets her lipstick on.

Butch Secret No. 9

The perfect butch would have the sandpaper tongue of a jungle cat, the mind of Audre Lourde, Martina's aerobic right arm, and the clothes of Macy's boy's department. In other words, she's just like you, only taller.

Femme Secret No. 10

Femmes know ourselves. We know we have personal quirks that we love. This might mean owning 20 pairs of black pumps, or hanging our earrings on lace scarves draped over the headboard. Your butch will boast about these things with reverence. Femmes will look at you with that knowing smile, and other butches will be amazed— then share their femme's eccentricities.

Butch Secret No. 10

Butches live in treehouses. Our furniture is made of bent sticks. Like Dinah Shore, the older ones still look 12 and the younger ones are getting more gorgeous every year. You will find us in *Who's Who of Amazon Warriors*. We will tear your heart out tenderly and savagely eat out your cunt.

Femme Secret No. 11

Butches don't have time to stop and think about how cool and unique they are— they're too busy lighting matches on their zippers or saddle-soaping their harnesses. They also don't have time to think about how important sharing secrets is to us—that's why I only got 10 instead of the promised 20 secrets from my butch.

ADDENDUM: If you don't get all the butch secrets, you're probably a femme. If you don't get all the femme secrets, butch, baby, study up!

Leslie Feinberg, Transgender Visionary

Interviewed by Athena Douris

When Leslie Feinberg, author of the award-winning *Stone Butch Blues* and *Transgender Warriors*, fell ill recently with CMV, doctors failed to make a correct diagnosis for 12 months. One doctor shoved his hands down Feinberg's pants; another screamed, "You people are disgusting." It's a chilling irony that the leader of the transgender movement in this country was denied proper medical care—and nearly disabled—because of transphobia, the fear and hatred of transgendered people s/he has dedicated hir life to eradicating.*

Feinberg and hir activist peers have transformed the landscape of current queer politics: They have introduced "transgender" (even into the mission statement of the National Organization for Women) as an umbrella term for any person whose gender expression appears at odds with his or her biological sex, including transvestites, drag queens and

"I've been thinking a lot about how to write a sexuality that's not necessarily masculine or feminine, or gay or straight."

kings, intersexed persons (i.e., hermaphrodites), "passing" women, transsexuals who choose sex-reassignment surgery and those who do not, feminine men, and masculine women. Feminist theorists introduced the distinction between "sex" (as biological sex) and "gender" (as the social expression of masculinity and femininity); the trans movement took this distinction to the streets.

Feinberg discusses hir struggle with the health care system in hir new book, *Trans Liberation: Beyond Pink or Blue*. Released in September, *Trans Liberation* chronicles Feinberg's career as a popular public speaker and collects the addresses s/he delivered to a variety of groups, from Gay Pride organizers to straight male transvestites. We spoke with Feinberg about why sexual freedom is impossible without freedom of gender expression.

On Our Backs: *Trans Liberation* was released this past September. Can you tell us about what you're working on now?

Feinberg: I'm deep into a novel titled *Drag King Dreams*. It's about a working-class, Jewish trans person who has a foot in both the diverse trans communities and also the lesbian, gay, and bi communities. It's a book about figuring out what "home" means and who your people are.

I'm also trying to write a fable titled "Tale of Two Hearts." It's really a love song to Minnie Bruce Pratt—my wife, my lover, and my friend. It's just one chorus of the love song I write to Minnie Bruce every day of my life.

On Our Backs: Your relationship with poet Minnie Bruce Pratt, thanks in part to her book *S/he*, is well-known. What is your advice to those of us seeking a long-term relationship as loving as yours?

Feinberg: I just know that for me, this is a relationship unlike any other I've ever had. I wasn't looking for a lifetime commitment when I met Minnie Bruce. I'd been dating nonmonogamously for quite a while, nothing serious.

Minnie Bruce and I both did a lot of work individually to grow up, get sober, and work hard at developing our political consciousness and activism. We were ready for each other. Ready to be loving, to communicate, and to listen.

On Our Backs: Pat Califia once wrote that she wishes there would come a time when we don't pick a sexual partner by his or her gender, but by other criteria, such as whether the person is a top or a bottom. In your ideal world, what would attract people to one another?

Feinberg: It's hard for me to hypothesize; I think more concretely. In the world we live in, individuals do organize their preferences around gender expression. But a spectrum of sexuality existed in ancient societies that predated state-sponsored repression of human love. That leads me to think that these preferences might continue to exist in future societies in which no form of sex or gender is outlawed or demeaned.

I don't think the problem today is preferences so much as prejudices. For example, I read personal ads in which people say "no druggies or butches need apply." Wow! That's prejudice. If you say in an ad that you're looking for someone feminine or androgynous or some other form of preference, that's very different from saying "no butches."

As more and more prejudices are defeated, and in a world freed from divide-and-rule bigotry, people will be freer to explore their preferences about gender and about individuals.

On Our Backs: Do transgendered persons have sexual representation—pornography, erotic fiction, videos—made for and by themselves?

Feinberg: Right now, there are many people trying to write erotica that bends gender. And I think it's very important. For many of us, it's very hard, never being able to identify with the sexuality we see everywhere in the dominant culture. [So] it was very important for me to write about sexuality in *Stone Butch Blues*. In the novel I'm working on now, I've been thinking a lot about how to write a sexuality that's not necessarily masculine or feminine, or gay or straight.

On Our Backs: What do you mean by "sexuality that's not necessarily masculine or feminine"?

Feinberg: I see masculinity and femininity as forms of gender expression. But a person's gender expression doesn't necessarily determine their sexuality. It doesn't determine whether you'll be attracted to someone of a similar gender expression or a dissimilar one. It doesn't mean you'll be sexually aggressive or submissive or both.

That's what makes me so angry when I hear people derisively refer to someone as "she thinks she's so butch, but she rolls over in bed." It's an assumption that masculinity translates into being a top sexually. It limits the range of sexual expression of masculine females. And it's a sexual attack on someone who is, by virtue of their social oppression, already sexually wounded.

On Our Backs: Both sex scenes from *Stone Butch Blues* were excerpted for collections of lesbian erotica. Did you intend the scenes to be sexually arousing for readers—to be erotica—when you wrote them?

196   **Feinberg:** That's such an interesting question. I have to say that when I set out to write the sex scenes, I began to be aware of internalized censorship: "Can I or should I write about this or that?" So I consciously blocked out any thought of readers with this odd mental trick: I told myself that whatever I wrote, I didn't have to publish it. First write it, then decide. By doing that, I discovered that I could write about the kind of

sex that I thought was true to the emotional makeup of the characters. If it was erotic for readers, I think it was because I was true to the characters themselves, so the sex was "real," if you know what I mean.

On Our Backs: Can sexuality exist without gender? Or is gender an essential component of sexuality?

Feinberg: Certainly everyone is gendered—quite complexly. And we infuse much of who we are, as gendered people, into our sexuality. But sexuality is so complicated by oppression right now that it's really hard to study it removed from its social soil. Jesse Helms defeated funding for a study that would have backed up much of what Kinsey revealed decades ago: that human sexuality is not two opposite poles—one normal, one not. Sexuality is on a spectrum, and many individuals move along that continuum during their lives. But lesbian, gay, and bisexual love is outlawed in the majority of states in the U.S. So how can a truly objective, intensive study of sexuality even be conducted? It's like doing a study on religious beliefs and affiliations during the Nazi regime in Germany.

So much of what we will learn about the relationship of gender and desire, as well as unraveling other questions about the matrix of sexuality, will be tied to the victories of our liberation of humanity from oppression altogether.

On Our Backs: In *Trans Liberation* you wrote about how frustrating it is voting in a two-party system when both parties are backed by big business. Do you vote? Should poor, queer and trans people even bother voting?

Feinberg: Well, politics is about more than voting. It's also about finding ways to move people to action. In a particular situation where voting on a issue in an election or a candidate can help advance the movement, I would. In general, though, I don't think voting for Republicans or Democrats—both supported by wings of corporate America as their parties—advances our struggle. I believe we need to build an independent liberation movement that's not tied down by waiting to see what happens in the next election. Everything our movement has ever won, including progressive legislation, has been won based on the strength of our struggle.

197

On Our Backs: Lesbians who accept transgender liberation in theory often balk at making alliances with transsexuals. Why is this so?

Feinberg: First and foremost, transsexual men and women helped build the modern lesbian, gay, and bisexual communities and movement. I know of at least one transsexual sister who fought the cops at Stonewall. They haven't always been recognized for their valuable contributions.

But I believe strongly that those in the lesbian communities who are opposed to building coalitions with the diverse trans communities are just one current, and very often a minority current. The question is: Which current of any movement will lead? Those who seek to narrow the movement, or those who seek to broaden and strengthen its collective power?

*In this interview, On Our Backs *refers to Feinberg with the pronouns "hir" (pronounced "here") and "s/he." We choose to do so because Feinberg has stressed that if society is to accept transgendered people, our language must expand as well. S/he gives the example of "Ms.," a common term now that was unacceptable before the women's movement.*

Femmes: A Love Letter

by Patrick Califia

The most surprising thing that testosterone brought into my life is a fresh, compelling, and sometimes distracting appreciation of femmes. I notice them before I notice anybody else in a crowd. There they are, looking fabulous, and here I am, wanting to do something dirty about it. Excuse me, Miss, do you come here often? Any interest in coming at all?

Maybe this surprised me because I bought into the idea that if you are a transsexual man, you must on some level have negative feelings about the female form. Instead I seem to have been set free of any inhibition, hesitation, or insecurity that I used to feel about savoring the sight of beautiful women. Victoria's Secret commercials put me in a trance. Cleavage and miniskirts can fascinate me so deeply that I walk into telephone poles. Lipstick and high-heeled

> **Cleavage and miniskirts can fascinate me so deeply that I walk into telephone poles. Lipstick and high-heeled shoes make me perspire and breathe funny.**

shoes make me perspire and breathe funny. I've always been drawn to butch men and women, but alongside that Big Fag streak in my libido is a new, happy highway, down which I have run full-tilt, full of girl crazy.

I may start a few unintended fires by saying I am an FTM with the hots for femmes. At least one butch dyke will be pissed off because, as one especially indignant butch put it at a forum I attended, "FTMs are stealing all the femmes" (as if the girls had nothing to say about it). One or more femmes will have angst because, as the lament goes these days, all of the butches are taking hormones and turning into men.

But I also know there are femmes who define themselves as women who eroticize masculinity, whether it comes in a butch, FTM, or bio-boy package. Some of these

Michele Serchuk

women think of themselves as dykes, some call themselves bisexual or queer. These are the femmes I love the most. Although I can appreciate a dolled-up straight babe, I am more turned on by women who are at least a 3 on the Kinsey scale. We have a community in common, a position as outsiders, an insight into how the system of sex and gender privilege operates.

I also think queer-identified femmes have a sharper sense of style, a more individual way of moving through the world. The assumption that a femme is mimicking a heterosexual role is wrong-headed. It's quite a challenge to manifest a publicly queer identity as a feminine female, but femmes manage this task quite well, if you're paying attention. (Hint number 1: Look for the short fingernails.) Femmes are fierce and radical in addition to being soft-skinned and nice-smelling. Their skirts usually have pockets, and sometimes they're carrying sharp objects in their artful little bags. While they might gladly pretend to be submissive, that is by no means a foregone conclusion. The patriarchy has much to fear from them, for they are no man's pawn. It's all about Power to the Pussy.

Why am I all of a sudden longing to peel a busty beauty out of her latex catsuit or insinuate my fingers underneath a pair of black satin panties? Polarization. The more masculine my body has become, the more comfortable I feel putting my skin against Her, She, the one with long hair or seamed stockings. I am intrigued by and drawn to femmes because their lives and desires are so very different from my own. And perhaps I feel an enhanced ability to give them satisfaction. I am no longer afraid that a femme will come into my life and be too much for me to handle. I am more grounded now, more settled in myself, and thus more able to deal with other people's needs. Especially if they are willing to sit on my lap, wiggle around a little, and call me a dirty old man.

I am also drawn to femmes because I think they "get" my unique masculinity. As time goes on, my ability to pass may increase, but I don't think I will ever have a simple and straightforward male identity. I am not likely to be strutting naked around the steam room at the gym any time soon. My body has taken so much criticism, both from other people and from myself, that I often feel as if I am carrying an injury that I want to protect. Femmes represent a potential refuge to me, a sanctuary from the uglier tactics of the gender police.

A loving femme understands that her lover has needs, strong needs, but she also has an intuitive grasp of the physical boundaries that can sometimes intrude. If I don't want to take my shirt off, she's not going to harass me about that. If I need to be touched on top of my clothes, that's OK with her. If I need to take my pleasure indirectly, without having her touch me, she doesn't complain. And if I do want to be more vulnerable with her, she doesn't shame me.

By taking pleasure from me, a femme confirms that I am not deficient. I think this is an area where butch and FTM experience overlaps. Both of us want to know that we can love our women better than those guys with XY chromosomes and phalluses of flesh. In some ways, a femme is my dick, because when she gets off around me, she makes what I have seem valuable to us both.

Femmes feel like natural allies to me because I know they have their own body-image issues. Girls always feel bad about some aspect of their physical appearance. Women are always being made to feel too tall, too buxom, too fat, not voluptuous enough, too old. Add to that the fact that many people assume anybody in a skirt is a straight girl, and you can see why many femmes feel alienated from the lesbian community and despair of ever feeling that they belong.

Femmes know, like I do now, what it's like to feel queer on the inside but look straight on the outside. The fact that we are sexual outlaws becomes a secret, unless I forget to pitch my voice low and start talking with my hands. She's often not very happy about this, and I'm not very happy about the fact that when we go out together, gay people avoid us, especially the men I would like to bend over and fuck. I want my bed to be a playground of delirious delight for her, and I don't want that joy to vanish during Gay Pride month.

I know that some of the women who are reading this essay will be furious that it appeared in a lesbian magazine. Some FTMs will wish that I had kept to myself my ruminations about transsexual desire. Butch dykes have many good reasons to feel competitive with men, and I know I could be perceived as just one more prick—despite my lack of one—who is poaching the Sapphic Fort Knox of lovelies.

But there's a difference between a straight man and me. For one thing, real men have no idea what it feels like to have a vagina, and they learned to eat pussy from watching porno movies. If there's a wet spot on the sheets when we're done, I didn't make it, but you won't have to sleep on it anyway. I'm a gentleman who treats women well because I used to be perceived as one, and I know how hard it is to be a woman in a man's world.

202

I also know it's a lot easier to achieve political correctness than it is to find good sex, let alone true love. We all fear the exposure of being seen as we really are by someone we deeply care about. Yet we also hunger for the reassurance of being understood. We want to know where we belong, to be adored, needed, soothed, defended, and challenged. The older I get, the less I care about how people label themselves and the more I care about how they label others. I understand so much more poignantly that the true measure of a man or woman is not between their legs. It is in the heart, which either dares to connect with others or shrinks from that glorious ordeal.

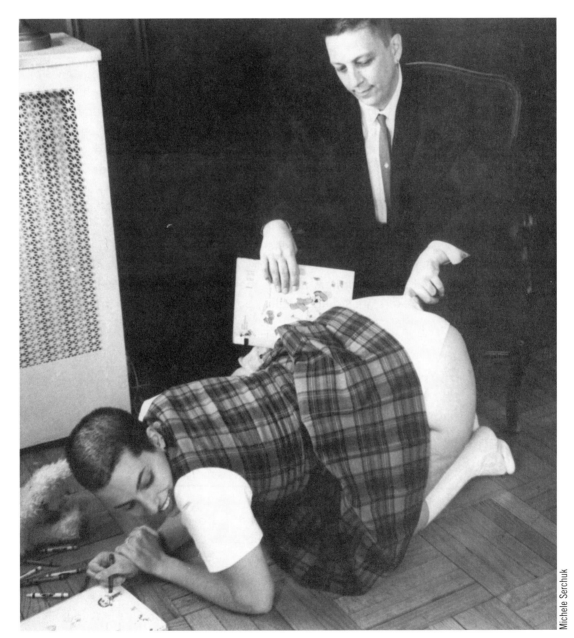

203

A Dyke's Guide to Fucking Genderfuckers

by Tristan Taormino

The emergence of a vital female-to-male (FTM) movement has created greater visibility, access to better healthcare resources, and more awareness through activism, organizations, conferences, and support groups. Awareness and education has led to more lesbians going FTM than ever before. As the lesbian and bisexual partners of FTMs struggle to come to terms with issues of identity and community, there is one issue that seems to be left out of the discussion: sex. Whether your partner has decided to transition, or you are ready to jump into bed with a fabulous new hottie who looks like a boy, sex might not be what it once was. You can't assume you're getting busy with just another really butch lesbian. If *he* identifies as FTM, then everything you learned in Sex With Butches 101 may go right out the window. The rules have changed, and here are some helpful hints as you navigate the terrain of trans sex. Remember too that these tips are not just for dyke partners of trans men—they may prove helpful for fucking all sorts of genderfuckers, including butches, boy-dykes, bois, and other specimens of female or not-so-female masculinity.

Communication is key as you negotiate sex with an FTM. Each person has a unique set of boundaries and triggers. Talk specifics as much as you can and listen to each other.

The Trans Spectrum

How does your partner identify? As trans, a dude, a boy, or just Jack? There are so many variables in gender, so many options available to people born with female identities who don't identify as women. Ask your partner what identity s/he claims, so you can better understand it and work toward embracing it. For example, some people do not identify as female *or* male because they don't believe in the two-gender system; they may call themselves transgendered or something else entirely. Some FTMs identify as male, continue to date lesbian women, and consider themselves queer, even though society may label them straight. As my friend Daphne says, "I identify as me."

Becoming FTM
There's no one way to be an FTM. Some folks identify as trans or FTM without altering their physical bodies in any way. Some decide to take testosterone but forgo any surgery. Others take testosterone and have "top" surgery, e.g. have a double mastectomy. And a smaller percentage of FTMs opt for testosterone, a mastectomy, and some form of "bottom" surgery to create a phallus. Don't assume that because your partner has facial hair that he's on hormones or because his chest looks flat that he's gone under the knife. On the other hand, don't assume they just because he has boobs he's not an FTM. Some people have a different bod than the one they were born with. Others are considering their options. And others don't have the money or health insurance to do everything they want to do.

Just Call Me...
Many FTMs want to be called "he," but other genderqueers may go for either pronoun. Some trans activists have ditched our two standards in favor of "s/he" (Riki Wilchins's choice) or "ze" (Leslie Feinberg's preference). Get a handle on the preferred pronoun, since some nontranny but boy-identified dykes still won't go for "she." Better to ask so you don't get it wrong in the heat of the moment.

Topping the Top
Tranny boys who don't have top surgery wear something to bind their breasts; it may be several Ace bandages, other athletic bindings, a really tight sports bra, or the infamous "frog bra" (designed by and for sportswomen who need major support, this apparatus compresses the breasts, making it a favorite among trannies).

Boxers or Briefs?
Trans men can be quite particular when it comes to underwear, and what goes on underneath it. Each one will tell you his tried and true way of creating the perfect package, whether it's with a softie dick in a jockstrap, a harness and packing dildo, or a firm cock in a pair of "tighty whiteys" that's always ready for action.

Second Skin
Whether it's a binder or boxer briefs, a harness or a "packy," tranny boys can be very particular about what they put on and what they take off. Be prepared for some of it

to stay on indefinitely, even once you get under the covers. Don't assume you need full nudity to be intimate and sexy.

Body Politics

Trans-identified people often feel a sense of discomfort or disconnection from specific parts or all of their bodies; their relationship to their own body can shift and change as they transition. Can you play with his tits and nipples or should you ignore them altogether? Does he prefer you touch his pecs, above his breasts, and leave it at that?

His Cock

One thing you need to keep in mind is something that's never far from his: his cock. Remember that his dick may always be there, even if there's no harness and cock strapped to his body. That's a difference between dykes and FTMs—dykes can take their dicks off; for FTMs, their dick is a part of their body, their identity, their reality. It gets hard, he jerks it off, he likes it sucked, it may even allow him to come inside you. Think about it, and go with it.

Understanding Stone

Some FTMs may have been stone butch lesbians, and their stone status remains after they transition. Or their new trans identity may have shifted their sexuality toward being the assertive "doer" in sex, but never the receiver. Stone may be a permanent way of being, a temporary safe resting place, or a sometimes flexible state of being. If your partner identifies as stone, realize that it doesn't mean that he is unable or unwilling to receive pleasure; stone butches and stone boys do get pleasure, they just do it without, um, getting done. Their desire is to give and to please and to bring forth writhing orgasms from their partners; they get off on getting you off. Honor their sexuality, do not shame or guilt trip them for it.

Doing a Boy

Just because he's a boy, don't automatically assume he doesn't want to get fucked. Find out where his comfort zones are and what places may be totally off-limits. Respect those limits, and make the most of what's available. I know boys who like to get fucked in the ass (since bio-boys can get fucked in the ass), but the other hole is not fair game. Also, make sure you are aware of how you talk to him during sex; nothing deflates a boy's ego like asking him if you are making him wet instead of hard.

The Place Formerly Known as Pussy

Speaking of off-limits, since most trannies do not opt for phalloplasty, a pussy is still part of the package, along with a much larger clit for those boys on testosterone. How does he feel about his cunt? Does he want you to touch or penetrate it at all, and if so, how? What do you call it—his hole, his dick, his member?

Do Ask, Do Tell

Communication is key as you negotiate sex with an FTM. Each person has a unique set of boundaries and triggers. Talk specifics as much as you can and listen to each other. Think of all the fun new ways you can give and receive pleasure. Don't let a change in gender identity prevent you from having the mind-blowing sex you both deserve.

FTM, Transgender, and Intersex Resources

FTM International www.ftmi.org
Intersex Society of North America www.isna.org
Gender Education and Advocacy www.gender.org
National Transgender Advocacy Coalition www.ntac.org
Gender Talk www.gendertalk.com
International Foundation for Gender Education www.ifge.org
New York Association for Gender Rights Advocacy www.nyagra.tripod.com
Harry Benjamin International Gender Dysphoria Association www.hbigda.org
It's Time, America! www.tgender.net/ita
The International Journal of Transgenderism www.symposion.com/ijt
TransGender San Francisco www.tgsf.org
Gender Public Advocacy Coalition www.gpac.org
Trans Art www.trans-art.com

208

An Interview With Joan Nestle

by Athena Douris

Joan Nestle is a lesbian national treasure. A Jewish working-class femme born in 1940, Nestle came out in the 1950s, marched for gay rights in the 1960s, and cofounded the Lesbian Herstory Archives in 1973. For the next 20 years—until they finally found a three-story home—Nestle housed the archives in her apartment. At Nestle's behest, the archives accepted controversial sex documents—including the papers of Samois, the first national public lesbian S/M organization.

Nestle was one of the speakers at the Barnard conference of 1984, a conference (and later an anthology titled *Pleasure and Danger*) that both sparked the sex wars of the 1980s and ushered in the "pro-sex" culture we take for granted today.

Nestle holds a special place in the hearts of femmes: She espoused butch-femme history and politics during a period when both identities were considered patriarchal. She wrote about femmes who carried dildos in their purses when they went to bars.

> ## "Femmes come up to me and say they consider me their mother. But I'm always a little sad that femme women need someone to give them permission."

She wrote *A Restricted Country* and edited *The Persistent Desire: A Femme-Butch Reader.*

Last year, when Nestle found herself in need of $5,000 to pay her chemotherapy bill, she mailed out a prospectus for a new work. Cleis Press was the only publisher to answer; they published *A Fragile Union* in November, almost 20 years after her last work.

On Our Backs: In *A Fragile Union,* you talk about lovers nine, 13, and 20 years younger than you.

Joan Nestle: I'm almost 60, and my present lover is 46. I can't say I don't have concerns about it, because I do. To me 60s and 40s is a very big difference. But it's not just that I'm 58; it's that I have cancer. It's not just that my body is 12 years older; it also carries its own mortality in such a marked way. It makes the sexual play in some ways even more powerful than it's ever been in my entire life, and more poignant.

With my younger lover it's not that I feel that I'm teaching her. It's more that in a way I'm showing her the possibilities of her own future. My present lover is a femme woman.

On Our Backs: You write about your femme lover in your book. Do you recommend femme lovers for femmes? Has it been healing for you?

Nestle: I'm at the point where I know I can't talk for all femmes. As I get older it all gets more personal for me. If it makes sense to anyone, I'm glad. It started out, butch women were the bridge to my own sense of beauty. It was butch women who said, "Joan, you're a beautiful woman"—a statement I've never believed. But they gave me the gift of myself.

It isn't just that my new lover, Diane, is a femme woman—she's also a larger woman. The first time I set out to make love to her—I was so nervous, it was like starting all over again. Believe me, I understood what performance anxiety was about. Because she had been with butch women too. I was afraid I wouldn't be enough for her.

The first time I held her in my arms it was like everything just stopped. She didn't feel fat, she didn't feel ugly. [*Pause*] She felt so beautiful to me. For the first time I understood what my butch lovers had held in their arms when they held me. I felt something of value.

That may come as a surprise. How can I put this? There are so many levels on which we have sex. There are so many different experiences of self-acceptance or self-rejection that go on at the same time. I guess I had never realized, in my whore self and in my femme fatale self (well, I consider myself a low femme, so I was never a femme fatale) that such a dissonance still existed. I didn't realize such self-hatred still existed between me and my body. And I couldn't rely on the butch adoring me to give me back myself. No, I had to find myself. I don't make love to my femme lover as a butch. I've discovered another position; I'm not quite sure what it is. We engage in some wonderful fantasies.

On Our Backs: Can you give me an example?

Nestle: Wait till she sees this in print! For example, we were having dinner in my apartment, and she wears short skirts. I as a femme have never worn a short skirt; I just don't feel comfortable in my body that way. She came to dinner and she just did this thing: She lifted her leg so her skirt rode up, and put it on the edge of the chair, and she wasn't wearing any underpants. Now, I've played with all kinds of things, but never like this. Because butch women wouldn't do that. I have taken cocks out of [women's] pants—but this was a woman doing this to me. And I almost fell off the chair. I mean, I've played with others, but no one had ever played with me.

For a brief time, I took money for sex from women. I also worked in prostitutes' rights. Being a whore is more than a fantasy—it's a resonance, it's something that's always present in my sexuality. And she reversed it on me.

On Our Backs: Our sex culture grew out of a political organization that didn't have room for sex. After Matthew Shepard's death, I worry that our sex culture doesn't have the means or the organization for any political movement. What can we do about this?

Nestle: First, I just want to say that *On Our Backs* is political work, even though it seems to be cultural work. But cultural work is political work when it's about taboo, or when it's about any area of shame. Shame is a great controller of a people's dreams. And when you take on that shame, you're freeing people up for political struggle.

You know, the pendulum has gone many swings. Now I think we're in a position to really combine these two movements: the fierceness and the political savvy (and I hope, not the mistakes) of the women's liberation movement of the '70s and the queer-culture movement. And yours is the generation that can do that. It can start with a mailing list of 20 sex radicals, forming a group, "Sex Radicals for the End of Violence Against Gay People."

I think that what we did as sexual writers was a political act in itself in the beginning, but now I think everything has moved up a notch. I'll put it this way: I no longer trust some of the largest gay organizations, such as the Human Rights Campaign. I think that new political voices coming out of the queer sex radical world—such as Leslie Feinberg's—are incorporating the insights of feminism that work and can be tremendously powerful. And we're going to need tremendously powerful voices, because of the forces on the other side.

211

Our Backs: Do you think that things are better now for femmes than they were 10 years ago?

Nestle: More and more femmes are announcing themselves, and there's a kind of joy in these femmes. At the same time, we're living in a time when lesbian masculinity is tremendously popular, more so now than ever.

One of the goals of my work was to destroy myths about femmes. Femmes come up to me and say they consider me their mother. But I'm always a little sad that femme women need someone to give them permission. Femmes need to do a lot more work— finding the language, the political positions, the thinking that is unique to us, separate from butches. For instance, butch women have soft [butch], stone [butch]. I'd like to see those different levels for femmes.

There was a time in my life when I didn't consider myself a femme unless I was on the arm of a butch. Now I know that I have a whole world I carry with me. It's there to share with another person, another butch, if I choose to share it.

On Our Backs: The few femme-femme spreads we have done at *On Our Backs* have been the most unpopular. Do you have any ideas of how we can showcase femmes?

Nestle: I think deeper analysis would be interesting. I wonder if it's just reminding the viewer too much of straight porn. Could we present femme-femme in a way that does-n't bring up those resonances? I remember looking at *Nothing But the Girl* with Jill Posener. Susie Bright couldn't be there for some reason, so I was the femme stand-in. I remember looking at the book and I saw there wasn't a femme chapter. There were all these other chapters but not one for femmes. And I asked Jill Posener about it and she said to me—and this I will never forget—"Because a femme by herself is not sub-versive enough. She's just a woman." I'll never forget that.

As for a femme-femme spread in *On Our Backs*...maybe an older femme and a younger femme, with something that marked them as femme. Maybe some kind of teacher-and-student scenario. That would upset a lot of people!

212

On Our Backs: You write that, after having to face surgery for cancer, you made a promise to "never again betray myself." Would you mind sharing the story of one time you betrayed yourself?

Nestle: I have always been searching for butch women who would allow themselves to penetrate another woman. In the old days penetration was taboo; lesbians wouldn't do it. Some of the things I've written have celebrated my great hunger for penetration. The flip side of that, from time to time, has been too much self-sacrifice. I prolonged a relationship in which it was clear that "it" no longer existed. I couldn't stop the rush of need to really think about what was good for me.

Maybe I'm talking about femme loneliness. The lover of mine that I lost—the manner in which she left was harsh. She was driven by her passion, which I can understand. Being alone is not the worst thing in the world for a femme. But not taking care of oneself is. I'm not talking about self-indulgence. I'm talking about *survival.*

Butch on Butch

by Desai

My first inkling that butch-on-butch wouldn't be as straightforward as I'd hoped came when I met Rae. Red curly hair in a D.A., tailored clothes, light-blue eyes, a honeyed Southern accent, lean but with a sweet woman's ass. Everything I liked in a butch in one package. And she could dance. So one hot summer night, as we danced together somewhere in the West Virginia mountains, I asked her if we couldn't do lying down what we did standing up. She stepped back and frowned at me in my Levi 501s and man's tailored shirt.

"What on earth are you suggesting?"

My moves withered on the spot. I looked back at her, trying to picture what she saw when she looked at me—someone who looked like her mirror image.

"What do you think I'm suggesting?" I asked her, trying not to feel defensive. I put my arms around her again and tried to pretend we were just as we had been before my fateful words.

Carrie stood in the bed of her pickup truck, pulling nails from a two-by-four. I'd had my eye on her for months. I liked her strong arms, her fearlessness, her willingness to attempt anything.

She let me embrace her again but stopped moving her hips. Finally, she murmured, "Honey, you don't understand. It just wouldn't work."

She was right. I didn't understand. Two years passed before I got any more information from her about what my gaffe had been. By that time the flirtation had matured into a friendship, and I didn't lie awake at night trying to figure a way to win her. I wasn't going to, I could tell that much, and though I didn't know exactly why, I knew it had something to do with…

214

The Ultimate in Same-Sex Narcissism

As if not already queer enough, butches who pursue other butches occupy an unexplored cul de sac in the world of same-sex relationships, a subset of a subset. They are elusive as the unicorn, a myth that you pursue down blind alleys. Women you might be sure were in butch-on-butch relationships perceive themselves as being a well-balanced mix of butch and femme. "Well," such women might say, "you're barking up the wrong tree. Marianna's a stone butch, and I'm kind of more femme. Except on alternate full moons, then we switch. And on the first Sunday of the month…"

Hooray for versatility! But what about me? I like butch women, and unfortunately for me, most butch women I've pursued, like Rae, perceive me as being butch, or too butch for them—and they "don't do butches." So where do I go to get me jollies?

Beyond Emily Post

Rae was a setback for me. After Rae, I didn't quite dare to approach butch women with the carefree naïveté I'd had with her. I became conscious of a thick book of unwritten rules, rules that were obscure to me but that I couldn't get any satisfaction about simply by asking. Because if I asked, people looked at me with that blank stare.

The things I wanted to know about seducing butches were hidden by thick blankets of etiquette. When I first came out, butch/femme was considered to be an ancient throwback that enlightened feminists had moved, fortunately for all of lesbiankind, far beyond. No questions could be asked or answered about its subtler permutations.

Another unspoken credo was that you had to learn everything you wanted to know about anything queer by yourself, because no one was gonna tell you a thing about it. A certain type of gay experience had to be gained, grain by grain, distilled through bitter experience.

Time Passes and I Make a Detour

When I moved to California, I decided that in the greater interest of getting laid, it was time to put the clit-throbbing fantasies of butch-on-butch on the back burner. I pursued and achieved women, femmes all, though the meals were too to satisfy me.

I even tried my hand at camouflage, but a frilly shirt and glitter earrings could not disguise from a canny butch the essential facts that I was not a femme and my m.o. not the least femme-like.

By now, old Rae and I were friends. Once, when she came to visit me during this period, I asked her point-blank to explain to me why "it" wouldn't have worked between us.

She thought it over. It occurred to me as she sat thinking that she was as much bewildered by the fact that I'd had to ask the damn question as she was by the question itself. Finally, she said, "Honey, don't you know?"

I shook my head.

"I just can't imagine what we'd have done together. That's all. We're too much alike. We'd have been fighting for the same...territory."

"No, we wouldn't have, " I protested.

"We would have to know what to do. Give and take, possession and surrender, were possible in all terrains, not just the most familiar one. But the image in the back of my mind of what two butches might do together trembled and winked out. Finally, we went to sleep in separate beds.

That night, lying awake, I finally figured out what I had done wrong with Rae: I had co-opted her sense of control. Making the first overt move was a prerogative she reserved for herself. She wanted a femme to pursue her.

A butch friend of mine told me once that what she expected of femmes was to pursue obliquely.

"They plot things for butches to fall into," she told me once. "They're smart. They know how to play a butch. They might say no, or keep you at arm's length. They act coy."

By Rae's code, I had been stupid, inept, abrupt, and brusque. I hadn't led the chase, as Rae expected—I had done the chasing.

I Meet a Willing Butch and Don't Avail Myself of an Opportunity

Carrie stood in the bed of her pickup truck, pulling nails from a two-by-four. I'd had my eye on her for months. I liked her strong arms, her fearlessness, her willingness to attempt anything. But I didn't have much hope. I'd already made my most overt overtures to her and been rejected. Not exactly with Rae's same look of bewilderment and disbelief, but she had hidden from me for several months.

But somehow, I couldn't quit chasing her. She pulled nails from the other end of the two-by-four.

"Give me the hammer," I ordered her. "I'll do these."

She looked up, cocked an eyebrow at me, and said, "I love it when women talk to me that way."

My stomach somersaulted. I played her words over in my mind, disbelieving what I'd heard.

"Say that again?"

"I said, 'I love it when women talk to me that way.' "

"I thought that's what I heard."

217

I went back to the nails. We finished the two-by-four. Carrie went her way, I went mine, dazed and erotically charged by the exchange. I thought a lot about her. What did she mean? Was it a come-on? Was she telling me something I needed to know about her?

Then I thought, "What if that was my chance and I didn't take it?" Fool! But my pride and sense of rightness had taken a beating, so I couldn't be sure I'd heard what I'd heard. I let it lie there, unresolved.

More time passed. I saw her other places, being her usual butch self. I wanted her, I wanted not to discover the same old disappointments, hear again that "it just wouldn't work." She made a wonderful fantasy and would be a cruel disappointment. I'd had too many of those. Better to admire her form afar, I decided.

Finally, she ended a relationship she'd been in for several months—with a femme, I observed somewhat cynically. I was too miserable for pursuit, even if I'd had the will. But one night I comforted her when she was feeling depressed about how things had turned out for her and the other woman. I invited her out for a drink and told her that anyone who'd leave her didn't have the sense they were born with.

Having gotten that far, I spilled all the beans. I told her I intended to make a serious move on her, as soon as she was ready. She looked astonished, but not bewildered or mystified at the subversion of this natural order of things. She was pleased by my interest.

We Make Love and the Butch Confesses

"I was butch in the womb," Carrie tells me. "I was really upset when they forced me to stop playing touch football with the boys. I never deferred to boys. They liked playing with me because I was bigger than them and liked playing the same games."

I ask her why she's always been with femmes.

"I've always been attracted to butch women," she says. "In every couple where there was an obvious butch and a femme, it was always the butch that caught my eye."

"So why have you always been with femmes?" I persisted.

"Aggressive femmes would always swoop down on me before anything else could happen," she responds with the helplessness of a woman desired intensely by others and always pursued. "They assumed I was butch in bed because I'm butch in my life. One lover I had wouldn't ever penetrate me because I was the butch and that just wasn't supposed to happen. I did what they wanted me to because I wanted to be a good lover. But I was always mildly frustrated because I wasn't getting my fantasies fulfilled. It was serviceable sex."

"So does that make me an aggressive femme because I swooped down on you?" I asked.

She laughed. "No femme could take me the way you take me. I love being had by you. I like the way you take your pleasure from fucking me. I used to have to get off with whatever was left lying around. I wasn't supposed to be the centerpiece. I didn't like that. Being on my back doesn't compromise the integrity of this butch."

"I ain't baking cakes, but I do like to spread my legs," I told her. "No one's ever going to come up to me and say I'm a femme."

"I love your strength," she said. "I love it that you can wrestle me to the ground. I've always been the biggest and the strongest, and you match me. I also like it that you're butch without stomping around. You're a different layer of butch and that interests me."

A Few Words by Way of Conclusion

Most of the fantasies I've read, most of the butches I've talked to, resolve themselves eventually into the butch/femme format. One butch to whom I put this "butch on butch" question said, flatly (before moving on to the topic she was most interested in—femmes), "I don't know too much about it. I know it exists."

Another said, "I've had butch women be attracted to me, but I look for femmes on purpose. I don't bother with butch women. I just don't fall in love with them."

Others looked at me as though I was a little, you know, weird, and said stuff along the lines of, "Well, you know, I'm not putting it down or anything."

Maybe most butch-on-butch couples are the kinds of couples who say, "Role? What role? We're not playing any roles." Denial is rampant. Whereas two femmes together might be seen as a kind of quintessentially lesbian-within-a-lesbian experience, and a butch/femme combination reflects the "normal" yin/yang balance, two butches together are unlesbian. Two "boys" together can seem more like an affront to the natural order of lesbianism.

Butches who like to get fucked by other butches, butches like my lover, are basically women who like using the right tool for the right job. Their genitals happen to be the right tool for the job of getting off, and they'll happily get on their backs to do it right. Along with her power tools, her toys, and her cunt, this elusive butch lover of mine craves my butchness to hone her strength against.

The Happy Ending

Last night she made the first move. I let myself come for her. This morning, when I got up, long after she had gone to work, I found this note.:

219

Ahh! You were so delicious last night, the elusive butch bottom—what a taste treat! P.S. I love you for your mind too.

An Interview With Kate Bornstein

by Lindsay McClune

Transgender writer and performer Kate Bornstein, author of *Gender Outlaw* and *My Gender Workbook,* has been questioning and researching gender all her life. Bornstein's work examines a world that insists there are two, and only two, genders, and that doesn't encourage us to develop the gender that feels right for us. Bornstein has written and spoken extensively about this imposed two-gender system, helping people question what is a "real" woman or a "real" man?

"I was born male and raised as a boy. I went through both boyhood, and adult manhood, went through a gender change, and 'became a woman.' A few years later, I stopped being a woman, and settled into being neither." This space of "no-gender" is perhaps one of Bornstein's most provocative ideas, and she recognizes the difficulty inherent in trying to identify where gender is and moving away from it. *On Our Backs* spoke with Bornstein about how the two-gender system is a part of the lesbian community, why she identifies as a dyke, and how S/M brought her back to her body.

On Our Backs: How has your sexual practice changed throughout your gender travels in terms of how it feels emotionally and physically for you?

Kate Bornstein: I had an outie, and now I have an innie. Sex now, being touched now, is a lot less of the penis and a lot more the connection. When I had a penis that was an outie, you didn't really have to question much about sex. It just felt pretty damned good any way you did it; it was pretty easy. It was right out there, all you had to do was rub it, and it wasn't too hard to do that. With my new equipment, which is neither-here-nor-there equipment, it looks "girl," but feels very, very different. It just feels so much different now that everything is inside. I am having to explore. So the actual act of sex is not as unthinking as it was. I am thinking a lot more, and there is a lot more humor in it. I am curious of what produces sensations now. Sex is almost a scholarly act.

OOB: Does your attraction to men and women differ, and if so, how?

KB: It kind of does. With my attraction to women, there is almost always accompanying it the possibility that, "Oh, my God, what if that [sex] really happened?" Whereas with guys, I am much more comfortable with my attraction in fantasy. I have not really had that many encounters with guys where the reality lived up to the fantasy.

OOB: I have heard you identify as an S/M dyke. Why it is important for you to claim that identity?

KB: When I went through my gender transition from male to female, "lesbian" was both a sexual and a political identity. Over the years it has become much more of a political identity based a definition of a "real woman." "Dyke" never seemed to need that. I first ran into [the term] "dyke" in San Francisco in the early '80s with the S/M group the Outcasts. I like it because it embraces the idea of butch and femme. It's brave enough to proclaim its own queerness. "Dyke" is not trying to mainstream into the gender system, meaning the bipolar gender system.

OOB: What sorts of reactions have you had from the lesbian community?

KB: When I first went through the gender transition—again, male to female—it was in Philadelphia in the late '80s. I came out into the lesbian community, and you know you've got to learn all this girl stuff fast. Not only did I have to learn girl stuff, but I had to learn lesbian stuff. And not only did I have to learn all that stuff, but I wasn't really allowed to do any of my guy stuff. Not that I particularly wanted to, but it would kind of poke out. And I was just "bumping into" people. And I think for that reason, there were a few lesbians and dykes in Philadelphia who are not all that pleased when my name is mentioned. I am sad about that, and I've been working on it.

I think any kind of "What's the reaction of the lesbian community?" question can *only* be answered in the personal because, by golly, lesbian is only one of many identities someone has. When I find that I can't connect with a quote-unquote lesbian as a quote-unquote transsexual, then we find another pair of identities that we can connect with.

221

OOB: You have said that we all face underlying rules and stereotypes about gender. In what ways does the lesbian community still encourage these gender rules and stereotypes?

KB: When I am talking about the lesbian community, by that I don't mean all dykes. But in its very backing of the system that depends for its livelihood on the existence of two and only two genders, through supporting that system, [the lesbian community] backs the bipolar gender system. Very, very little queering of gender goes on in the lesbian community.

OOB: How do you see femme and butch as "queering gender"?

KB: The way femme and butch are done—the way I know of—is much less a this-is-what-I-have-to-do-in-order-to-get-on-in-the-world, and much more of a choice. It queers the lesbian identity by taking what's sacred and reowns it for itself; it takes what's sacred in the culture. Whereas the lesbian agenda—by and large the assimilationist lesbian agenda—would be "don't ask, don't tell," butch and femme proclaim. They don't have to wait to be asked. It's in that proclamation that I think comes the queering.

OOB: Could you describe your femme identity?

KB: I came into this femme identity of mine through Leslie Feinberg's *Stone Butch Blues.* It was the first time that I read a description of a femme that was anything but weak. Seeing femme through the butch's eyes like that was such a treat, it was breathtaking. I think if I had real role models within the lesbian community, it would be the femmes in Seattle. There was a bunch of good, good, good femmes of all ages up there, and each one had her own specialty. We would trade femme secrets, like how to do it. Because, again, it is a studied thing, and after a while you get to realize that, well, of course you are never going to be femme enough. That's only for fairly few folks. It's the same with butch: There is always going to be someone bigger and badder or whatever. And at that point I was just able to start smiling and enjoying it.

Butch and femme is like a dance. When an old-school butch starts flirting with me, it's a recognizable dance, it's in my blood. And I just follow myself there, I follow her and she's just...that's... Oh, man, it's the hardest thing to put into words because it is a dance. It's a dance of identities, and a very, very structured dance. Like any great dances, you have to learn the steps.

222

OOB: So are the butches the ones that drive you wild?

KB: Old-school butches. Every single time they make my knees totally, totally, like, floppy. It's that dance thing again. It's like, "Ah, someone who knows the steps." And it's very, very, very body-level for me when a butch flirts with me, even when I just *see* an old-school butch.

OOB: In an interview, I heard you say that we tend to describe our sexual orientation based on the gender of sexual partners, rather than their age or sexual activity. I have often felt that I have more in common with a very sexualized gay man than with an antipenetration vanilla lesbian. As an S/M dyke, have you found the S/M world to be a place that is freer for you to develop your sexual expression?

KB: I got into S/M—and I've been into S/M for a while—in the late '80s and early '90s. But I got into it particularly heavily when I broke up a pretty hard relationship. It was a wonderful relationship, and I am still in touch with the person, but when we broke up it was really hard. I was not feeling good about myself; I wasn't feeling good about life. The last thing I wanted someone to do was to look at my body. I wasn't feeling very good about my body. But I was feeling weirdly sexy, weirdly horny, and didn't know where this was coming from. I was getting involved with some women who were into S/M in Seattle. I got more and more heavily involved with them, and found a way to express sexiness again, that energy, the power of sex, in a way that wasn't necessarily [found] in fucking. Certainly not all the time. It was certainly erotic. And having learned that, I was able to work my way back into body-level sex, and tantric-level sex, and other ways of doing sex. And I still like the occasional piercing stuff. I like blood.

OOB: Do you ever find that the power dynamics and role-play found in S/M is a way of playing with gender?

KB: Well, yeah. Gender itself is an expression of power, and so the interaction of any kind of power would shed some light on gender. What I've found in S/M is the rawest expression of power: I am, you're not. I do, you receive. It is a constructed binary that is honored by both of the participants. When you give yourself consciously to that sort of thing, it's like any other discipline, you achieve an ecstatic place from that.

223

OOB: You have been such a strong role model for so many women. Did you have any important role models?

KB: My mother. I have never really said that before. I have written a lot of pieces about my mother. She's quite an amazing woman, imperfect in every way. But she was a strong thing in the '50s, when women were all supposed to be in the kitchen after the husbands came home from war. Instead my mom put herself through school, got a teaching degree, and taught for 20, 30 years. She was quite radical in that way. If anyone were to play her in the movies, it would be Barbara Stanwyck, a kind of a tough-girl thing. She was a major femme. I've got this picture of her in crinolines with a cigarette in one hand and a martini in the other, and a big smile.

OOB: What is the best way for individuals to educate people about transphobia?

KB: To be human is the best way to do that. Because there is so much comedy inherent in the notion of transsexuality and transgender, why not use it? And the comedy that is inherent in these identities is that we are fools. Like, "Golly, look how foolish we are. Look at how silly we are. Look at how powerless we are." Just by embracing that [powerlessness], the opposite is true, and there you have the nature of camp. If you have the drag king and drag queen humor, and their whole idea of embracing their own foolishness, it's kind of cool. The whole idea of stepping down, giving up your own power, admitting that you don't have it. Because the fact of the matter is that I don't [have power]. I have got white privilege, and a certain blond privilege, whatever that is. But boy, oh, golly, when they find out I am a tranny, all the rest of it kind of goes out the window. So I might as well just have some fun with it.

OOB: What is the most respectful way to approach a trans person if you want to have sex with them?

KB: On your knees. But if you don't feel up to that, if you don't feel up to crawling over there and pleading like a worm, then with respect. And I'm not saying don't treat someone like a sex object. Personally, I love being treated like a sex object. But first you should approach someone with respect—I mean, how would you approach anyone you were seriously interested in having some good sex with?

Dating FTMs: Should Lesbians Stand by Their Men?

by Jackie Cohen

These days it seems like many dykes are transitioning—from female to male. And their lovers face the prospect of losing their identity as lesbians if they stick with their partners.

"When you're walking around on the street, everyone thinks you're heterosexual," admits Annie Sprinkle, who documented her romance with a transsexual male in the controversial film *Linda/Les Loves Annie* back in 1989. "So when I was with Les, everyone assumed I was with a man, especially 'cause he had a beard. That was a little uncomfortable."

Naturally, these fears are even harder for the FTM person to deal with. Jamison Green, one of the original founders of FTM International, recalls that it took him decades to get the courage to go through with the transition to maleness—even though he experienced gender confusion from day one. By the age of 20, he realized he was

> "When the relationship is a good one, I mostly see people choosing to stay together and strategizing to make it work. True love is not that easy to find or that easy to give up once you've got it." —Patrick Califia-Rice

most likely a transsexual. But that truth was frightening: In the 1970s, transsexuals were practically invisible. Very few transsexuals, especially of the FTM variety, were out. When a dyke friend announced that she was becoming a he, Green felt conflicted: It didn't jive with the feminist ideology he'd embraced as part of dykedom. Yet the lesbian scene wasn't a perfect fit for him either, especially as his self-awareness grew.

"The very first time I made love with my girlfriend of 14 years, she said, 'I don't know how to tell you this, but I feel like I was just with a man,'" recounts Green, who replied at the time, "I don't know how to tell you this, but I think you just were with a man." Over the years, "she was very cool about it, but when I began transitioning to male, she said, 'Do what you need to do. I'll support you, but I don't know if I can stay with you.'"

About one in 100,000 females opt for a sex-change operation, according to the *Diagnostic and Statistical Manual of Mental Disorders*. But the actual number of FTMs is much higher, since the vast majority just take testosterone and get mastectomies, without genital reassignment.

"The FTM community is a lot more visible and accessible. There are female-bodied people transitioning now who 10 years ago would have remained in the lesbian community all their lives," says Patrick Califia-Rice, who spent 30 years in the lesbian community before coming out again as FTM.

Visibility and awareness have grown, thanks to the rise of groups such as FTM International, a several-hundred-member support, education, and advocacy group, with a Web site and regular meetings. And as similar organizations continue to pop up around the world, the Internet has been enabling more transgendered people to find these communities. In addition, there are growing ranks of therapists and surgeons who address these issues, armed with better knowledge and medical techniques. And as public awareness increases, some states, municipalities, and employers are implementing policies to protect the rights of transsexuals.

But of course there are still a lot more people who have trouble adjusting comfortably to transgender identity. "I knew that some of my lesbian friends were not very happy about my transition, but they usually did not talk about those feelings of grief or anger with me, so it was hard to be sure exactly how many were disapproving or upset," says Califia-Rice. "About 10% of my lesbian friends have grief about the part of me, the lesbian identity, that's gone. And people like my landlord and the folks at the grocery store are puzzled. What happens the most is that people get their pronouns mixed up."

With all of the social taboos, deciding to take the plunge is difficult. Most physicians require at least one letter of recommendation from a therapist before they will administer testosterone. Before they can qualify for surgery, trans men must tell at least
226 a few friends and/or family members of their decision as well as take hormones and live in their gender of preference for at least a year. These prerequisites and other ethical guidelines are detailed in the much-touted Harry Benjamin International Gender Dysphoria Association's *Standards of Care for Gender Identity Disorders*, first drafted in 1979 and recently republished in its sixth revision.

The association's executive director, Bean Robinson, notes that these guidelines have eased up a bit, as the association has in recent years adopted the attitude that there are more than two absolute gender categories. "More and more of our patients are choosing a place somewhere along the continuum—hormones but not surgery, for instance," says Robinson. "Some want to have mastectomies but not genital surgeries, preferring to wait until better techniques become available."

Surgeons and therapists increasingly consider patients' readiness for surgery on a case-by-case basis. "Not everyone needs to see a therapist first," says Michael L. Brownstein, a San Francisco–based surgeon who's been performing sex changes since the late 1970s. "If someone has been living in the male role for 20 years, and just now has the money for surgery, I don't see any reason for them to have to go into therapy just to get the magic recommendation letter."

But that's not to say that none require therapy. "Some of our patients do have mental health problems and may suffer from depression, and sometimes it gets better with the treatment for the gender dysphoria," says Robinson.

Things may or may not improve for the partners of FTMs once they begin the transition, depending on how the couple chooses to label themselves and on other interpersonal dynamics. So, is it worthwhile to stand by your woman after she tells you she wants to become a he?

"I wouldn't advise anyone to be politically correct about this," says Califia-Rice. "What is PC is to support people for self-actualization, but that doesn't necessarily mean you need to date them. The first thing you need to do is clarify your own boundaries. If you identify as lesbian, and your partner wants to transition to a male identity, the relationship might not work. While a separation under these conditions is bound to be painful, I think it's a legitimate reason to end the relationship. There are FTMs who want to hang on to part of their dyke identity, however. Partners of FTMs may identify as lesbian, bisexual, or heterosexual. They can also label themselves as queer since transgendered people and their partners fall under that large umbrella. There are many possibilities. When the relationship is a good one, I mostly see people choosing to stay together and strategizing to make it work. True love is not that easy to find or that easy to give up once you've got it."

ELEVEN

BEYOND THE BEDROOM:
LESBIAN SEXUAL HEALTH AND KNOWLEDGE

Hot and Healthy

Which Sexually Transmitted Diseases Do
Lesbians Really Need to Know About?
by Cara Bruce

I'm a lesbian, so I'm safe from sexually transmitted diseases. Only women who sleep with men are at risk for HIV. Oral sex won't give me anything. I'm not dirty and don't use drugs, so I can't get hepatitis.

These are common myths in the lesbian community about sexually transmitted diseases (STDs). And myths can shape reality: Ziadee Whiptail, Education Manager of the women-owned sex toy store Good Vibrations, says that not one lesbian group has requested a safer-sex workshop from her in over 12 months.

But STDs don't discriminate by sexual preference. Diseases don't care whether you're gay, straight, or bi. By definition, an STD is an infection that is primarily spread by sexual contact: oral, anal, or vaginal, either by skin-to-skin contact or by exchanging bodily fluids such as blood, vaginal fluids, or semen. If you're performing oral sex on a woman, then you're exchanging body fluids: her vaginal fluids, your saliva, and everything that

STDs don't discriminate by sexual preference. Diseases don't care whether you're gay, straight, or bi.

lives in them. No matter what Bill Clinton thinks—and lesbians know this from experience—sexual contact isn't just penetration. Yet we seem not to be able to translate this into our understanding of STDs. If you have human papilloma virus (HPV or so-called genital warts), you can touch yourself, give your fingers to your girlfriend to suck, and potentially transfer it to her. Think of a virus as a tiny, mobile organism. Now think of what it's like to burn the roof of your mouth on a hot piece of pizza. If it gets the chance, that virus is going right into the tears created by that burn. So whether you're having full strap-on sex or just teasing her with your fingers, it pays to know your STDs.

HPV
HPV, the human papilloma virus, may be the most common STD. It can be passed from

231

woman to woman by skin or mucous membrane contact and can cause genital warts and cervical neoplasia (precancerous or cancerous cells). An estimated 70% of the adult population is infected. If you don't know your partner's entire sexual history, I'd recommend you protect yourself. There's no treatment for the virus, but if warts develop they can be burned off with liquid nitrogen (which often takes more than one treatment). This procedure doesn't sound like fun, so be careful. I'd rather lick a little latex than have liquid nitrogen anywhere near my clit.

HPV can be passed by fingers, so if you like a good hand job, finger-fucking and fisting should be done with gloves. Some experts think that it can be passed by inserting toys, so to be safe use a condom and clean all of your toys with antibacterial soap. Just like all women, lesbians need regular Pap smears and checkups, in part because Pap smears can detect HPV and cervical irregularities. Frequent Pap smears are particularly important if you are sleeping with a woman who is infected with HPV.

Bacterial Vaginosis

Bacterial vaginosis (BV) is one of the most common STDs among lesbians. It is associated with having multiple sex partners, douching, or using scented products. It is passed by means of vaginal secretions. Often there are no symptoms, or women will mistake BV for a yeast infection. Women may experience a thin white or gray discharge, an unpleasant or fishy odor, burning while peeing, or itching in the vagina. If BV goes untreated, it can cause pelvic inflammatory disease and may increase the risk of contracting other STDs, including HIV.

Chlamydia

Chlamydia is another very common STD. According to the World Health Organization, 89 million people are infected, and there are four million new cases each year. Because chlamydia often shows no symptoms, it is called a "silent epidemic." Chlamydia has been around for quite a while; it was first documented in Egypt on papyruses and was first seen under a microscope in 1907. It is passed by oral, anal, or vaginal sex. It's easily treated with antibiotics, and people who have chlamydia often have gonorrhea. Sharing a dildo or sex toy—another reason to use condoms on your toys—can pass chlamydia. Untreated chlamydia can cause long-term problems, including pelvic inflammation, swollen or scarred fallopian tubes, and chronic pain.

Hepatitis

Hepatitis means "inflammation of the liver." There are many different strains of viral hepatitis. The most common are hepatitis A, B, and C. Hep A and B are not usually chronic, but hep C becomes chronic in about 85% of those who are infected. Hep A is transmitted via fecal matter to the mouth, so rimming (licking a partner's anus) is especially hazardous. More flexible, hep B lives in all body fluids, including semen, blood, saliva, and vaginal fluids. It can be transmitted by any sexual contact. Hep C, transmitted only by blood, can be passed by sharing needles (or any intravenous drug paraphernalia), straws (e.g., for snorting cocaine), razors, and even toothbrushes.

Hep C is a tiny and potent virus. Some experts believe it can live outside the body for up to three months. Although hep C is not considered a sexually transmitted disease, you should still be careful. If you have cuts on your mouth or bleeding gums, you can contract hep C by performing oral sex on a woman who is menstruating. Likewise, if you have cuts on your digits when you are fingering a woman on her period, you are at risk. There is no vaccine and no cure for hep C. Currently the most effective treatment is a combination of two drugs, pegylated interferon and ribavirin, but these drugs can cause severe side effects. All treatments for hep C are relatively new, because the hep C virus was only discovered in 1989. Blood banks didn't screen for it before 1992, so if you or your lover received a blood transfusion before 1992, you may be at risk for hep C.

Hep A and B usually cause recognizable symptoms (such as jaundice), but hep C can remain asymptomatic for years. People can live with it for decades and suddenly find out that they have cirrhosis or fibrosis (scarring of the liver). This is why it is also called the silent epidemic. One in 50 Americans is infected with the hep C virus. There are probably many more who don't know they have it.

HIV

h women reported other risky behaviors, usually injection drug use. Although female-to-female-transmission of HIV is rare, there is still some risk. The inside of your mouth is a mucous membrane. If you have sores or cuts that come in contact with vaginal secretions or blood containing HIV, you are putting yourself at risk.

As with HPV and hepatitis, dental dams, condoms, and latex or polyurethane gloves can block the transmission of HIV during sex. But one of the top ways of preventing HIV transmission is to know your partner's status. Get tested. And watch out for risk factors: IV drug use, sex with men, and "multiple partners" are usually considered risky. But remember too that if you're practicing safer sex with all your partners, polyamory is actually *less* risky than unprotected sex in serial monogamy. Women in monogamous relationships, in fact, are sometimes more at risk. If they cheat, they may be less likely to practice safer sex because they're not used to it, they're in denial about the affair, or they didn't think ahead to buy condoms or gloves. People who have an STD are two to five times more likely to contract HIV.

Know Thyself (and Her)

Millions of people are infected with STDs; many don't even know it. Some STDs can remain asymptomatic for years. So how do you know? The best thing you can do is get regular tests by your gynecologist. A few things to watch out for are: discharge from the vagina or anus; burning or pain when you urinate; itching or irritation of the genitals; warts, bumps, sores, blisters, or rashes around the genitals; redness or swelling of your genitals; bleeding between periods or after sex; pain in the abdomen; nausea; vomiting; fever; persistent sore throat; and jaundice (yellow skin and eyes). Many of these symptoms sound like the flu, but the key idea here is persistence. If a symptom doesn't go away, you should get it checked out.

Finally, if it's true love you're after, you should really know your partner. Don't be afraid to ask questions. Communication is the key to any happy, healthy relationship. Many lesbian-identified women weren't always, and unfortunately sometimes the past comes back to haunt you.

Sex, Drugs, and Getting Off

The Hidden Cost of Treating Depression
by Victoria A. Brownworth

"If someone offers you your life or your sex life, it's not *that* difficult a choice," says Laura McMahon.* "When you're suicidally depressed, the last thing you're thinking about is having sex. It's only later, when the depression starts to lift, and you're having problems reactivating your sexual self, that you question your decision."

McMahon, a 31-year-old New Jersey construction worker, is one of the 50 million Americans diagnosed with depression each year. Four years ago a series of personal crises catapulted her into a depression she couldn't snap herself out of. "The day I was standing on a girder at work and thinking how easy it would be to unsnap my safety harness, I knew I was in deep trouble. I was at the doctor the next day and on meds within 24 hours. I have to say it saved my life. It also changed it. I can still have sex, I can still come, but I just don't want it the way I used to, before the meds."

Each day Americans see an average of 20 advertisements for antidepressant medications. Magazines, particularly women's magazines, promote a range of antidepressants available to a market increasingly eager for them. Women with depression outnumber men with the illness three to one, and antidepressants are used not only to treat depression but also to treat premenstrual syndrome and menopausal symptoms.

In the voice-overs to the commercials or the small print attached to the advertisements, one side effect may stand out: sexual dysfunction. Many consumers interpret that as male impotence, which can be a sexual side effect for male users. But for women, lack of sexual desire, inability to reach orgasm, and other changes in sexual functioning occur in the majority of those taking the drugs.

Flipped by a Drug
"I *used* to be a top." Dani Nelson, a 35-year-old political consultant on the West Coast, laughs wryly. "I was out there packing every weekend, hair slicked back, leathers absolutely impeccable. I'd been out since high school, and the only time I was ever on my back was to get a blow job from a chick. Now I couldn't top if an S/M goddess had a gun to my head. I just don't have that top drive anymore. I just want to lie there and spread my legs. Put *that* in the commercial for what antidepressants did for me."

Jules Connelly, a 22-year-old college student on the East Coast, shares Nelson's sentiments. "I was in the process of coming out and questioning if I was trans as well, all while heading into my senior year," she explains. "The conflicts and pressures really pushed me to the edge, and I just totally freaked. After some craziness where I lived, my friends got me to see someone, who put me on antidepressants in a nanosecond."

Connelly adds, "It certainly helped the depression, which was pretty rough. It really strung me out. In some ways it steered the course of my sexuality too, because after I was into the drug, I was out of the sexual thing completely. I no longer asked if I was a boy or a girl; I asked if I was a eunuch. All my sexual desire just went *whoosh*. Gone. I don't want girls, I don't want boys, I don't even want to masturbate."

As a psychologist in private practice, Dr. Barbara Stein has treated depression for more than two decades. A majority of her patients are women, including a large lesbian clientele. Stein asserts that sexual dysfunction is a by-product of depression but needn't be a result of medical intervention.

"I couldn't top if an S/M goddess had a gun to my head. I just don't have that top drive anymore. I just want to lie there and spread my legs. Put *that* in the commercial for what antidepressants did for me."

"Drugs are evolving every day, and most women don't have to suffer with unpleasant side effects," Stein said. "The standard medications we used to treat depression when I was first practicing, tricyclics, have been overshadowed by serotonin re-uptake inhibitors, the Prozac family of drugs, as it were." Stein notes that the newer drugs such as Prozac, Zoloft, Serzone, Effexor, and others have far fewer side effects overall than their predecessors and have less impact on sexual function than self-medicating through alcohol, marijuana, or opiates.

236

"Antidepressants aren't a one-size-fits-all classification of drug," she explains. "They have to be chosen with the individual patient, her particular medical and personal history, and degree of depression in mind. Some patients are clinically depressed, in a state of low-level, lifelong depression, which must be managed like any other chronic illness. But many more are suffering from episodic depression brought on by severe stressors. Those patients will generally be on medication for about a year, maybe more, while also engaged in talk therapy. This means any sexual dysfunction they are experiencing should be temporary."

Not always, say some who have been on the drugs. "I have been off medication for a few months after taking it for about two years," said Nelson. "But I think I am a bottom for life now. It's like the medication flipped me and I can't get back to where I was before. It's very frustrating for me because it feels like I lost my identity along with my depression. I talked to my therapist about it, but she says there's no data on just what sexual changes happen from these drugs and how they are reversed. I mean, I'm not sorry I went on it. I was in really bad shape and really needed it, but I can't help feeling that it really changed who I am by changing the sexual part of my life really radically."

Culprit: The Drugs or the Dumps?

For those like McMahon, who has learned she suffers from chronic depression and will need medication for life, sexual side effects are a component of treatment that can't be waited out. "I used to be able to come like *that*," she says, snapping her fingers. "Now it's this agonizingly endless process, and a lot of the time I just pass. It just seems like work to me. Plus, there's a lot of pressure in my relationship to come in bed. I'm not that bothered by not coming myself, but it drives my girlfriend crazy because it's important to her to get me off. So my not coming has created some problems between us. It's that rock-and-hard-place dilemma: I need the drug to keep from getting so depressed I'm suicidal but I need to be the sexual person I used to be to please me and my girlfriend."

Inability to achieve orgasm, less-satisfying orgasms, and a general dulling of sexual sensation are common side effects of the newer medications—as is sexual languor, what Nelson calls "just wanting to lie there and spread my legs." The desire to be an active participant in sex dissipates in women experiencing this side effect.

Not every woman has negative sexual experiences while on antidepressants, however. For some, the depression is what killed their desire, not the drugs to treat it.

"When I was depressed, I had no desire whatsoever, I just felt sexually very flat and numbed out," says Marla Levin, a 44-year-old New York artist. "So actually, I have to say my sex life has improved significantly since I've been on the medication, because it reignited both my desire and my enjoyment of sex. I had sex when I was depressed, but it wasn't satisfying. I don't know exactly how long I was depressed— a long time before I realized that's what it was—and so it was an extended period of lessening desire. Now I get excited normally, I get aroused when I'm touched by or touch my lover. It's made sex so much better for me; I'm grateful to feel so much again. The drug gave sex back to me after the depression stole it."

For those who feel their sexual desire has diminished or altered because of antidepressants, Stein recommends asking one's doctor for a change in medication. "Sometimes the loss of sexual functioning or a shift in the kind of sexual functioning one is used to is just unbearable, because [sexuality] is so intrinsic to who we are as women," she says. "That's going to create stress that will just add to problems connected to the original depression. So it's important to talk to your doctor about trying something else or adding in another medication that counteracts the sexual side effect aspect of the antidepressants."

Experiencing satisfying sex is part of maintaining a healthy psyche, Stein believes. "Diminished sex drive is actually one of the first warning signs of depression," Stein says. "It's normal to want to have sex in your life; it's important to have that intimacy. Most women can tell if it is the depression or the medication that is making sex difficult or different for them. Don't suffer with it, don't assume there are no alternatives, because there are."

*All names of individuals in this article have been changed.

238

Sex and the Disabled Dyke

by Victoria A. Brownworth

Next time you strap on or strap in for a night of sexual play, consider the following: One in six Americans has a disability; the disabled are America's largest minority group and also the most invisible. Thousands of lesbians are disabled. Their disabilities can be physical or mental, visible or hidden, congenital or late-onset. Some use assistive devices like canes, wheelchairs or oxygen tanks, others do not. Some look nondisabled while others present obvious disability. Concomitantly desexualized by society and sexualized by men excited by their (seeming) helplessness, medicalized by doctors, often limited by their particular disability, these lesbians frequently find themselves shut out of the sexual marketplace.

"It can be daunting," explained Lana Young, a 26-year-old graduate student from Boston diagnosed with chronic fatigue immune dysfunction syndrome (CFIDS) and multiple chemical sensitivity disorder (MCSD) three years ago. "I had just broken up with my girlfriend and got what I thought was the flu compounded by allergies. Except I never got better."

Young spent eight months in bed before she was sufficiently improved to return to school and job. "By the time I was back at school after taking a year's leave of absence, I had basically been branded as a malingerer," she sighs. "No one believes you're really sick. In fact they constantly say, 'You look so healthy,' in a really insinuating way. They think you're trying to avoid work and responsibility. And that's your friends!" she laughs wryly. "Try finding a girlfriend under those circumstances. Every other personal ad you read states plainly: Must love hiking, sports, and long walks on the beach. I'm lucky if I can walk to my car from my front steps. It takes energy to have a relationship—even to have sex—and energy is what I *don't* have."

Many disabled dykes share Young's frustrations. "I have been on SSDI (social security disability insurance) for two years," says D. Kirby, a 33-year-old former industrial worker from New Jersey who was partially paralyzed in a forklift accident. "I used to be such a big butch daddy. Now I feel like I should just put on the lace and read the femme manual. Well, almost," she jokes. "But when you're used to being in control, in charge, it's hard to adjust. Hell, you don't know how to maneuver. In rehab they don't teach you how to fuck a femme when you can't move from the waist down. And while you might be able to figure that out on your own," Kirby adds, "you need the self-confidence to go there."

The Catch-22 for many disabled lesbians is that self-confidence often comes from being in a sexual relationship post-disability. Maureen Horowitz was 37 when she lost her right arm and leg in March 1999. A New Yorker transplanted to Kansas, Horowitz acknowledges that she was fortunate to meet her partner, who is nondisabled, after her injury. "I thought it would be months before I could have sex [post-amputations]," Horowitz admits. "I had spent so much time in the hospital and then rehab being poked and pushed around, my body didn't feel like my own anymore. But Chris has been so patient and gentle with me, she's helped me recover some of my sexual self."

But Horowitz is quick to acknowledge she's the exception. "My partner says people don't know what to do with us [disabled lesbians]," she explains. "People think lesbians are all about sex, and disabled people aren't supposed to have sex, so—where does that leave us?"

It leaves some lesbians choosing self-pleasure by default. "I am single and my disability has impacted my sex life to the point that I haven't had so much as a date in 14 months," admits Kathleen, a 43-year-old consultant from Sonora, Calif. "I'm afraid to even start with the whole thing—the explanations and so forth."

Like many lesbians, Kathleen's partner left after she was diagnosed with MS. "I was unable to go for walks on the beach with her, indulge in strenuous athletic sex, travel without ice, meds, sanitary pads, change of clothes for incontinence, wheelchair, ad nauseum, ad infinitum. I had to put down towels or pads before sex, because I sometimes lost urinary continence, and that turned her off."

"My disability has interfered with my ability to have an orgasm with a partner," Kathleen explains. "I am only able to do it alone now. I have a very hard time asking for what I need sexually. Either it just 'happens,' and I'm swept away by emotions and physical desire, or just fricking forget it."

The lesbian playwright Carolyn Gage, who has suffered from CFIDS for years, has written extensively about what she considers the insensitivity of many nondisabled lesbians toward those with disabilities. In an essay titled "Hidden Disability: A Coming Out Story," she states with her usual clarity and directness that nondisabled dykes need to be more accommodating, less dismissive, and more accepting of disability.

Disability should be viewed like race, Young asserts. "It used to be I was overly sexualized by other women because I'm Asian," she notes. "Now it's like I don't exist.

My wheelchair is like an anti-sex force field. Girls who would fall all over themselves to include me because of my race now *exclude* me because of my disability."

Young adds, "I *want* to have sex, but I can't go to bars. Most venues aren't chemically friendly or aren't accessible. And then if I do date someone, she doesn't take me seriously when I tell her scents make me ill, or she expects me to have boundless energy. It's maddening."

Being in a relationship makes sex more available, but problems remain. "I'm just clumsy," Horowitz notes. "I mean sexually—you want to have a little grace." She also feels less attractive. "I'd always been thin," Horowitz explains. "But since I've been in the wheelchair, I've gained a lot of weight. And then the stump looks very ugly [to me]—it looks like a slab of raw meat. Chris says it just looks like a scar, but not to me. So you constantly feel different things—relief that someone loves and wants you but a deep sense of loss for who you were and what your body was."

Some women have found ways to accommodate their sexuality and disability. When Jane Bennett, an English teacher from the Pacific Northwest, was diagnosed with MS at 30, she was very active: a rock-climber who taught martial arts. She has been with Elaine for 11 years, since just before her diagnosis. "Sex has always been about strength and vitality and spontaneity for me," Bennett asserts. "I really like the power of sex. MS made me feel less powerful."

She explains how disability "changes what I can do. Changing positions is harder. I'm spastically orgasmic, and my muscles will go into spasms."

Body image isn't an issue for Bennett, however, nor does she have problems topping her lover. "I don't feel less desirable. Sex is all about desire—giving and getting what you want. Desire lives in that place where two people meet. It's not desire per se until it clicks on somebody else." Bennett and her partner "have a lot of sex. Lately it's become quite bawdy and fun."

Finding ways to maintain sexual power and identity is important, these women attest. Bennett notes that she recently cut her very long hair quite short and dyed it. "I realized I had somehow begun to equate my helplessness against MS with femininity," she acknowledges.

"I need women to understand the chair doesn't make me less butch," states Kirby. "I'm still the same daddy inside, but I think when femmes see the chair, they can't see butch, they see powerlessness."

"No one expects to become disabled," adds Young. She wants other lesbians to know she is still a sexual being. "Just because I get fatigued really easily doesn't mean I can't be sexual, can't give and take pleasure," she asserts. "Am I a little more high-maintenance than other dykes? Maybe. But I'm the same sexy Asian chick I was before this disease. If I could say one thing to other dykes, it's this: Look past the disability. If you became disabled tomorrow, that's what you'd want."

Breaking New Ground for the Mentally Disabled

Even more than their physically disabled counterparts, mentally disabled lesbians face tremendous difficulties in acquiring sexual partners and even expressing their sexual preferences. Many mentally disabled adults live with parents or in independent living situations where their caregivers can be resistant to the idea of any sexual involvement. These living arrangements can also be outright homophobic, stifling any opportunity for sexual expression.

The Gay and Lesbian Community Center in New Haven, Conn., founded the Rainbow Support Group in 1998 under the aegis of John Allen. Funded through Easter Seals in Connecticut, it provides a social and semi-therapeutic space for developmentally disabled LGBTI folks. According to Allen, agencies servicing mentally disabled adults have been calling and bringing clients down. The basic goal of the Rainbow Group, the first of its kind in the U.S., is to allow queers who are classified as developmentally disabled or autistic to meet and engage in supportive friendships and relationships with other mentally disabled queers.

Judy Tompkins, founding facilitator, is heterosexual herself but considers sexuality a natural part of adulthood—regardless of mental ability, though she acknowledges this isn't a common perspective on the mentally disabled, who have frequently endured forced sterilization, chemical castration, and other sexual restrictions. Tompkins has worked for the group since its inception and tries to create an atmosphere where queer developmentally disabled adults can meet other people, find a partner, be with other queers, be comfortably out.

Tompkins was shocked to find the level of homophobia mentally disabled queers were dealing with, in particular, attempts to force lesbians or gay men to date members of the opposite sex.

The program has been so successful that now many caregivers bring their clients to the meetings. Allen hopes the success of the Rainbow Group will encourage other communities to address disability issues.

Desire and Fulfillment

Sex Over 40
by Victoria A. Brownworth

There they were: Three single East Coast dykes—one butch, one femme, one undecided—having dinner on a Saturday night. As they shared Asian food and perused each other's cookie fortunes the talk made the natural turn from politics to sex.

Paloma, 47, and Blair, 40, had each broken up with their lovers of nearly 20 years within the past six months. Mira, 44, had broken up with her lover of over a decade a year earlier. Paloma admitted she and her ex hadn't had sex in nearly five years before the final split, and that lesbian bed death was both a symptom of problems in their relationship and a contributing factor in their breakup. Blair and Mira had been actively sexual with their girlfriends until the final days of their relationships.

"I don't miss having a girlfriend, but I do miss having sex," Blair acknowledged, while Mira asserted she'd like to have sex with strangers but knew a little too much about STDs to do it other than virtually.

Despite media and medical hype to the contrary, sexual desire rarely decreases for women as they age.

The three discussed sexual histories, desires, and fantasies. Mira had had numerous sex partners, including group sex, and had tried everything on the sexual spectrum, including S/M. Blair had only had two sexual partners in her life, and her sexual experience was limited to their rather rigid preferences. Paloma's experiences were broader than Blair's but also limited by her partners' inflexibility.

Of the three, only Mira masturbated. The other two were somewhat aghast at the idea of solitary sex, but by the evening's end Blair and Paloma agreed to a trip to the sex shop with Mira as their guide. Not having partners shouldn't inhibit their sexual desire or experience, Mira explained, and off to buy vibrators, dildos, and other accoutrements they went. Partners would come in time, but lack of partners shouldn't keep them from coming in the interim.

We've heard about it for years: Women's sexual drive peaks in their 40s. One of the cruel jokes of heterosexuality is that men's sexual peak hits 20 years earlier. Thus, it doesn't take a leap of logic to presume that women would be far more likely to find sexual fulfillment with other women, no matter what their age, based on physiology alone.

But 40 is also the age when menopausal changes begin in most women, often lessening desire. And more breakups occur between couples in their 40s than at any other age. In addition, a significant percentage of women—so many that there are Web sites and message boards for "late bloomers"—discover or acknowledge their lesbianism in middle age. Which means that 40 and beyond can be a sexual minefield for many women.

Lesbian sexuality is a minefield that noted photographer Tee Corinne has traversed for decades. Her *Cunt Coloring Book* is still being banned two decades after its initial publication, and many of her books of erotic poetry and stories have been banned as well. Her erotic photographs of lesbians, sometimes engaged in sex acts, have also sparked controversy.

Now 57, she has lived in the Oregon woods with her 50-year-old partner for over a decade. For most of Corinne's sexual life she has preferred monogamous sex, though that "sometimes included going to group sex parties and getting it on with my monogamous lover."

With her art and personal life sexually charged, Corinne sees the two melding often. "There is a relationship between sexuality and creativity," she explains. "The initiating impulse often seems the same to me—making love and making art." Corinne notes, "A sexual/sensual awareness is present in much that [she and her lover] do together, not just the sex itself, which is regular," Corinne says.

Aging has brought some sexual changes, however, Corinne states. "My sexual desire has changed, especially since passing through menopause. It isn't so much that it has decreased as it has become more diffused and less goal-oriented. I also don't feel so driven by it, which I did, at times, in the years between 13 and 40."

244   Contrary to some women's experience, it has been in her middle years that Barbara Grier, 67, cofounder of the world's largest lesbian publisher, Naiad Press, has had the most desire. Monogamous for the 28 years she has spent with lover Donna McBride, 59, Grier—who pioneered writing about lesbian sex in the 1950s in her publication *The Ladder* and made lesbian sexuality the focal point of the novels

published by Naiad—has been intensely sexual since she announced to her mother at age 12 that she was a lesbian.

"From age 40, when I had a complete hysterectomy, my sexual desire increased steadily until about five years ago," Grier asserts. "While it has not subsided, it has not continued to grow stronger."

And like Corinne, Grier discounts the idea that sex becomes less important or less fulfilling as women age. "Sex is a continually more pleasurable activity with each passing year," Grier says. "I suspect that may stop being so at some advanced age, but I have no idea what age that might be."

Lifelong femmes, neither Corinne nor Grier has felt any desire to change sexual

Navigating and Negotiating

With age does not necessarily come experience. One of the startling statistics of the past few years is the rise in new AIDS cases among people over 50. Women are as likely to contract the disease as men are, but lesbians often think safer sex isn't an issue if they aren't involved with men.

The older you are, however, the more sexual partners you are likely to have had. The same is true for your partners.

Only a small percentage of lesbians have never had sex with men. Late bloomers are most likely to have had sex with men recently—and thus more likely to be at risk for a range of STDs. The myth that lesbians don't contract STDs is just that: myth.

Negotiating safer sex isn't necessarily easier when one is older, but it's just as important at 50 as at 15.

"I have trouble discussing safe sex with new partners," says Terri McCormack, 49. "I intend to practice safe sex, but a lot of women my age think if you want to do safe sex that either you have an STD or think that they do. It can be a big turn-off. I've actually had women just leave, telling me they didn't want to hear from me again."

The language of safer sex may seem to be only for Gen Xers and their cohort, but the stats prove there's no age limit on catching herpes, chlamydia, hepatitis, or HIV. So as you expand your sexual horizons, keep the latex close at hand.

roles since menopause, but some women do. Paloma, just entering menopause, has always had butch partners, but now feels herself shifting gears toward a more assertive top role.

"I feel more aggressive, more desirous of being in control, on top," she explains. "I spent 20 years with a woman who never allowed me to initiate sex, and that is what I want now—to be able to do that."

Shifting sexual desires post-menopause can also force women out of the closet. Fleur, a 53-year-old New Yorker, had been a ballet dancer, but although her career revolved around her body, she was in "a barren sex life with a man for years." Then in her mid 40s she met "an adorable sort of butchy older lesbian, and I was so turned on I went into some type of sexual psychosis and was hot and horny all the time," she admits. "Being practical, I left the well-respected doctor for a certain Miss W and had the hottest, most satisfying sex ever."

Now Fleur can't get enough of lesbian sex and age hasn't lessened her desire one iota. "My experience is that I get better and better at responding sexually, more intense in my focus and desire and better at seeking out and negotiating sex with a prospective partner," she explains. "Now I find that the more I give sexually, the more eroticized I become."

Hong Kong–born author and athlete Kitty Tsui is known as an erotic darling, her stunning athletic physique having graced the cover of *On Our Backs* as well as her own erotic book, *Breathless,* and won her gold and bronze medals in the Gay Games.

Currently single and living in Southern California, at age 48 Tsui finds her sexual desire and her desire for sexual exploration have both increased. "Exploration is great," Tsui notes with enthusiasm. "Sexual territories can be extraordinary adventures, and I am a confirmed adventurer and risk-taker, though I've practiced safer sex since 1988 so I don't take risks in that area."

Like many other dykes, Tsui's sexual predilections have altered slightly as she's gotten older. She identifies as a "butch top and have most of my sexual life. When I was younger I was mostly attracted to other butches. As I've gotten older, I've mostly been attracted to femmes. But I've been with both femmes and butches, and what I find irresistible is a woman who is both butch and femme." Single for over four years by choice, Tsui is now dating "and finding no problem with willing participants."

Like Tsui, Mississippi attorney Diana Hart has no dearth of willing sex partners but says finding a serious relationship is increasingly difficult. Hart just turned 40 and finds that although her level of sexual desire has remained constant since her 20s, she is now "far more open about communicating that desire to a partner and more willing to explore sexually and take risks"—if her partner is also willing. Describing herself as "pretty much butch to the bone, but willing to be both top and bottom," Hart says bondage, anal sex, and light S/M are among her most compelling fantasies but says "small-town Southern life doesn't lend itself to fulfilling these fantasies. Most women I meet would run screaming from the suggestion alone."

So despite media and medical hype to the contrary, sexual desire rarely decreases for women as they age, though availability of suitable partners may, particularly for women seeking monogamy. But fulfillment of sexual desire needn't be a fantasy.

"I used to have to avoid my sexual desire because there was no release for it," notes Fleur. "Now I embrace it, myself, the sexual journey I am on. Sex is wild, spiritual, emotional, sensual, visceral. It's everything it never was when I was younger."

"Age has brought a heightened awareness of my being," says Tsui. "All my senses are engaged in sex. I take more time and am as focused on the journey—making love—as the destination—orgasm."

"I am learning that desire is the foundation for fulfillment," says Paloma. And age is no barrier to either.

Intimate Disclosure

Seven Women Talk Sex and Class, Part 1
compiled by Laurie Toby Edison and Debbie Notkin

We knew when we began this conversation that we were stepping into unexplored and unexamined territory. We expected basic surprises. We found two, neither of which is surprising after the fact. First, although as queer feminists we're all pretty comfortable talking about sex, this country and this culture are so silenced about class that all the articulate women in this roundtable (including ourselves) had trouble getting started, and the conversation often seemed to lag. As Elena said at one point, "Class issues are more intimate and involve a lot more self-disclosure than sex for me." Nonetheless, we gathered far more material than can fit here. For instance, we had to cut everyone's explanations of their class backgrounds.

We also didn't anticipate the extent to which sex and class intersect with women's abuse histories. The threads of class are twined with all the history of our lives, but the particular threads of class and abuse seem to be woven together in ways that require one to contemplate the woven fabric rather than try to unweave it. If you try too hard to separate the strands you may unweave a reasonably whole truth into something less true.

Finally, we started off with Debbie as a "nonparticipating moderator," but when members of the roundtable objected to having someone who was listening to the conversation but not taking equal risks, she joined in as a participant.

The Roundtable
Elena: My mother explained sex: "It's something disgusting that you have to do to make a baby. And if you're married, because that is part of your duty as a wife, to let your husband have sex with you whenever he wants to. Because he pays the rent." Later on she complained about my dad's sex drive. I said, "I thought sex was something that was bad, Mom? Huh?" She just seemed ashamed.

Betty: I assume that my mother and father had sex, because they had four kids. That was my only clue. They never slept together. My mother never, ever discussed sex with me, not even, or maybe especially, when I told her that I thought I'd just been fucked by her uncle. All I ever got from her on the subject was pursed lips and a cold shoulder.

248

Laurie: Everything that happened inside my house took place in a bubble that was separate, silent, and apart from the world. There was a force field I walked through every day, and the girl on the outside of the door was raised to never get pregnant, always have boys treat her with "respect," be terrified of the possibility of getting pregnant (this is way pre–legal abortion).

Debbie: My parents' tolerant liberal politics was very much a class stereotype. I had access to birth control pills as soon as I wanted them. My father helped me find a safe illegal abortion for a friend. My parents never made me feel that sex was bad or evil, just unimportant and not directly discussed.

Marlene: I was raised on the kid's stories published in *Ms.* magazine. I grew up having *Our Bodies, Our Selves* in the house. My parents told me sex was a good thing, but complicated enough that one had to wait until adulthood to make decisions about it. The fact that they did everything they could to turn me into a "decent, sensitive man" is one of the things I value most about how they raised me. All of those lefty ideas about sex and gender contributed greatly to my ability to face my problems with my gender rather than continue to hide from them.

Lydia: I had exactly one conversation with my mother about sex. [She] came into my room, sat down on the bed, and said, "You know, Lydia, sex is a marvelous thing, in the marriage bed. It's wonderful, a gift from God. And even if some of the things you do feel degrading, well, as long as it feels good then it's fine. Within the marriage bed, I mean." And then she left. Sex was dirty. Sex was wonderful. Sex was the ultimate sin. Sex was a great gift God gave to man (not woman). It was also nearly unmentionable, and certainly not by its name. Homosexuality was completely unmentionable, but referenced obliquely in a lot of my father's sermons.

Jewelle: I was raised by my great-grandmother, living on welfare, and she said almost nothing about sex, ever. She didn't even let me know about menstruation until it had already happened!

With my father and stepmother's working-class background, there was little overt discussion of sex. But sex was a natural part of their lives; they insisted on their privacy for it without embarrassment.

My father asked my stepmother to make sure I had birth control info when he realized I was having sex with men, when I was about 20. Their ability to make desire and satisfaction an honest part of themselves and their relationships gave me a much easier time.

Elena: Usually sex was something my cousins did, but they were "trash." I guess my mom forgot that she was related to them, somehow. They had babies [with] no fathers. She did, too. But she had been deceived, so it was OK for her. When I did have sex, my cousins were much nicer to me. Like I'd come over to their side, or something.

Early on I got that white, upper-class women did not like sex. And white upper-class men didn't know how to have sex. Now the lower classes, both white and brown, were good at sex, and liked it. This made them "breed like animals."

Betty: I learned about sex from the paperback books I read and then masturbated in my bedroom.

Laurie: The clean "pretty girl" who lived on the outside of the force field used being a "lady" to make herself safer (and it worked…it was the '50s) and enjoyed the power her looks gave her over boys and men, while being careful to use it only in ways that were useful to her. This feels very middle-class to me: being "clean," using power that came from the promise of sex withheld. I didn't have "real" consensual sex until I had a diaphragm firmly in place, and by then I was well out of high school.

Betty: I didn't have consensual, know-what-I'm-doing sex until I was 23. At 12 I knew I was a dyke, but I fucked a lot of guys, proving it to my sister and my new therapist I got when I went to college. Fucking can be fun when you no longer give a shit, and my mother was dead by then, so I didn't give a shit.

On Various Kinds of Coming Out…

Jewelle: I think that the working-class lives of my folks made me feel easier about sexual desire, difference, and sexual expectations. Gays, for instance, were patrons in my father's bar, etc., and it wasn't a scandal or problem.

My grandmother told me once she'd made a conscious decision that sex wasn't that important anymore to her. I thought that was amazing in that it highlighted how important sex had been before that.

My father actually had two "wives" at the same time (after he split from my mother), and they knew each other and were friends. I understood that he had a sexual life and that his social circumstance was unusual. That also helped me adjust to being an outsider as a lesbian. On one hand, I had romantic expectations, and on the other I didn't expect anything in my life to be like anything else I'd seen.

I think my background made me very flexible. Sometimes that was an advantage; other times it left me with no articulated standards in order to check on my safety.

Elena: Coming out wasn't hard for me, but it was hard to tell my parents. I had to give them the silent treatment before they learned to behave themselves around me. Mainly because my mom worked in the jail and the only lesbians she ever saw were the ones who were drunk and disorderly or in a fight over some girl. To this day she calls them "bulldaggers." I laugh when I think of myself as a "bulldagger."

Betty: My family thinks that being a dyke is weird, but they also know it keeps my outsider status in place, regardless of my salary or my education. I actually think it keeps together what upward mobility could have torn apart. Of course if I were closeted and/or trying to pass for middle class or thin it would probably all be blown out of the water and either I'd disown them or they'd tell me to go fuck myself.

Lydia: I found out, in my year at the massage parlor, that I didn't want to play the odds that living "the life" required. Too many of the girls there had lost more than they'd won, and I didn't have the flexibility or the reflexes for it. But it still looks attractive, vivid, sharp. Turning tricks wasn't usually an isolated craft, a job you could work from 8 to 8, or anything like that. It was integrated into the whole set of accommodations, risks, and gains that living there requires. Some days it's fun, some days it's scary, some days it's just what you do.

I worked at the parlor out of curiosity, not need. I actually turned only one trick. The rest of the time, I only offered hand jobs. I didn't mind the physical services that much, but I hated the role-playing that was required. If the customer had wanted just the mechanics of sex, that would have been fine, but he never did.

Marlene: When I was 13 I had sex with a girl for the first time. When I was 15 I had sex with a boy for the first time. When I was 12 I got drunk for the first time. I drank and did drugs because I was uncomfortable with myself, my body, my gender.

It wasn't long before I was having sex with older men for drugs. Because of the various social conventions of the gay male bar scene (especially the fact that I wasn't sissified), the men I slept with thought of me as rough trade. I got more and had to do less if I left this fantasy undisturbed. If I wanted to get fucked, if I pretended to be conceding something reluctantly, I got more.

As I got a bit older, I stopped going to the bars and started going to clubs. The difference between the bars and the clubs was class, not between the buyers, but between the sellers. In clubs I made more if I looked expensive. If somebody wanted rough trade, they'd go looking in the places I had been tricking in before. It was expected in the clubs that I would get fucked when I went home with someone. It was also assumed that I was actually queer rather than just broke or strung out.
I don't know about how these stereotypes manifest themselves outside the gay male world. I've never sold sex as a woman.

Debbie: I never conceived of myself in any felt way as a sexual being until I was well into my 20s (and certainly no longer a virgin). I never masturbated to climax until years after I'd been living with a lover. For most of my growing-up life I ignored my body as much as possible, and had no idea that anything was missing. Marlene's account of a sexually active and risky life before she was 20 makes me think, "Wow, that would be like living on another planet." Does this have anything to do with class? If so, I haven't been able to tease it out so far.

Intimate Disclosure

Seven Women Talk Sex and Class, Part 2
compiled by Laurie Toby Edison and Debbie Notkin

Queer communities often pride themselves on the ability to talk about sex, feeling smug about the facility with words and desire. From homophobia and fear of gender transgressions to plain old cultural repression, there's a lot of pressure to be quiet. When we're loud and lusty, we're making revolution. But that doesn't mean there isn't more to do. Laurie and Debbie organized a cyberspace conversation on the theme of sex and class. What came up in those interviews shows how wound together—and how largely unexplored—the sex and class dance is. What are the various prices we pay, dependent on our class and race, for being sexually visible? How does class get into bed with us, or against the kitchen table, or in the back seat of our car? —Susan Raffo (author of *Queerly Class*)

On Cross-Class Relationships...

Laurie: I had a 20-plus-year relationship (off and on) with a woman from my own background with whom I was deeply in love. We didn't make it simple and she cared way too much what people thought (in the midst of her outrageous life), and I still miss her. This is a story as much of time as class: We were both '50s girls, and our stories often lack happy endings. I had a long relationship with a woman who identified as under-class and wanted very badly as time went on to pass over into middle-class visuals and manners (at first mostly for work). Even when she was working on assimilation, her good, clear class politics were open and out much of the time. She taught me a lot, and loving her taught me a lot. As she got better at passing, she became less vivid, and I missed that part of how she had been before. I eventually lost her to her assimilated choices. That's happened to me more than once. I'm not a good choice for a girl on the way up: can't afford enough things, don't appreciate people being "understanding" about it, and don't appreciate "up" a whole lot. As a working artist, I like my "unimproved" life.

Elena: I have a long history of loving working-class men and middle-class women. Very strange. Although I do have to say that I am attracted to working-class women,

253

but often they are scared off by those initials [Ph.D] at the end of my name—they make me the enemy.

Betty: One of my pet peeves is being sexualized in private, or semiprivate, in a sort of titillating way, but then being shunned or censured for it in other settings. I often think I'm doomed to fall for women who want to stand by their man—or their butch, as the case may be. I like middle-class women, or women with middle-class values. It brings out a hostility in me that is sexually exciting. It also touches upon a core of gentleness that I don't often find in myself. I had a middle-class lover. I think she was also trying to "save," shelter, or protect me in some way, or at least "excuse" me. She understood when I didn't buy her flowers because she assumed that as one of the poor poor, even though I had money now, I wouldn't think of such things—and she "forgave me because of it."

The sex was fun. It was the expectations we each had about coupling, courtship, romance, etc., and how honest and up-front about all of this stuff we could be with each other—as well as the social implications of it all. In retrospect, I never really felt as if I were her lover; it's more like I was her girlfriend prop. She'd buy herself the flowers and prop me up by her side as the girlfriend. I was as much a prop as the flowers were in making up a picture of her life.

Marlene: I'm kinky, queer, and transgendered. The kinds of kinky I tend toward are more of the serious pain variety than the silk-scarf-bondage type. I don't like being exoticized for my gender, and I don't like feeling that my lover is being "a good person" by "understanding." It's been a lot of years since I've slept with anyone who hasn't discarded close to all of what they were raised to believe about sex and relationships. By the time I get someone, they don't exhibit a lot of expectations about this stuff that I can identify with any kind of class origin. I'm anxious that this sounds like the American middle-class myth of class not being a real issue, which is not what I'm trying to describe.

Debbie: For many years I lived with a (male) lover who was far more upper-class than me, and who carried a deep sense of prudery around sex that I never found myself able to either understand or sympathize with. In particular, enjoying sex for its own sake seemed wrong to him; it was only OK to enjoy sex if you were doing it for a purpose (not necessarily breeding, but to forge a bond with someone or solve a fight). Enjoying just the sex was not OK.

Betty: Sometimes when I'm with middle-class S/M dykes I forget I'm with middle-class dykes and that while someone may be dressing like a slut and acting like a slut and may even be getting off on being treated like a slut, you ain't never, ever supposed to forget that she's a lady. Sometimes I feel as if I walked into a costume ball, only nobody told me and I have to figure out for myself who is wearing a costume and what it all means and when they have their mask on or off. I know how to play the bad girl. What I don't know is how to play the good girl playing the bad girl. It's like to fit in I'd have to unlearn too much of what I already know, and it's just too much.

On Courtship, Money, and Presents...

Elena: I learned to write or draw or create something of myself, because I didn't have a lot of money. Sometimes, though, it really, really hurts. When I was living on $583 a month and my lover's birthday came around, I gave her a massage and got her some little presents, including a little jar of Baby Bee lotion. She had bought this big jar of the same brand and was hiding it because she didn't want me to feel bad about my gift. I kind of sat up. I didn't feel bad about my gift, but I did then. It wasn't because she got herself something better, but that she felt she had to hide it to protect me. I felt really vulnerable. I think the biggest way in which my class affects me is that I hate to receive presents. It unnerves me and makes me embarrassed. I never know what to say. Thank you doesn't seem to be enough.

Lydia: Money was just so weird in our house. It was the Victorian unmentionable, especially in social settings, but it was constant threat and promise and bone of contention as well. When I was down to nothing, owed the landlord rent, no food in the house, no job, not eligible for assistance, my parents gave me a dollar and a quarter with which to buy toothpaste. I guess I'm still very bitter about how money was handled in my family.

Laurie: I like food in courtship, at home and out. Eating with someone is an important piece of courtship to me (Jewish, middle-class, immigrant, New York City, I don't know.) I also like the whole food-after-sex thing: scrambled eggs or ramen or whatever. It's the post-sex food hunger and eating together in bed. I have problems if a lover doesn't understand that shared food can be a form of love.

255

The Panel

Betty Rose Dudley is a fat, white dyke who comes from a working-class background but currently makes a decent salary. Although she grew up in small-town Missouri and not rural Tennessee, *The Beverly Hillbillies* was one of her favorite TV shows as a child, so she moved to California—San Francisco, not Los Angeles. She now lives in Oakland and hopes to one day win the Lotto, after which she will have a big car and a big house done up in bold, primary colors. There is very little pastel in her personality.

Laurie Toby Edison is an internationally exhibited photographer. *Women En Large: Images of Fat Nudes* (with her photographs and Debbie Notkin's text) was published in 1994. Her current work in progress is *Familiar Men: A Book of Male Nudes*. She is also a jeweler and sculptor. She has two daughters and lives and works in San Francisco. She has at various times been a member of the Gay & Lesbian History Project, Queer Nation, and other queer activist groups.

Elena Escalera earned her Ph.D. in Social Psychology at the University of California at Berkeley. She now teaches social psychology, as well as being a massage therapist in San Francisco.

Jewelle Gomez was raised on welfare in Boston and now leads a middle-class activist life in San Francisco. She was on the original board of GLAAD and is on the national advisory board of the National Center for Lesbian Rights. She writes about black lesbians in the past and the future. Her six books include *The Gilda Stories* and *Don't Explain.*

Marlene Hoeber lives in San Francisco with a cat, a lizard, a snake, a girlfriend, and a few fish. She tries to make beautiful/dangerous things for a living, and failing that, she does miscellaneous light industrial work.

Lydia Nickerson lives in a polyamorous household in Minneapolis known as Blaisdell Polytechnic. She earns her living doing clerical and secretarial tasks for doctors, and helps organize science fiction conventions for recreation.

256 **Debbie Notkin** divides her time between social change work and making a living by editing and multimedia instructional design. She wrote the text for *Women En Large: Images of Fat Nudes* and is chair of the mother board for the James Tiptree Award, which honors works of science fiction and fantasy that explore and expand gender roles. She lives in Oakland when work doesn't force her into long periods in New York City.

Sex for Sale

Why Some Dykes Do Sex Work
by Deborah Addington

The sex industry produces goods or services meant to enhance the quality of sexual experience: things like books, videos, magazines, music, exotic dancers, peep shows, and prostitutes. Given its longevity, the sex industry meets a need, and its prospects seem to only be getting better.

Women have niche markets, but most of the products of the industry, in general, are intended for and consumed by men. And there's no way to control who consumes the product after it's on the market, so even stuff not intended to give guys a hard-on might end up doing so.

There's little social support for the institution or the humans that give us shower nozzle masturbation material. Why would a lesbian run the legal, personal, and social risks associated with being engaged in such a popular yet culturally complicated industry?

> **"If a female customer does come in and wants to tip me, I make a big show of it. It's my way of saying, 'Yeah, that's right. I dig chicks, and you boys are paying for looking at something you can never have!'"**

Many people assume it's for the money. Miranda, a 36-year-old professional dominatrix in the Bay Area who earns around $65,000 a year, would agree. She's also very happy with the flexibility of her work. "I set my own hours, I answer to no one except my clients, and they know my limits when they contract with me for services." Regarding her pay, she says, "Just like a regular building contractor, I'm skilled labor. I deserve to be paid for my skills, and well-paid too. I have a small fortune invested in equipment and my own training.

"Some days, I can't believe there aren't more lesbians doing this for a living," she adds, "but if we [sex workers] were easier to find and we had more legal room, there'd be more of us, and it could even become a buyer's market." Miranda says it's now a seller's market, "and people want what I offer."

Lou, a 22-year-old prostitute who got her start because she was tired of "squat daddies" wanting pussy for free, disagrees with the money as motivation angle. "I started tricking because I thought it would be an easy way to make money," she says. "I was giving it away in exchange for safety, so I figured I might as well make a buck." She fantasized about being saved by some rich sugar mama. "I think I expected to pull some *Pretty Woman* stunt and go live happy ever after. I was really, really wrong about the money thing, but I found I like the work." Most of her clients are male, and she finds it easier that way. "I fuck men, mostly, because that makes it easier to separate work from pleasure. I keep doing it because I love my job."

Lou also gets off on the control that sex work gives her. "I work hard. I'm good at what I do. I like taking advantage of my skill in bed, especially when it comes to men. I control them when I'm rocking their world. I like the hours compared to a regular 9-to-5 job. I put in less time to make the same amount of money, even though the money can't touch the risks involved. But I like risk."

And there are many risks, no matter how careful you are; STDs aren't the worst of it. Many prostitutes face physical danger at the hands of tricks, with no protection from police. "I'm very careful. But one hospital bill after being beat by a trick and there go your profits for the next couple months, and we can't exactly get worker's comp," Lou tells me. "This is hard work, and almost no one I know supports me in it. If I was struggling with college classes or a tough boss in an office, I'd get a lot more support."

Like other kinds of activists, some of us take it to the streets; others take it indoors. Lisa, 27, responded to an ad for "models." It turned out to be an audition for a strip club. She had no intention of joining the industry, but was lured in by the starting pay of $18 an hour. After doing it for a year, she has this to say: "I love my work. I love to be watched, and I get paid for it. It's perfect. The guys can say whatever they want, but not one of them can touch me. Some clubs make you do lap dances, and they try to touch you then, but not where I work."

Lisa enjoys being a dyke and dancing for men. "If a female customer does come in and wants to tip me, I make a big show of it. It's my way of saying, 'Yeah, that's right. I dig chicks, and you boys are paying for looking at something you can never have!'"

Even for women who love the industry, there are challenges. And not just for the sex worker. Lisa says, "I think stripping is a lot harder on my girlfriend than it is on me. She catches shit for having a girlfriend who is an object of male lust. A lot of her 'real' lesbian friends think of me as a sellout, and that puts stress on our relationship."

I asked Lisa's girlfriend, Kelly, how she felt about Lisa's work. "I worry about her," she says, "but not nearly as much as I would if she was actually fucking her customers. Yeah, some of my friends give me hell because of what she does, but that's their problem."

Anti-prostitution activists might change their minds if they saw things the way Kelly does: "Lisa's not being exploited by what she does—she's exploiting. She's working those men, and she knows it. I've seen her do it, and I love watching her do it." In addition to the rush of excitement, Kelly gets something more personal out of the deal. "I know Lisa," she says. "I know how much she loves being the total center of attention. She gets her fix, comes home horny as hell, and I'm the one who gets to make her scream at night."

Kelly sees sex work as a business, and a good-paying one. "Sex is big business. Beats flipping burgers, and she doesn't smell like someone else's dinner when she comes home."

Amber, 47, makes porn for women. She says, "So much of what's considered attractive by the media has no appeal whatsoever for my audience. I don't want to see some boob-jobbed twit with dragon lady fingernails flicking her tongue in the general direction of some other girl's clit."

Money, control, personal gratification, politics: It's all part of why lesbians work in this industry. Every time I think I've heard, done, and seen it all, I meet someone who bends my brain and body around some new delight.

"I don't really care if some guy gets off watching me," says Amber. "I like knowing that he wasn't included in the creative loop when the film was made. I'm doing this to get women off, and to make a living is a secondary—but very wonderful—thing. I make a statement and I make a buck. What a great country."

Jasmine, 23, does amateur, girl-next-door-style live video for the Internet. She works at home in a modest apartment in Oklahoma City. "I don't expect this to lead into a career; I expect my education to do that. I do my site because it makes me enough money to stay in school and support my girlfriend and myself comfortably." Jasmine got the idea for this type of work from watching a talk show. "I think it's a great medium, and it's all about the supply and demand. I can make money from home, in bed, making love to my girlfriend."

259

The majority of Jasmine's customers are male. "As long as there are credit cards with men attached to them, there will be a market for what I produce." She thinks her work is fun and can't imagine working an office job. "Can you think of anything better than lying around in bed, getting laid, and making a living at it? I can't."

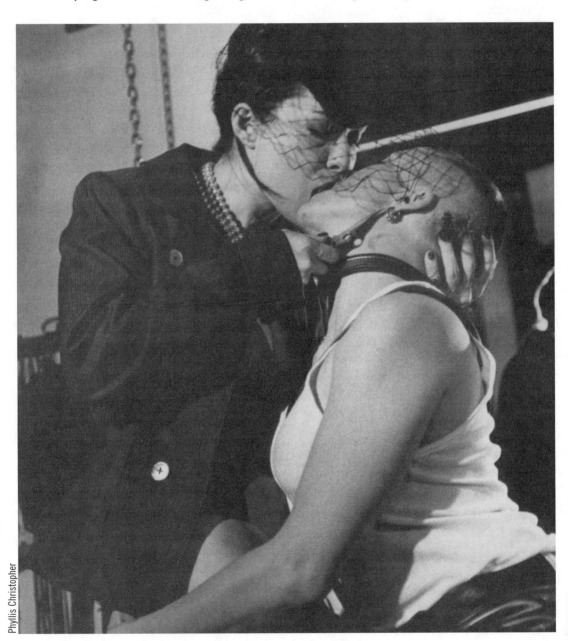

No Ass, No Tail

Uniform Festish Aside, Real Military Dykes Aren't Getting Laid
by Myriam Gurba

In 1993, Bill Clinton passed the "Don't Ask, Don't Tell" (DADT) policy to protect gays and lesbians by prohibiting discussions of sexual orientation, activity, and gay marriage. According to Clinton, DADT was introduced to give "decent regard to the legitimate privacy and associational rights of all service members."

But gay and lesbian organizations point out that DADT is the only law in the country that forces people to be dishonest about their lives at the risk of being fired or imprisoned. The Human Rights Commission has called the policy nothing more than an excuse to keep gays and lesbians out of the military.

The number of gays and lesbians discharged has actually increased since 1993, and lesbians have been disproportionately hard hit. Although women make up only 15% of the armed forces, they represent nearly one third of the discharges that have occurred since DADT went into effect. Several Defense Department and Senate reports state that women servicemembers, regardless of their sexual orientation, often fear reporting sexual harassment because they believe they will be accused of being lesbian and lose their careers as a result. The threat of a discharge, court marshaling, or even imprisonment is very real.

Many baby butches imagine the military to be a butch haven, a place where their budding masculinity will be appreciated. "Joining the military seemed like a way to be masculine with no questions asked. I didn't see many other options, especially for a fledgling butch in Iowa. You serve an important purpose, and that's a very powerful feeling. I was in love with the discipline and the physicality of it," recalls Trina Dewey, who enlisted in the army at age 18.

Puppet, an ex–Air Force servicemember, was shocked at how straight her military experience was. "The military is stereotyped as a dyke haven. I was shocked at how many women were joining the military that were not dykes. I believe I was the only dyke out of 60 girls in my basic training flight." Puppet remembers the rampant homophobia among her fellow female officers, which made her a target for attack. "The straight women in basic training were afraid I would hit on them and reacted by desperately trying to get me kicked out for things like cursing too much or accusing me of being sexual with some of the girls. I wasn't interested in any of them sexually." Basic training became a nightmare for Puppet. "I think living in close quarters with 60 women was actually one of the most dreadful experiences I've had to endure."

Pulp novels used to portray women's barracks as sizzling with lesbian sex after lights out, but in reality the opposite is true. Puppet found herself constantly monitored for signs of sexual misconduct. "Sergeants were always looking out for the signs of homosexual behavior," she says. "We couldn't spend too much time with one person, and we had to make sure we were all in our assigned rooms during bed checks. All of us had to be very secretive, so a lot of the time the dykes wouldn't even be seen together. That way if anybody got caught you wouldn't be associated with them and they wouldn't try to get you next. Any camaraderie with the handful of people who knew what you were going through was really out of the question."

One Air Force doctor—we'll call her Major Smith—who is dating another female officer describes similar feelings. "Our general would only have to catch one person to start an entire domino effect," says Smith. "I don't like being watched like a hawk. I've worked hard to get where I am. I'm in a respected position, as is my girlfriend, and neither of us like the idea of cameras in our bedrooms just to see how straight we are."

"Sergeants were always looking out for the signs of homosexual behavior. All of us had to be very secretive, so a lot of the time the dykes wouldn't even be seen together."

Unlike the tomboyish dykes, femmes seem to fly under the radar of homophobic concerns. "As a pretty, femme, young, model-minority woman, and a squared-away soldier, I think I simply went undetected," says Midori, who is now a kink educator and writer. "I simply did not threaten authority or masculinity. This is one of the few advantages of being a second-class citizen."

Dykes who were out before they enlisted must deal with reentering the closet. "It was difficult to jump back in, especially after I'd been out all through high school, but I just had to remember why I was there and that got me through," says Puppet. While many in her squadron chose to remain closeted, Puppet recalls one woman who made a point of not hiding her sexuality. "She was really into wearing her pride gear and trying to make a big statement about being a dyke in the military," says Puppet. "A lot of us didn't like her because we felt she joined for the wrong reasons and she was going to take down a lot of other dykes with her. She would go to the mall off base and hold hands with her Navy girlfriend. Nowadays, I can see that happening more often, but only a few years ago it was frightening. You didn't just get kicked out if you got caught, you got sent to military prison."

Although it's extremely risky, it's common to find curious or questioning women using their time in the military to experiment. Most of the women Puppet slept with were straight-identified before joining the Army. "Many of us were just out of high school, and there were plenty of women who wanted to experiment. The girls I had sex with had never been with girls before. The sex was pretty vanilla," she recalls. Midori also says that her unit had a "sexually charged atmosphere" but that back then she "was hardly sexually aware, much less out." "I did have a mad, mad crush on a couple of Marine Corps female officers during a joint combined exercise. They looked so cool, controlled, and oh-so-fabulous in their uniforms!"

Sexual contact on the base is dangerous and happens very infrequently. "My girlfriend and I have kissed on base twice, but it wasn't something like those passion-filled kisses you read about in novels," says Smith. "It was quick and brief. I visited her in her quarters to check up on her when she wasn't well and that was it. Not exactly a happily-ever-after thing, I guess."

Puppet describes sex on base as fast and furtive. "It never involved any toys, because they always checked our lockers and that was too dangerous. Basically, it was quick and quiet and didn't get much past the typical finger bang."

Smith has been with her officer girlfriend for two years. She explains that maintaining a relationship for long is very difficult. "Being a sexually active dyke in the military is stressful and very lonely at times. You're always paranoid that your commanding officer is going to suspect something, especially when you're having relations with a fellow officer." The worst part, she says, is that "it's tough to act straight when all you want to do is be with the girl you love. We make love whenever we get the chance, but usually when we have sex it's somewhere that is not in any way connected to the Air Force," says Smith. "We are both active members of the 'mile high club,' sometimes the back row in the last week of a bad movie, and just about anywhere else that we like where we won't get caught."

Trysting off base is still risky and often takes the form of anonymous encounters. "Once, I went to a Melissa Etheridge concert in New Orleans. I started hitting on this cute girl. We spent the rest of the concert making out. Afterward, she offered my friends and I a ride back to Mississippi. I took her back to our hotel and we had crazy sex all night, and then I never saw her again," recalls Puppet.

While all experiences may not be positive, at least dykes get a souvenir worth keeping—the uniform. "I have to admit that even to this day, girls are intrigued when they hear I was in the military," says Puppet, "but what they really want to know about is the uniforms." As a femme and a budding fetishist, Midori delighted in her uniform. "I wasn't aware of this when I enlisted," explains Midori, "but today I recognize that I have a pretty deep uniform fetish. It explains why my gaze was always drawn to sharply attired soldiers." Midori frequently draws upon her military experience in her personal and professional life. "The military has elements of power exchange, dominance and submission, rank, order, and purpose that are very attractive to me," she says. "This attraction has been consistent throughout my life, and it's certainly obvious today."

Tantra for Dykes

Haute Sex and Consciousness Joined at the Hips
by Colette De Donato

Tantra is the ancient Indian practice of using sex to increase, improve, expand, and explore your spirituality. Tantra teaches that sexual union is the key to bringing harmony to relationships, to the household, and to society. This doesn't translate simply as "a well-laid person is a happy person," though there might be no denying that. Tantra sees sex as a tool that we use for personal growth, and the theory is that our individual enlightenment will ultimately improve the community around us. Today, tantra practices have expanded to include sexual healing as well—from pain, violence, and erotic neurosis.

Tantra had its renaissance in the 1980s, in the form of workshops, books, and videos aimed at giving couples something deeper and more fulfilling in their sex lives. Some came to tantra through massage, feeling that slow, conscious touching was something they desperately needed. Other people wanted to learn how to get turned on by the slightest movements and to have a better, longer, harder orgasm—an orgasm that came from places they didn't know orgasms could come from. Couples who had lost the time to have sex in their hurried lives turned to tantra to reconnect with each other and discover how to slow down.

Learning about tantra taught women how to ask for what they wanted, how to honor their own personal goddess and to see the divine in their partners, how to bring a sense of playfulness into their lovemaking. It also taught them how to have hot, haute sex. But there was one problem: Most of the tantric workshops and videos were focused on heterosexual couples in a classic male yang and female yin paradigm. Lesbian and bisexual tantric practitioners see beyond the simplified notion that man holds the yang and woman holds the yin, and through sexual union the energy is balanced. They believe that each of us has yin and yang, male and female energy, contained within us.

On Our Backs founder Deborah Sundahl discovered tantra through the practice of yoga, witnessing her libido burst forth through mediation and recognizing the divinity inherent within it. Annie Sprinkle had mastered every form of kink and fetish possible, yet felt fucked-out, so to speak, and wanted something more satisfying, something

265

metasexual, that would bring her to new heights of ecstasy. She calls what she practices metamorphisex: neo-tantra or queer tantra. Barbara Carrellas also came to tantra in the mid '80s, when the New York Healing Circle had formed in response to the AIDS crisis. "We were dealing with sex, death, grief, and healing, and we wanted to explore the nonphysical dimensions of sex. Really, we wanted to get as high as we used to, safely. But we learned how to make it juicy too!"

Today, Carrellas, who teaches tantra to lesbians and queer-identified people in New York City, calls it "urban tantra," or "tantra for the rest of us." "It's tantra for the modern world, not just for people who live in cities, in case you were feeling left out already. This is conscious sexuality," Carrellas explains. "We slow down, pay attention to how we are touching, with more attention to the edge. We are working on the male and female—whatever that means anymore!—in each of us. We're simultaneously expanding the definition of tantra."

Carrellas's workshops focus on bringing tantra into any relationship: Whether it's feathers or floggers, hard-style or soft-style play that gets you to pay more attention to your sensory experiences, tantra can be the path that deepens our relationship with ourselves. "We're all living 99 lives and doing so much these days. We are more armored now than ever," says Carrellas, in a typical moment of enormous enthusiasm about the subject. "In tantra, we learn how to drop the armoring, how to move sexual energy around in the body, immersing ourselves in it."

In tantra the goal is not to be goal-oriented, so you need to let go of focusing on an orgasm. One of the most basic and core tantric exercises is eye-gazing. We sit with our partners and look into their eyes for an extended period of time. Evalena Rose, who teaches lesbian tantra in Northern California, describes eye-gazing as seeing into your partner's original innocence. "Because many women come to tantra to heal the wounds in their body, eye-gazing helps us to imagine seeing who we are before the wounds, to teach us that we are not our stories."

Other tantric exercises might include following the energy path in your lover's body by using your tongue. Start at the vulva, up across her belly, between her breasts, up her throat to her brow, and then stop at the crown of her head. Giggling is allowed, as this may feel funny for the first time. Include a little masturbation, and the entire experience gets higher. The important thing is to focus on the way the energy moves around in our bodies.

Rose wants to show women how to live from their heart and how to become "their own beloved," whether they choose to be sexual or not. "In tantra, we learn about freeing the kundalini energy in the body. We work with what Tantrika Margo Anand calls the 'inner flute,' the central channel in our bodies where energy flows. We use our breath to come into this flow, and learn how to have a 'valley orgasm' (as opposed to a peak), where the sensations are moving through every part of us. Homophobia has made lesbians feel protective of their sexuality. I want to bring it forward, explore the lost avenues, open the doors again," says Rose.

In the ancient Taoist tantric texts, there is considerable instruction in locating the "hidden jade moon," and "the heart of the lotus bud," or what we 21st-century girls know as the G spot. Known in Taoist texts as the yin, or the hidden side of the yang (the external clitoris), the G spot serves as a great point of exploration. The Taoists also talked about the nectar of the moon, the copious fluid women produced in their internal ejaculation. It was recommended that it be tasted to absorb the deep, cool, yin essence from it.

If it's so good, and so full of useful knowledge, why has tantra gotten so lost and marginalized? Why doesn't every women know about Jawala's book, *Sacred Sex: Ecstatic Techniques for Empowering Relationships*? Why doesn't every sexual being log on to tantra.com for advice? Most likely because of the radical—and yes, still taboo—idea of mixing sexuality with spirituality. In fact, all Western religions, dominant in this country and in this community, strictly *oppose* the coupling of sexuality and spirituality. And while it's true that we don't live in the India of 900 years ago, where these practices originated, we still have difficulty merging the two.

For some women, spiritual sex means letting the concepts of organized religion enter into our sexual vocabulary. For others, especially spiritually identified women, there's too much pressure to also be searching for enlightenment during hot sex. And maybe the idea of finding the oneness of everything in an ecstatic sexual state sounds too New Agey.

Yet mystics tell us that sex is a great source of power. And who doesn't feel potent after a good screaming, writhing, rousing, fiery fuck, frolicking on a higher plane with someone we trust and feel safe with? Many contemporary tantric teachers tell us that tantric states are more powerful than any drug they've ever experienced, a psychedelic journey to outlast all the others. Better than Ecstasy, tantra helps you interact with the world in a different way, to taste it deeper. Ready to show you the incredible range of emotions in the vagina and teach you that the G spot is connected to the part of the brain where consciousness resides, tantra gets you beyond the superficial, beyond the personality, and lets you reclaim your lost erotic energy.

267

TWELVE

ON-SCREEN SEX: VIDEOS TO GET YOU IN THE MOOD

How to Take the Drive-In Home

by Victoria A. Brownworth

Alas, the drive-in—the American standard that mixed sex and movies into a perfect hormonal cocktail and turned heavy petting into a high art—has passed from the cultural landscape. But don't despair! Bring the drive-in, with all its sexiness, home. Renting a porn video can turn couch potatoes into Cassanovas with the flick of a switch. Here are some pointers to help you get the E ticket of your dreams.

Know What You Want
Don't just grab the first box on the shelf. Choosing porn videos is just like choosing any other film. You have to know what you're in the mood for. Comedy? Thriller? Action? Romance? Soft-core? Hard-core? Something in between? Short or full-length? There's everything a boi or girl could want out there in Porn Land, and then some.

The Play's the Thing
The whole point of playing with porn is to get hot and get off. Think 1930s Bette Davis movies for setting and 21st-century technology to complete your mise-en-scène. Prepare. Have everything you need for hot sex to a hot flick with a hot chick. Nothing spoils the mood like let-me-hit-the-pause-button-while-I-go-and (fill in the blank). No boy hoping to score ever went to a drive-in without a condom in his wallet and a pillow in the backseat. You'll want low lights (or no lights), whipped cream instead of popcorn (salt can be so painful), champagne or a nonalcoholic equivalent (bubbles heighten the senses), and any other accoutrements you might need: pillows, strap-on, condoms, lube, etc. All should be discreetly—and handily—within reach.

271

Know Your Audience
Don't forget the company you'll be keeping. Are you viewing with your favorite fuck-buddy, staging a seduction with the girl of your dreams, or trying to pump some heat into that half-dead lesbian marriage bed? Or do you just want a nice, hot evening with

yourself to the right accompaniment? You know what turns you on, but do you know what turns on (or more importantly, what turns *off*) your partner? This info is essential to making your video pick. You want to rev her up, not cool her down.

Check It Out
Plan to spend a half-hour or so by yourself just looking at what's available in your local video store. This part can be a little daunting. Most video outlets have the proverbial back room filled with porn videos, and most also have the moral equivalent of a neon sign above that room flashing PERVERT. So be prepared to get a stare or three from both staff and other clientele as you cross the threshold. Once in the room, you will likely be the only X chromosome there, but any guy present will be just as squirmy as you are. Porn room etiquette demands that everyone ignore everyone else. Once you're feeling more adventuresome, you and your sex partner might want to go together and pick out a video. Perusing the porn room with your girl can be as much of a turn-on as the videos themselves.

Word of Mouth
Porn stores are separated by proclivities. Het, homo, lesbo, trannie, threesomes, S/M, B&D, anal, masturbation, black, white, Latino, Asian, mockumentaries, comedies, thrillers—it's *all* there. Read the boxes. They're pretty explicit about the video inside. You should be able to tell by the cover art how sleazy or refined the camera techniques will be—shot through gauze or lit by a 150-watt bulb hanging from the ceiling. If you have questions, ask the video staff (the men will inevitably know more than the women and be more willing to share). Be brave.

Warning
Again, the point of porn is to get hot and get laid. That said, nothing can dampen ardor like a raw scene in the wrong place. If your video is meant to seduce that special someone, you might want to preview it first. Many otherwise extremely hot videos have rape scenes inserted in them, or what looks like a lesbian video can suddenly become a girl-meets-girl, girl-loses-girl-to-guy movie. Some chicks find watching dick enjoyable, but others find it unpleasant, even though they're playing with yours. Feel out your partner before you plan to feel her up.

Infomercial
Don't be afraid to use your video choices creatively. If the heat has started to evaporate from your relationship—or even if its purring along just fine—one way to get things up

272

and running is to use porn videos to tell the story for you. (See honey, we could do *that*.) It's also a way to clue your partner in to something that intrigues you that she might not have tried before, like S/M or B&D. Seeing it in a context where the participants are enjoying it may help allay any fears or trepidations she might have about trying something new or outré.

Ignition

Above all, have fun. Porn videos are raunchy, raw, and ribald and are far less expensive than many other sex aids out there. Plus, they can get you hotter than you ever thought possible. Find the one that best suits your needs and play to your heart's (and parts' and partners') content.

Pulp Friction

by Laura Weide

Femme fatales with leopard cat suits, waist-high panties, and flame-retardant bras that turn breasts into nuclear warheads—our contemporary notions of the bad girl were born in the '50s. Hard-edged women with angelic faces, their kohl-lined eyes squinting through cigarette smoke—these images of seething sexuality smeared an indelible lipstick mark on the index of female sexual expression. Their feisty delinquency is with us today, as the cat-fight lives on in campy lesbian sex fests, dyke porn noir, and stylized art smut.

History of the Blue Movie
dir. Alex de Renzy
[Caballero Classics, 1970]

A unique documentary, *History* shows clips from some of the earliest sex movies and takes us through the 1960s on a tour of the stag movie (porn's predecessor), with an emphasis on its social and legal context. My favorite is a transgressive Italian clip from the 1940s in which a nun sheds her habit and masturbates with a vibrator. You'll see the burlesque styles that preceded the advent of Irving Klaw's Betty Page movies; after that, a substantial part of the video is dedicated to Klaw's classic work establishing the genre of fetish film. Like Marilyn Monroe, Betty Page was a kittenish pinup girl whose iconic sexuality became larger than life. All those leopard bathing suits? You'll learn that Betty sewed them herself—and see some of the classic rope bondage and catfight scenes that have become a contemporary retro reference.
Bottom line: history lessons with homework to beg for

Voluptuous Vixens
dir. Sadié Foxe and Sadie Valentine
[Sex Positive Productions, 2002]

I love this lesbian ode to pinup girls for its colorful palette, diverse cast of super sexy big

girls, campy decadence, and exuberant sex. A welcome respite from the inescapable hyper-thin body standards that pervade today's mainstream media—and porn. With more curves than a grand slalom, Voluptuous Vixens features fierce femmes in four vignettes. If tail fins get your motor running, you won't want to miss the H.O.T. masturbation scene in a classic car—but unlike the Backseat Betties of yore, who only wiggle and pose for the camera, star Celestina Meow Meow is all about ensuring her own orgasms. The '60s lounge environs, complete with magenta faux fur and lava lamps, set the stage for a sizzling strap-on scene. Later, fur flies in an S/M-ish catfight. The whole show is overlaid with an original soundtrack, which I find preferable to the usual porno music. However, I did miss the slap of palms against ass cheeks and the moans of orgasm: the aural titillation of porn.
Bottom line: supersize, sexy, and stylin'

Box of Laughter: Dueling Pages
dir. Maria Beatty
[Bleu Productions, 1998]

Maria Beatty's film craft is head and stiletto heels over most pornography. Her Box of Laughter series is a fetishistic exploration of the delicious, devilish torture of tickling. The black-and-white Dueling Pages features two Betty Page look-alikes in a sexy remake of the old Irving Klaw movies, but with a postmod twist. Two Betties help each other dress up in heels, classic fishnets, and '50s-style lingerie. A catfight ensues. From the mirror images emerge a Top Betty and a Bottom Betty, who wrestle in the inimical blue movie style. The Betty on the bottom becomes helpless and gets hog-tied and tickle-tortured. Top Betty takes a nap (odder things happen in porn), and when the sleeping beauty awakens, the tables have been turned. Also on the tape is more of a meditation on bondage, beauty, and laughter: A series of beautiful women appear in the same simple set, each tied to a chair. Faceless hands appear, and the tickling begins. We don't hear the screaming sounds of their laughter, but their expressive faces are mesmerizing. In the expulsive, whole-body experience, there is something suggestive of orgasms.
Bottom line: fetish tickle-me-lesbo

Take Her Down: A Lesbian Oil Wrestling Party
dir. Sondra Goodwin

[Fatale Video, 2002]

You won't find campy wrestling suits or Eartha Kitt references, but this production by the pioneering Fatale Video shares a vision with the early bondage genre in its extended focus on sexy women as they grapple and try to pin one another to the floor. The similarity ends there. A bevy of sexy athletic lesbians gather for a pool party and make-out fest in beautiful outdoor New Mexico. The vibe is flirty and playful. Next, the party moves indoors and gets down to business—the business of wrestling, that is. The loving eye of the camera dotes on the curves of flexed muscle, greased-up ass cheeks, and moves that get more suggestive as they go. These women are definitely having fun, and if you are on the lookout for lesbian porn that offers more buildup and body worship than your standard plug-away video, this is a title for you. Few of the scenes include explicit sex, but the story climaxes in a sexy strap-on shower scene. **Bottom line:** WWF, move *way* over.

Porn That Bites

Vampire Sex That Will Suck You Dry
by Laura Weide

Insatiable, cold, sharp, carnal, and imperious, vampires are the sexiest monsters. These demi-gods of the undead aren't just serial killers with orthodontic issues. Vampires inspire speechless swooning in their sexually overpowered victims. It would seem, from books and movies, that the best sex the victims have ever had was the full-bodied orgasm that came with a pierced jugular.

What explains the eternal rock-star status of Dracula? Vampire eroticism speaks to our desire to be transformed by sex and reminds us of the connections between sex and death. (Talk about life-threatening exchange of body fluids!) If you've ever felt a clench in your cunt from a well-placed love bite or dreamed of sharp objects pressing into soft flesh, you're probably already a believer.

Dracula Exotica
dir. Warren Edwards
[VCA, 1979]

A young Jamie Gillis is the priapic Count whose hopeless love for a cloistered virgin drives him to rape and debauchery in this classic '70s porn. His punishment: eternity as a blood-sucking Romanian ghoul who can't get off. A hundred years later, his castle is nationalized and turned into a tourist trap by communist bureaucrats. It's off to America, where he is suspected of being a commie spy. It's a clever spy-meets-spy Cold War subplot. The amazing Vanessa Del Rio serves up searing scenes and clearly enjoys her voracious fanged afterlife. Unlike other porn, which crumbles like stale cake when the plot thickens, this production has no trouble managing complexity. But it's not for the thin-skinned—violence, rape, age play, necrophilia, and countless murders provide edgy material. Like other films of its genre, it serves up good writing and wry humor without the badump-bump timing of many contemporary porn flicks.

Bottom line: sanguine and sexy classic

Ladies of the Night
dir. Maria Beatty
[Blue Productions, 1999]

Maria Beatty is my favorite pornographer. She makes gorgeous, crackling movies, works of art that capture the drama of the dungeon. In this black-and-white silent film, made in the style of early "talkies," a young schoolgirl wandering the empty streets of Paris is swept away by gleaming-eyed, high-femme lesbian vampires. Just the words "lesbian vampire" induce visions of S/M—"vanilla vampire" is an oxymoron. The schoolgirl is put through the paces in the torture chamber and is transformed by the devilish ministrations into a demonic bottom.

Bottom line: a toothsome, tribade-filled treat

Dark Angels
dir. Nic Andrews
[New Sensation, 2000]

Gloriously gloomy, slick, and sexy, this hot horror thriller was a big winner at the 2001 AVN Awards. Gorgeously filmed and edited, *Dark Angels* is my top mainstream vamp flick. Sydney Steele leads the sizzling pack of dominatrices of the undead, who fuck the living daylights out of men and then tear at their jugulars with sizable incisors. This one really isn't for the faint of heart—there is a gruesome coroner's report and lots and lots of blood, and let's not forget the ritual virgin sacrifice. Crackling latex and PVC costumes and the smoky atmosphere create a compelling backdrop for some truly inspired sexual performances.

Bottom line: gore plus a haunting lesbo scene

Sex Flesh and Blood
dir. Christopher Lee
[Producers Christopher Lee and J. Zapata, 1999]

A rocking goth-punk porno. Hot and sexy trans man Angel and a band of bad boys have down and dirty sex. The fiendishly erotic Jade Blue Eclipse haunts cemeteries and nether places for fresh meat, hot and cold, and finds it in a mausoleum three-way. As the box cover says, "a hard-core tale where leathermen, vampires, transpecies, and cadavers collide."

Bottom line: first-rate queer monster mash!

Forever Night
dir. Michael Ninn
[VCA, 2001]
Michael Ninn's porn has been compared to MTV music videos—rapid-fire edits and tooth-aching eye candy. *Forever Night* offers an homage to *Dracula Exotica*, Jamie Gillis again is the Count (22 years later), looking a little worse for the wear. He's been condemned to an eternity without sexual gratification. The voyeur at the edges of surreal acrobatic wall-to-wall sex scenes, Gillis watches as silicone-enhanced porn stars suck and fuck. There's no vampire action, but Jill Kelly has an electric encounter with a greasy looking demon with sharp teeth, fun toys, and a nice dungeon. There are no realistic female orgasms, but lots of come shots and facials.
Bottom line: This one really sucks.

Les Vampyres
dir. James Avalon
[Metro Productions, 1999]
A trio of vampires is cruising California, fiercely fucking men and then biting off their dicks and draining their lifeblood. Jewel Valmont plays the girl next door, whose inexplicable craving for hard jugular chewing during sex with her fiancé leaves her befuddled about her true self. The production values are fabulous—gorgeous film quality, great sets and costumes, first-rate editing—but unfortunately, the script is painfully weak.
Bottom line: flushed lesbian sex scene, bloodless script

Voluptuous Vixens on Video

Real Bodies Really Doing It
by Laura Weide

Nonenhanced. What a strange term we've come up with to describe women who haven't undergone plastic surgery. To me, there is something weirdly unnatural when hair, breasts, and hips stay perfectly still through the motions of sex. People are supposed to jiggle when they fuck. While Hollywood and Simi Valley standards of hyper-thin, siliconed female beauty prevail in the images we receive, there are an extraordinary number of people who want to see themselves and their desires reflected in the rutting bodies on their screen. In my years hawking sex products I've heard innumerable women and men searching for natural bodies in porn. Body hair, love handles and belly rolls, wrinkles, variably sized and shaped breasts, and penises on men that don't look like they spent a week with their dick vacu-locked in a penis pump are all in demand. For those who like straight porn, the biggest complaint about the male stars is that penis size is more important than overall good looks. And the majority of women never get to see themselves reflected as sex objects in movies, on TV, in magazines, or in skin flicks—and so it is with pleasure that I recommend the following titles.

Slide Bi Me
dir. Felice Amador
[Sex Positive Productions, 2001]

An insurance company picnic turns into a big bisexual orgy. *Slide Bi Me* breaks the two-buff-guys-and-a-girl bi porn mold in every way. Artsy camera work; a truly multicultural cast of fresh, fine, and enthusiastic performers; physical diversity; and an emphasis on full-body pleasure ensure the group-sex scenes, trios, and pairings are hot. The guys are cast for their overall good looks and sexual enthusiasm more than for their penis size or ability to shoot big wads of splooge across a room. Personally, I loved that the girl dicks were the largest members in the scenes where women strapped it on. The buildup of arousal is a delight to watch, and the director captures a dynamic and full-bodied experience of orgasm rather than the standard focus on the end product. And the sex is sweet: There are more smiles, giggling, and exchanges of sweet looks than you'll find in other porn movies—or at any white-collar picnic.

Bottom line: luscious bi romping, no remote needed

Please Don't Stop: Lesbian Guide to Giving It and Getting It
dir. Oriana Bolden
[Sex Positive Productions, 2001]

Kudos to Sex Positive Productions for making the first-ever, all-lesbians-of-color dyke sex video. This how-to is one of a kind. Smart-sexy friends share their experiences, ask questions, and get right-on sex information—which they immediately put to good use. If you're looking for a flick to accompany a pussy-petting session, you might be disappointed, as the educational sections are extended—in other words, there's lots of talking. But the sex scenes are worth waiting for. The heated opening will keep you glued to the screen, and the sexy vignettes—a couple's anal play first, a sexy masturbation strip, and hot, squirty sex in a mechanics garage—show the women applying their newly learned lessons at home. *Please Don't Stop* conveys the sex information that many dykes are looking for without succumbing to the hackneyed and boring "talking heads of the experts" format.

Bottom line: hot demos, too much talking

Fat Chicks in Bondage Nos. 1 and 2
dir. RedBoard Video
[Red Board Video]

If you can get over the offensive tone of the title, you're in for a tasty serving of enthusiastic and intense canings, role-play, catfights, hot wax, and more. Unfortunately, these movies are low budget; the sound and lighting are pretty poor. My favorite in this series is number 2, as it captures a number of exquisite moments: A punky top brings out sweet little-girl energy in her big, beautiful bottom; an acolyte receives severe ministrations of clothespins and hot wax from a pagan high priestess.

Bottom line: enthusiastic, big-hearted BDSM amateurs

Big Girls
dir. Sara McCool
[Fat Girl Militia, 1999]

This is not a porn flick, but rather a documentary about big beautiful women in the sex entertainment industry. Powerful, luscious beauties talk about being prostitutes and models in a racist, fat-phobic world. McCool offers statistics on the difference between pay rates for thin, virtually all-white models in men's magazines and what big women and women of color make doing the same work. McCool is a great documentarian and elicits insightful interviews about the workings of desires and the economies of sex work.

Bottom line: powerful documentary, fierce subject

Dyke Sex on the Big Screen

The Best of Film Fest Porn
by Laura Weide

How often have you watched explicit dyke sex on the big screen? I'm not talking about Violet and Corky mussing up some sheets or close-ups of cramping toes, I'm talking real dyke action. If you have a penchant for independent queer sex cinema, your big-screened voyeuristic thirst might be quenched only once a year at GLBT film fests—if you're lucky. Fortunately, the highlights of this year's explicit festival fare are available on video.

Sugar High Glitter City
dirs. Shar Rednour and Jackie Strano
[S.I.R. Video, 2001]

"It's the future. Sugar is outlawed, and cane-addicted dykes will do anything to get their fix. Even sell their own bodies," intones the smoky voice of narrator Honey Lee Cotrell (of 1980s *On Our Backs* photography fame), guiding us through the sticky, seamy world of Glitter City. Sugar whores get shaken down by dirty cops and trade tricks for treats with whomever is holding. S.I.R. Video serves up sex-drenched scenes—with candy-swirled muff diving, femsicles sucking off butch-pops, genderfucking, squirting, and a caramel glaze of dirty talk—in their latest all-dyke-produced skin flick. Fucking is their forte; scene after scene of sugar-coated sex will get your molars aching and your pussy wet. Usually when porn is described as "diverse," it means there is one person of color and maybe one actress with a hint of hip handles. Happily, the stars in this juicy fuckfest represent a range of female pulchritude, and half are women of color. S.I.R's insistence on portraying authentic dyke sex means the stars are turned on and clits get serviced center-screen. Hot scenes starring real-life lovers light the match to this toothsome flambé. The filmmakers get it on in front of the camera, in a down and dirty three-way with the pretty Josephine X; newcomer Aimee Pearl purrs her way to getting what she wants with the suave and sexy Charlie Sky;

283

and Simone (the honey-dripping scene-stealer from *How to Fuck in High Heels* with the herstory-making tongue) and her coolio dealer, Hella Getto, radiate heat and intimacy in a multi-orgasmic finale. Butches don't wear makeup in my fantasy life. But I found their stagey glitter makeup tolerable for its B-movie futuristic effect. Finally, you'll want to avoid this flick if you think there's nothing sexy whatsoever about drugs, and that lesbians who think otherwise need a 12-step meeting: Coke powder–cum–pixie sticks are snorted, er, rather, lapped up in scene after incisor-rotting scene.

Bottom line: Satisfy your oral fixation with S.I.R.'s decadent production.

The Pain Game
dir. Cléo Dubois
[Cléo Dubois, 2000]

The Pain Game is the most compellingly authentic portrayal of S/M I've seen on film. While filmmaker Maria Beatty has made gorgeous bondage films that artistically convey the steely grace of a top and the beauty of a bottom in pain, few have truly captured the ecstatic energy between tops and bottoms—till now. Well-filmed and edited, Cléo Dubois's pièce de résistance is both explication of BDSM and demonstration of supercharged play between seasoned players. The two featured scenes carry distinctive moods and connections; it's not just that you'll witness a diverse set of activities—flogging, severe nipple clampings, and genitorture on the handsome older male, and play piercing and wickedly beautiful double-clothespin zippers on the lithe female bottom—but you'll witness unique emotional responses as the bottoms soar to ecstatic release. Mainstream porn's canned portrayals of S/M shrivel in comparison. Dubois's topping is a joy to watch: skillful, graceful, and finessed; her discussion of sadomasochistic motives, negotiation, and boundary-pushing is also edifying.

Bottom line: S/M-curious or a regular player, watch Dubois push the edges of her bottoms and make them fly.

Afterschool Special
dir. Aprilicious
[Fatale, 2001]

284 Garage bands are lovable for their unadulterated passion for rock and roll. Garage porn can feel similar—the sound might suck, the editing might leave something to be desired, but the spirited enthusiasm and purity of nonpackaged sexual creativity shines through. So it is with *Afterschool Special*, winner in the Shorts category of Fatale Video's XXX Real Lesbian Sex video contest. Bostonian baby dykes made and star in

this black-and-white sexcapade of a gang of bad girls who ambush a group of good girls, mess 'em up, abduct one, and fuck her so well she wants to join the bad girls. Nan Kinney of Fatale calls it guerrilla porn, "where the act of making porn is itself empowering"—these dewy-skinned dykes exude excitement, and they're clearly having a blast.

Bottom line: Won't scorch your knickers, but amateur aficionados should check out this rare real-lesbian production.

Fresh Doms and Subs

Bondage and S/M Videos Get Better—and More Lesbian
by Greta Christina

Decent BDSM videos are extremely hard to find, even harder than decent vanilla-sex videos. And decent lesbian kink videos are like two-headed goats, they're so rare. So I take unusual pleasure in telling you about three—count 'em, three—new lesbian and lesbian-inclusive kink videos that are worth checking out.

Tie Me Up!
dir. Cléo Dubois
[Cléo Dubois Academy of SM Arts, 2002]
Screw saving the best for last. I'm eating dessert first. A video how-to guide on BDSM (emphasis on the B), *Tie Me Up!* is aimed at folks just starting with kinky play. On that level, it definitely works: The information is solid and clear, with excellent insight on why and how people do kink. But that's not why I'm raving about it. I'm raving because it's so fucking beautiful. Poignantly, spectacularly, impossibly beautiful. The players in *Tie Me Up!* are totally enthusiastic about what they're doing. They show passion and delight. This video does a top-notch job of capturing what it actually feels like to do kink; the connection between Cléo and her bottoms (two women, one man) leaps out and grabs you by the heart and the crotch. And the production values are terrific, not flashy, but clean and professional.

Personally, I'm not much into actual bondage. I don't have the patience for it; I always want to get to the hurty stuff right away. And watching other people do bondage is usually like watching a lovely bit of paint dry. But *Tie Me Up!* wasn't like that at all. It was compelling from beginning to end.

Bottom Line: Bet you'll get roped in.

Whipsmart
Dir. Laura Plotkin
[Sex Positive Productions, 2002]

Good ideas often occur to several people at once, which is probably why two different "BDSM for beginners" videos were released within two months of each other. *Whipsmart* is probably more useful as an actual how-to guide. Made by the video production arm of Good Vibrations, *Whipsmart* is a very solid piece of video sex-ed. The information is excellent, thorough, and well-organized, and Mistress Morgana is an intelligent and articulate narrator.

I'll be honest, though: *Whipsmart* is an important, useful video whose time has come, but it didn't make me run down the street raving about it. The scenes are perfectly fine, and they do a good job of illustrating the principles. But when "perfectly fine" is the highest praise I can muster for a kinky video, well, enough said.

To be fair, *Whipsmart* is aimed at beginners, totally brand-new beginners who've never done bondage and submission. They may never have heard of S/M. So the scenes (some lesbian, some hetero) are pretty mild. *Tie Me Up!* is aimed at beginners too, but it assumes more, and while the scenes aren't super-heavy, they also aren't tamed-down to avoid scaring people. And because the scenes in *Whipsmart* have been scripted to convey particular concepts, they lack *Tie Me Up!*'s energy and immediacy. So, for pure information, get *Whipsmart*; but for pure joy, go directly for *Tie Me Up*.

Bottom line: more educational than erotic

The Seven Deadly Sins
Dir. Maria Beatty
[Bleu Productions, 2002]

Speaking of the pure joy of watching bondage and S/M, Maria Beatty has a new video out. I love Beatty's work; she's a real artist, with a passion for both exquisite filmmaking and serious kink. And both passions come through vividly in *The Seven Deadly Sins*. Like many of her other movies, this one has an elegant, old-fashioned look, like a 1920s German art film or a naughty French postcard come to life. It doesn't have the raw immediacy of *Tie Me Up!*, but Beatty has a knack for creating beautifully framed iconic images, perfect moments of sadistic and masochistic fantasy. I didn't adore this one as much as, say, *The Elegant Spanking*, or *Ladies of the Night*, but that's probably more a matter of taste than anything. *The Seven Deadly Sins* is a fine production; it's gorgeous to look at, it's skillfully filmed, and

287

it successfully got my hand into my pants. (The culprit was the spanking scene with the shoe.)

Bottom line: exquisitely perverse

Bittersweet
dir. Alice B. Brave
[Alice B. Brave Productions, 1993]

No review of lesbian S/M videos would be complete without a mention of *Bittersweet*. Alice B. Brave's classic short isn't just my favorite lesbian S/M movie. It's not even just my favorite adult movie. *Bittersweet* is one of my top 10 favorite movies of any kind, up there with *The Godfather* and *Monty Python and the Holy Grail*. The filmmaking is stunning, with an intense artistic vision that makes me want to simultaneously weep and jerk off. And the women are focused on one another with a passionate intensity I've rarely seen in life, much less in videos. *Bittersweet* is hard to find (as far as I know, the company I work for is the only one that sells it), and it's only 18 minutes long, but it feels like a fucking epic.

Bottom line: beauty worth seeking

Gay-Boy Porn

Fag Sex That Will Make Your Dyke Dick Hard
by Laura Weide

On any given day, scads of dykes stride right past the shelves of lesbian porn for the gay boy flicks. They've seen the light and realized that gay porn offers up sweaty fuck-fests devoid of the fake breasts and long nails found in straight porn. And though lesbian porn gets better every day, compared to the hard-core action in gay material much of lesbian porn is somewhat tepid.

While dyke porn is rarely readily available, there are multitudes of gay porn titles and subgenres to choose from. There's tons of it, it's everywhere, and a lot of it is well-made. Since there are no females in gay porn, there's no troubling female objectification. You can turn off the sexism cop in your brain and stroke your petal without care.

And finally, it's no easy task to find lesbian fare that eroticizes masculinity. There are no all-butch-on-butch movies that I know of and only a handful of dyke-dude scenes. Whether you get turned on by masculinity or are yourself a masculine queer, you've probably already figured out that gay-male videos deliver the goods. Here are a few titles that deliver fag sex with dyke appeal.

Branded
dir. Kris Weston
[Falcon Studios, 2002]

In *Branded*, two men are hand-selected as new recruits for an elite club whose sole purpose is the pleasuring of men, by men. All members bear the branded mark of the Falcon. Only one will become a member, and they must compete to see who can pleasure the gang of men and win a skin-searing scar.

Hats off to the cinematographer. This is one of the best-shot porn films I've seen. Though the plot is simple, the sex is well-choreographed and hotly paced, delivering balanced frames and aesthetic appeal while maintaining the intense energy of the action. Even the come shots are artistically filmed. The sets are nothing special—and

289

someone should have tossed a sheet over the Crayola-colored bedspread in the first scene—but the ecstatic anally receptive bottom boy and well-shot penetration scenes will keep your attention off the rainbow decor. Hairless, tan guys feed one another huge mouthfuls of cock with gusto, and the directors show as much of an anal fisting as is possible without risking obscenity charges.

Bottom line: Butter up your cheeks and press Play.

Mardi Gras Cowboy
dirs. Rico de la Playa and Vidkid Timo
[All Worlds, 1996]

Who says gay porn is just bulging pecs and blow jobs? *Mardi Gras Cowboy* offers humor, heart, and sweet connections—*and* blow jobs. Movie-star-handsome Jim Buck is a country bumpkin with a pierced penis who moves to sin city New Orleans to make his fortune as a gigolo. Although he's "straight," it seems that queer tricks keep coming his way. A comedic spoof on the classic flick *Midnight Cowboy*, the Jon Voight and Dustin Hoffman knockoff characters fall in love and have sweet, romantic sex. I'm a sucker for the French Quarter—I'll even watch stupid car commercials for the pan of those wrought-iron balconies—but it's not just the Mardi Gras backdrop I appreciated. This well-made spoof breaks the cookie-cutter mold of gay skin-flicks, with stars who don't eat steroids with their Wheaties, goofy humor (the movie opens with Jim Buck singing "She'll Be Coming Round the Mountain When She Comes" as he masturbates in the shower), and characters who say "I love you."

Bottom line: sweet

Night Walk
dirs. Michael Ninn and Gino Colbert
[VCA Interactive, 1995]

MTV-style editing, moody surrealism, and special effects have won Michael Ninn a top-dog spot in the porn industry. *Night Walk* is a surrealist sex trip featuring colossal gargoyles who come to life and have monster sex. If life is a cabaret, you'd want to be in this one. You'll even find a musical number with a Marilyn Monroe look-alike and tuxedo-clad dancing boys—lots of show, beautiful men, snappy editing, and special effects, plus cool sex.

Bottom line: sex spectacle at its well-made best

Fallen Angel
dirs. Bruce Cam and Robert Kirsch
[Titan Media, 1998]
Thumping industrial music, crafty editing, and cock-hungry men drive this well-paced, glistening testosterone fest. A voyeuristic, otherworldly winged creature drops from the sky into a sharp-edged Gotham full of gym-toned leathermen. There it witnesses mean uniform sex, abduction, domination, and all manners of sucking and fucking in a gay bathhouse. Uniforms, hoods, and sex-club scenes give this one a cold and hard feel. These men aren't having relationships; there's little talking beyond barked orders and orgasmically howled epithets. *Fallen Angel* offers all the style of S/M, without the substance or dynamics one would expect with real play.
Bottom line: gay porn meets MTV

Mainstream Porn That Delivers

by Greta Christina

Ever since dykes started making our own dirty movies, we've tended to scoff at the mainstream porn industry's "girl-girl" videos. They're typically dismissed as fake, a version of lesbian sex made by and for men, starring women who wouldn't know their way around a pussy if you gave them a road map. And the criticism isn't entirely unjust.

But there is a fair amount of mainstream lesbian smut with performers who are clearly having a blast. Whatever other objections you may have to these videos, it's obvious that the sex is real: The women take intense pleasure in one another's bodies, and they come and come and come.

So where does this charge of inauthenticity come from? I think it comes from the idea that femmes aren't real lesbians—unless they're with butches, of course. One of the most common critiques of the girl-girl genre is that "real lesbians don't look like that." But some lesbians do look like that, and femme-on-femme isn't just a hetero male fantasy. More to the point, some of us like *any* porn with women genuinely getting off on one another.

I love lesbian-made, butch/butch, and butch/femme porn. I just don't think it has to be an either/or thing. We can have lesbian porn with women who look like truck drivers and with women who look like Marcia Brady. If they're having fun with one another, it's real enough for me.

But enough of the soapbox. Let's get on to the dirty movies.

The 4 Finger Club No. 11
no director credited
[New Sensations, 2000]
Now, here's a first-rate example of what I'm talking about. Yes, the video was made by men, almost certainly for a male audience. But it doesn't matter. Because the sex

in this video is amazing. It's enthusiastic, exuberant, energetic…all those good words. The most telling mark of its genuineness is how much the women are into one another's pleasure. When Phoenix is finger-fucking Bailey, the intensity and delight on her face is as vivid as the joyous abandon on Bailey's.

It's not a lucky accident either. There are off-camera instructions before each scene like, "We want real orgasms. Do whatever you want to get there." And while the camera crew are no Fellinis, they know enough to keep the camera on a woman's face when she's coming. Women having fun coming with each other is the whole point of the video, and it makes the point extremely well.

Where the Boys Aren't 6
dir. Ernest Greene
[Vivid Video, 1995]

Where the Boys Aren't 6 is more typical of the mainstream girl-girl genre. The sex is a bit more staged, without the spontaneous *oomph* of *The 4 Finger Club No. 11*. But the women are still having a good time, and a lot of it is hecka fun to watch, with long stretches of real passion and pleasure. I often watch faces in porn more than other body parts, and while *WTBA 6* does have your seasoned porn professionals' fake thrashing-and-gnashing, it also provides many unmistakable looks of genuine rapture—especially in the group scenes and especially from Jeanna Fine. Boy, does that woman love to fuck. And while *WTBA 6* isn't as sweet as *4 Finger Club No. 11*, it's rougher and wilder, with a slightly kinky flavor. I'm never going to argue with that.

Real Girlfriends Vol. 1
dir. Ron Richardson and Lydia Swartz
[Millers Work Inc., 2001]

I'm not sure this exactly qualifies as "mainstream." It's from a small, independent company, with a labor-of-love vision. But it is male-produced lesbian smut, with a male/female directing team, from a male-owned company that mostly makes hetero videos—albeit with real couples in real relationships, having the kind of sex they enjoy in their real life. It's as authentic as any by-lesbian smut I've seen. They basically turned the cameras on and let the women do their thing, with no staging or direction, and the result is sweet, passionate, intimate, enthusiastic, and very real indeed. And if you want "real bodies," *RG1* has tremendous body-type variety—more than most by-dyke smut, to be brutally frank. They even put their fat-girl couple on the cover.

293

San Francisco Lesbians 5
dir. J. Jones
[Pleasure Productions, 1994]

Here's the final paradox of mainstream girl-girl porn: It occasionally looks like authentically homegrown indie dyke smut. *San Francisco Lesbians 5*, for instance. The women in this video could easily be in a by-dykes-for-dykes production. There are butches, big girls, punks, bikers, all having a ball doing one another. The video even has a dyke director (also one of the video's performers). And the sex has a "bad girl" transgressive quality (transgressive for 1994, anyway), with dyke cock sucking and butch-on-butch action, touches of kink, and a strong tranny flavor. It's a pretty low-budget, low-pretense production, and while it's hot and nasty and fun, it doesn't break any sound barriers. But if it didn't open with cheesy phone-sex ads, you might not know it's a mainstream production.

A Dyke's Guide to Het Porn

by Greta Christina

I love dyke smut. I wouldn't be here if I didn't. Apart from the obvious reasons—I'm a dyke, I love smut—there's a lot to like about the growing cottage industry of by-and-for-lesbian sex videos. The authenticity, the labor-of-love quality, the attention to female pleasure, the freedom from mainstream porn formulas all make dyke porn a pleasure to watch. Even apart from the "women having hot sex with one another" angle.

But while the field of lesbian porn is certainly expanding, there still isn't much of it. So what do you do when you want that dyke-smut flavor but you've seen all the dyke smut? Well, you can watch straight porn. Sure, some of it is mediocre, but there are sweet spots, with plenty of the qualities that make dyke porn so special. Some of them are produced and/or directed by women, and some even have hot lesbian sex scenes. Here are a few of my favorites.

Revelations
dir. Candida Royalle
[Femme Productions, 1992]

Yes, Candida Royalle's videos are romantic. Yes, they're sensual. Yes, they're pretty. And you know what? They're also hot as hell. True, they don't fill my head with nasty fantasy images the way raunchier porn does. Instead they remind me of what it feels like to have sex, actual non-fantasy sex, with the kissing, and the fondling, and the getting lost in flesh and skin. The slow, sensual pace feels like foreplay to me, or like being teased and tantalized.

My favorite Femme Productions video is *Revelations*. I like the story, an Orwellian cautionary tale about a young woman in a sexually repressive totalitarian society who discovers a cache of illegal sex films. And there's a lesbian scene that's so tender it made my chest hurt. But if you don't like politics with your porn, Royalle has plenty of lighter fare. I've

never seen a video of hers that I haven't liked, and I've seen damn few that I haven't loved.
Bottom line: Romance fuels the flames.

Deep Inside Chloe
dir. Veronica Hart
[VCA, 2002]

If what you want from porn is the sight of women who passionately love sex, Chloe's your girl. The woman comes like she's having a seizure. I've never seen anything like it; she shudders, twitches, convulses, all with a look on her face like she's having visions of the Second Coming. And even when she's not in the middle of a beautifully spastic orgasm, her enthusiasm for fucking shines like a searchlight. *Deep Inside Chloe* is a fine sample, a collection of sex scenes from different movies that catches her alert, assertive, engaged presence in a yummy nutshell. The scenes are mostly with men and are mostly pretty wild; but there's a girl-girl scene with Ginger Lynn that has a genuinely affectionate quality that is sweet without being tepid.
Bottom line: Chloe's a fucking phenomenon.

Urban Friction
dirs. Marianna Beck and Jack Hafferkamp
[Libido Films, 2002]

The most common complaint about straight porn is that it's cheesy and fake. And yes, sometimes when I'm watching another going-through-the-motions, fuck-and-suck-and-pick-up-the-paycheck session, I want to pull my own teeth out just to alleviate the boredom. But there are small, quirky, labor-of-love hetero porn companies that have made their name proving that you can have authenticity and artistry in the same bit of smut. Libido Films—and their latest release, *Urban Friction*—is one example. The less-kinky sequel to *Thank You, Mistress, Urban Friction* has that all-too-rare combination: style and heat. The performers were obviously having a good time, and the camera and lighting people were obviously having a good time. And miracle of miracles, they weren't having it at one another's expense.
Bottom line: the right chemistry

Rocco: Animal Trainer
dir. Rocco Siffredi
[Evil Angel, 1999]

Rocco: Animal Trainer is from a big mainstream company, with a big-name porn star as its chief selling point. It wasn't directed or produced by women, and I'm damn sure it wasn't made with the "women and couples" market in mind. It's exactly the sort of thing that the "porn is violence against women" crowd complains about. It's nasty and rough, with a heavy dom-sub tone; women get slapped around, and there's a recurring theme of choking blow jobs and gagging actresses. And yet, in an unscientific survey of five or six acquaintances, it was the men who were freaked out by the video and the women who were leering and drooling and shoving their hands down their pants. I'm not sure what's to be learned here (apart from the fact that the women I know are big perverts). But I, for one, am sick to death of male porn actors who play it so cool you have to thaw them in the microwave. Rocco is the opposite of cool; he fucks like he's deranged, completely engaged with his raunchy, perverse thrills. And I can't think of anything sexier. Once again, authenticity is the key, and it's out there in hetero porn if you know where to look.

Bottom line: less politics, more pussy

Slumber Party Pornos

by Diana Cage

The mere mention of a slumber party invokes visions of Sapphic experimentation. What's not to like about a group of scantily clad young girls, all bedding down together in one room? Of course, the slumber party theme has been often exploited by mainstream porn, but the *Shane's Slumber Party* series is about as good as the genre gets. Completely plotless, the premise is simple: Shane invites a bevy of very young and enthusiastic hotties to spend the weekend with her in some sex-toy-stocked exotic locale. The camera follows the girls as they pair off for extended impromptu sex sessions.

The actresses are what set these videos apart from other all-girl mainstream titles. Most of them have natural bodies; implants are the exception rather than the rule. And they seem to sincerely like one another. No, they aren't all authentic lesbians, but they definitely have a good time getting down and getting one another off. There's lots of screaming, gushing orgasms—often multiple—and a few of the girls are ejaculators. Not every video is as inspired as it could be, so here are few to check out.

Slumber Party 8
[Odyssey Group Video, 1999]

Palm Springs is the setting in this somewhat spotty but overall good installment. An abundance of oral sex scenes and genuine chemistry between the actresses give this video an authentic lesbian feel. In one scene, a cute brunette with endearingly bad teeth and a European accent ejaculates repeatedly after some dildo and pocket rocket–induced orgasms. Stunned and envious, the other girls deify her and beg her to give them squirting pointers. It's genuinely useful information if you've never done it, and as proof, after the lesson one of the other actresses gives it a whirl and drenches the bed. A stunning, aggressive redhead and a beautiful Asian woman have really hot, enthusiastic sex during the orgiastic finale.
Bottom line: Squirting 101

Slumber Party 11
[Odyssey Group Video, 2000]

This party has good, strong sex scenes, lots of strap-on fucking, and raunchy behavior, but there's absolutely no dialogue or connective material before the fucking begins. This works fine if you usually fast-forward to the good parts anyway, but if you're looking for foreplay this video will disappoint you. The girls are really into what they're doing, and there is one very long, very hot hard-core strap-on scene on the pool table. Skip past the gratuitous shot of one gal stuffing a billiard ball into her pussy and attempting to shoot it into the pockets. This video also has some great ejaculation sequences.

Bottom line: hit and miss

Slumber Party 12
[Odyssey Group Video, 2000]

This time around we have a beach theme. The girls head down to Mexico for Spring Break. The video opens with all the actresses wearing bikinis and riding around on ATVs. To be honest, I was far too worried that someone would get hurt to find it erotic, but the girls seem to be having a good time—maybe the seats vibrate. The opening sex scene takes place on the beach. Blond, tanned surfer girls have some really exciting old-fashioned lesbian sex—no toys, just mouths and hands. Then two women in the shower have extremely hot sex, until one of them explodes and the camera zooms in on her pussy as it spasms in amazingly strong and visible postorgasmic aftershocks. Wow.

Bottom line: for outdoor enthusiasts

Slumber Party 13
[Odyssey Group Video, 2000]

In number 13, the beauties hang out at a pool party. Someone starts passing around a bottle of tequila, and before you can say "orgy" they're doing body shots off one another's nipples. I have the sex drive of a teenage boy, so I thought this was great. If you're more mature than I am, you may want to fast-forward. A poolside three-way has some of the dirtiest sex talk I've heard between two women in any video, lesbian or mainstream. And the woman wielding the strap-on in this scene has clearly done it a few times before.

Bottom line: poolside pussy-lickers

299

Slumber Party 18
[Odyssey Group Video, 2002]

Slumber Party 18 is just plain silly. The first 10 minutes of this video has the girls inhaling helium balloons and making funny voices for one another. I'm trying to imagine who might be turned on by this. Helium fetishists? Then they begin wrestling. Not in any sort of sexually suggestive way, just wrestling. And they're bad at it—though one of the actresses wears pink marabou-trimmed panties and bra that gave me lingerie-envy. Next we're treated to a group scene that, despite heavy reliance on toys, is truly inspired. Inexplicably, the subsequent sex scenes take place in a bowling alley. Really. Right there on the varnished maple floor. I'll tell you right now, no one gets done with a bowling pin, so you perverts might as well stop hoping.

Bottom line: more goofing off than getting off

Live or Memorex?

by Greta Christina

So there's this weird thing happening in lesbian video smut. It's getting harder to tell whether the tape you're watching is an authentic, by-lesbian-for-lesbian, transgressive reclaiming thing, or a fake, exploitative, male-appropriation-of-our-sexuality piece of mainstream trash. The line between the two is so blurry sometimes that if you skip the dork-wad phone-sex ads in the mainstream tapes you might not be able to tell which is live and which is Memorex. Some may find this trend unsettling. I think it's pretty darn cool. Here are a few examples.

Full Load
dir. Barbara DeGenevieve
[Fatale Video, 2003]
Butches, bois, FTMs, even a few femmes populate *Full Load,* the compilation of scenes from the popular dyke porn Web site sssspread.com being distributed by Fatale Video. Fatale is the by-dyke-for-dyke video smut company that pretty much started us all down this path of sin. (Me, anyway; my first smut appearance was in a Fatale video.) And their latest does a fine job of upholding the family tradition. There's lots of twists on expectations, and I don't just mean the gender identity stuff. There's the femme top who stays on top while she's getting fucked; the butches who keep their strap-ons strapped while *they're* getting fucked. The camera keeps focus on faces and body language while still giving you a good look at the goodies. And although the energy is uneven, it's mostly pretty high—fun and entertaining at least, passionate and electric at most.

    To be honest, *Full Load* didn't quite yank up my skirt and shove its hand between my legs. But that's probably because I'm not that into butches (with a few exceptions, and you know who you are). I'm usually good at telling when a video is tasty, though, even when it's not sending current down my personal wires. And I can tell, this is a tasty video.
Bottom line: Butch and FTM fans, snatch this up.

301

San Francisco Lesbians 9
dir. Cynthia Martin
[Pleasure Productions, 2003]

The thing is, this big-distributor tape doesn't look radically different from *Full Load*. There are no out trannies, but there are lots of butches, some of them pretty damn hard-core; plus there are big women and small-titted women and older women. Like *Full Load*, it's rather uneven; but the unevenness ranges from "reasonably fun" to "yowza," emphasis on the "yowza." And it's "yowza" for the same reason *Full Load* is: enthusiasm and passion, intensity and fun, real dykes having a really good time. It was even made by a female director, with an all- (or mostly-all-) female crew. In a way, the only difference between a video like this and a video like *Full Load* is who's putting up the money and doing the distribution. Not that that's an irrelevant question. But if that's not an issue for you, then go nuts.

Bottom line: more butches, mostly yowza

San Francisco Lesbian Bondage Club 3
dir. Cindy Martin
[Dungeon Video, 1998]

What is it with these "San Francisco" videos? Even the cheesiest mainstream producers—and both Pleasure Productions and Dungeon Video have produced some cheesy-ass videos—seem to get inspired by the sexual playground by the Bay. Like *S.F. Lesbians 9,* this video is a plotless wonder, with the production values of a high school play. But whoever did the casting was obviously paying zero attention to standard porn chickies and loads of attention to enthusiastic women skilled with the kink. They look like lesbians—there's a lovely variety of body types—and more important, they act like lesbians, seriously nasty lesbians, wailing on one another with energy and joy, with styles that range from sweet to ferocious. Hecka fun—and impossible to tell from homegrown.

Bottom line: energetic, no-frills dyke kink

Gallery Erotica
302 ### dir. Alpha, Kurt Hardy
[Passion Fruit, 2002]

Now this is a weird one. It's an independent by-women-for-women production that almost seems like it's trying to look like mainstream porno. It certainly has many of mainstream porno's common flaws. The acting is stiff and awkward, and the music is that grating, repetitive synth-shlock. And with a few exceptions, the outfits are cheesier than a Wisconsin picnic.

But *Gallery Erotica* does have a certain wonderful quality going for it. I know that when it comes to describing porn, *sensual* is often a code word for *boring*. But sensual is exactly what this video is. The sex scenes—the good ones, anyway—have a slow pace, a gradual buildup to the nastier bits, with lots of foreplay and a feel that's, well, real. The setups to the sex scenes are fake, fake, fake, but the sex itself feels more like real sex between real couples than most porn, even a lot of by-dyke-for-dyke porn. Some of it does suck. (The kink scene, for instance, is basically vanilla sex with a few kinky trappings.) But if you're sick of porn that races to the fucking like its ass was on fire, you might have a good time with this one.

Bottom line: mixed bag, good for foreplay fans

Why Nina Hartley?

by Greta Christina

As soon as you start exploring the wonderful world of porn, you hear about Nina Hartley. She was one of the earliest advocates for pro-porn feminism, and she's continued to be one of our most important sex educators and activists, speaking with intelligence and passion against the idea that porn actresses are coerced or brainwashed victims with no free will. She eagerly participated in the earliest lesbian video efforts. And she has a longevity that's extremely unusual in porn. She's been making dirty movies for almost 20 years now: no mean feat in a business that typically values novelty and youth above almost all other considerations, including talent. She has a slavishly devoted following among many serious porn fans—and here are some videos that will show you why.

Nina Hartley's Guide to Making Love to Women/Nina Hartley's Guide to Cunnilingus
dir. Nina Hartley
[Adam & Eve Productions]
If you want to see what all the fuss is about Nina Hartley, you actually might want to start with her educational videos. It may seem like an odd thing to suggest about such a prolific porn actress, but I think some of her best work is in her sex guides. They show her intelligence, insight, enthusiasm, compassion, humor, directness, cheerfulness, and general sex-positive philosophy to their best advantage. She has several of these guides out now, but the ones that'll probably interest lesbians most are and *Making Love to Women* and *Cunnilingus*.

304

For actual educational purposes, the cunnilingus video is probably more useful to dykes. It's packed with information (including anatomy and history) and ideas about techniques that should interest anyone who likes going down on women. And there are some very entertaining demonstration scenes, both hetero and lesbian.

But you get more of the Nina philosophy in *Making Love to Women*. And it's a metaphysics that's well worth a listen. The interesting thing about this video is that it doesn't focus on physical technique; it concentrates instead on emotional and cultural issues: how women are trained to feel about sex and our bodies and how this affects us in the bedroom. It's a refreshing change from sex-ed videos that treat women (and men, for that matter) as flesh machines that just need to be toggled in the right way to get them to perform effectively. The video does mostly assume that its audience is male (as does the cunnilingus video), but the ideas are useful for dykes as well. And her demonstration scene with Tina Tyler is way fun, sexy, sweet, and very giggly. They don't look like ordinary people having sex, exactly, but they do look like porn actresses having real sex that they're doing for pleasure.

Suburban Dykes
dir. Debi Sundahl
[Fatale Video]

On the other hand, if you want to skip the philosophy and just watch Nina having lots of dyke sex, *Suburban Dykes* might be your best bet. From the lesbian porn company Fatale Video, *Suburban Dykes* combines the authenticity of the by-dyke-for-dyke oeuvre with the experienced professionalism of Nina Hartley. (Her fellow performer, Sharon Mitchell, whom Nina's character hires to spice up her bland domestic partnership, is also a pro.) As always, Nina's enthusiasm and joy bubble up like seltzer. She is bisexual in real life, and it's clear in this video that her pleasure in doing other women (and getting done by them) is quite real. She has a remarkable ease with her body and with other women's bodies, a comfort and directness that comes not just from natural passion but from knowledge and experience. And she seems to be taking a special delight in doing a video that she knows is being made for dykes.

No Man's Land 10
dir. Wesley Emerson
[Video Team]

In addition to her other charms, Nina Hartley has a singularly useful talent: the ability to get her fellow performers revved up. Here's a fine example: *No Man's Land 10* is, for the most part, a fairly standard mainstream girl-girl video, the concept being a lesbian orgy celebrating Nina's 10th anniversary in the porn biz. Various couples get a headstart on the action before the orgy begins, with varying degrees of energy, ranging from fairly real passion to extremely rote sex. But when Nina comes to the door, the video lights up. All the women suddenly remember that they're there to have fun and get one another off—and they do, with verve and devotion. The sex starts all giggly and girly and ends up wild and thrashy and screaming. The orgy scene beats everything else in the video, and it sure looks to me like it was Nina's doing. She's not even on the screen a huge amount, since there are a whole lot of women for the camera to focus on. But her influence is unmistakable. With her enthusiasm, her delight, her huge infectious grin, she gets everyone else in the room worked up—and gives them a standard to live up to.

Beyond Suburban Dykes

The New Era of Lesbian Pornography
by Laura Weide

Since the last lesbian Fatale production was released in 1994, women have been scratching in vain at the doors of local sex shops for more dyke-produced skin flicks. Although many women are simply thrilled to see any authentic lesbian sex at all, there's a more discriminating audience beginning to develop. These viewers want porn with better acting (in terms of both sexual performance and dialogue delivery), less cheesiness, better production values, contemporary dyke aesthetics, and diverse casts of women who truly seem to be getting off. Well, our day is coming. Grab your remote and hang on to your hot pants.

Hard Love/How to Fuck in High Heels
[S.I.R. Video, 2000]
If you're going to treat yourself to one sapphic skin flick, this should be the one. This all-dyke-produced crowd-pleaser shoots straight for the hot spots with two movies in one box. S.I.R. Video's (standing for Sex, Indulgence, and Rock-and-Roll—the ruling spirit of these works) Shar Rednour and Jackie Strano capture great performances, and with strap-ons, fisting, mutual masturbation, anal sex, and dyke drama, they ensure there's something for everybody on this reel.

Hard Love is the story of two exes moving on in their lives—one in a sexy new relationship, the other with a one-night bar pickup—who still have some unfinished business of their own left. Plot-heavy porn often forces us to slog through at least 15 minutes of character and storyline establishment before getting to the sex. Not here. The horses are out of the gate and the sweat is flying before the credits are finished rolling. The mutual masturbation scene is truly notable. Here a butch/femme couple talk each other into a lather as they jack/jill off, Jackie working her silicone dick to a powerful butch orgasm. The relationship between the

307

exes is very well acted and their sexual performance gets my vote for the dyke-porn Oscars.

But if the plot of lesbians in the final throes of processing their tragic relationship doesn't move you, don't dismay. *How to Fuck in High Heels,* Shar Rednour's glamorama fuckfest, offers nonstop dirty talking, hip-thrusting, cunt-fisting, tit-fucking stiletto worship. Part porno music video, part pedagogical performance, but mostly sizzling, sparkling sex. If you like a rapid-fire change of scenes, people, bodies, and outfits, *How to Fuck in High Heels* will get your clit jumping in no time.

Such a Crime
[Wolfe Productions]

When I heard there was a new sex flick about radical lesbian eco-terrorists who hack into and steal from corporate polluters, I was psyched for some politically inspired creaming. While the filmmaking is better than most and the sexy opening promises erotic intrigue, the cardboard acting of the main character and unconvincing romance weakens the effort. I'd charge it with misdemeanor disappointment. Cheryl Newbrough's earlier video, *Goodbye Emma Joe,* is more successful, with a better script and better actors. If you prefer porn with a plot, more emotional complexity, and full-bodied shots to genital close-ups, then Newbrough is a dyke erotic filmmaker to watch out for.

Bed
[Willfully Perverse, 1999]

Evie Leder is a promising new dyke pornographer on the queer art film scene. Her beautifully filmed and edited short captures luscious butch/femme fisting. Grainy black-and-white stock, moody sound, and the motions of San Francisco nighttime streets and fireworks frame the sweet sex. The only flaw is a jolting jump shot from clit-licking and fingering to full fisting. Evidently Leder's camera was elsewhere during the penetration. Perhaps as if watching rare butterflies mate in the wild, Leder must not have wanted to startle her starlets and order a retake.

Ladies of the Night, Miss Tara's Finishing School
[Bleu Productions, 2000]

Maria Beatty is in a class all her own. Her edgy S/M videos are filmic gems, particularly her spellbinding black-and-white "silent movie" beauties *The Elegant Spanking,* *The Black Glove,* and her latest, *Ladies of the Night.* This crackling Gothic eye-candy tells the story of a French schoolgirl who gets abducted by sexy vampires. Teased and tortured with rope bondage, floggers, and glistening metal accoutrements, the willing schoolgirl (played by Beatty) is transformed into a demonic bottom.

A prolific pornographer, Beatty has nine titles to her credit. With an artist's eye and a pervert's sense of humor, Beatty explores territory other pornographers deem too risky. If teacher/student games get you itching for the sound of the hickory stick, then sit up straight, young lady, and pay attention to *Miss Tara's Finishing School*.

Resources

[Erotic Videos]
Fatale Video, www.fatalemedia.com
House O' Chicks, www.houseochicks.com
Passion Fruit Productions, www.passionfruitvideo.com
Sex Positive Productions, www.goodvibes.com
S.I.R. Video, www.sirvideo.com

[Erotica Books]
Afterglow, edited by Karen Barber (Alyson Books, 1993).
Bedroom Eyes: Stories of Lesbians in the Boudoir, edited by Lesléa Newman
    (Alyson Books, 2002).
Best American Erotica series, edited by Susie Bright (Touchstone).
Best Bisexual Women's Erotica, edited by Cara Bruce (Cleis Press, 2001).
Best Black Women's Erotica, edited by Blanche Richardson and Iyanla Vanzant
    (Cleis Press, 2001).
Best Fetish Erotica, edited by Cara Bruce (Cleis Press, 2002).
Best Lesbian Erotica series, edited by Tristan Taormino (Cleis Press).
Best Transgender Erotica, edited by Hanne Blank and Raven Kaldera (Circlet Press, 2002).
Black Feathers: Erotic Dreams, by Cecilia Tan (Circlet Press, 1998).
Body Check, edited by Nicole Foster (Alyson Books, 2002).
Bushfire, edited by Karen Barber (Alyson Books, 1991).
Electric: Best Lesbian Erotic Fiction, Volumes 1 and 2, edited by Nicole Foster (Alyson Books).
Faster Pussycats, edited by Trixi (Alyson Books, 2001).
Friday the Rabbi Wore Lace: Jewish Lesbian Erotica, edited by Karen X. Tulchinsky
    (Cleis Press, 1998).
Herotica, Volumes 1–7, various editors (Down There Press).
Hot & Bothered, Volumes 1–3, edited by Karen X. Tulchinsky (Arsenal Pulp Press).
Lip Service, edited by Jess Wells (Alyson Books, 1999).
Macho Sluts, by Pat Califia (Alyson Books, 1989).
The Mammoth Book of Lesbian Erotica, edited by Rose Collis (Carroll and Graf, 2002).
No Mercy, by Pat Califia (Alyson Books, 2000).

On Our Backs: The Best Erotic Fiction, edited by Lindsay McClune (Alyson Books, 2001).

Once Upon a Time: Erotic Fairy Tales for Women, edited by Michael Thomas Ford (Masquerade Books, 1996).

Pillow Talk, Volumes 1 and 2, edited by Lesléa Newman (Alyson Books).

Queer View Mirror, Volumes 1 and 2, edited by James C. Johnstone and Karen X. Tulchinsky (Arsenal Pulp Press).

Ripe Fruit: Well-Seasoned Erotica (erotica for women over 50), edited by Marcy Sheiner (Cleis Press, 2002).

Set in Stone: Butch-on-Butch Erotica, edited by Angela Brown (Alyson Books, 2001).

Sex Toy Tales, edited by Anne Semans and Cathy Winks (Down There Press, 1998).

Shameless: Women's Intimate Erotica, edited by Hanne Blank (Seal Press, 2002).

Skin Deep: Real-life Lesbian Sex Stories, edited by Nicole Foster (Alyson Books, 2000).

Switch Hitters: Lesbians Write Gay Male Erotica and Gay Men Write Lesbian Erotica, edited by Carol Queen and Lawrence Schimel (Cleis Press, 1996).

Tough Girls: Down and Dirty Dyke Erotica, edited by Lori Selke (Black Books, 2001).

Uniform Sex: Erotica Stories of Women in Service, edited by Linnea Due (Alyson Books, 2000).

Wet: True Lesbian Sex Stories, edited by Nicole Foster (Alyson Books, 2002).

Zaftig: Well Rounded Erotica, edited by Hanne Blank (Cleis Press, 2001).

[Internet Resources]

Alyson Publications (LGBT book publisher), www.alyson.com

Bella Books (lesbian book publisher), www.bellabooks.com

Cleis Press (publisher of many LGBT titles), www.cleispress.com

Erotica Readers & Writers Association, www.erotica-readers.com

Federation of Feminist Women's Health Centers, www.fwhc.org

Lesbianation (news, personals, and entertainment), www.lesbianation.com

PlanetOut (a community of LGBT people worldwide), www.planetout.com

Queer America (directory of local and national LGBT groups), www.queeramerica.com

Technodyke (news, personals, and entertainment), www.technodyke.com

[Magazines]

The Advocate (gay/lesbian news magazine), www.advocate.com

Bad Attitude (lesbian erotic magazine), P.O. Box 390110, Cambridge, MA 02139. $7/issue or $35 for a six-issue subscription.

Curve (general interest lesbian magazine), www.curvemag.com

Girlfriends (national general interest lesbian magazine), www.girlfriendsmag.com

On Our Backs (lesbian sex/erotic magazine), www.onourbacksmag.com

Philogyny (lesbian erotic magazine), Amie M. Evans, P.O. Box 1732, Cambridge, MA 02238-1732, $2.50/issue.

[Nonfiction Books]

After the Breakup: Women Sort Through the Rubble and Rebuild Lives of New Possibilities, by Angela Watrous and Carole Honeychurch (New Harbinger, 1999).

Alive & Well: A Workbook for Recovering Your Body, by Rita Justice (Peak Press, 1998).

Beginnings, edited by Lindsey Elder (Alyson Books, 1998).

Bi Lives: Bisexual Women Tell Their Stories, edited by Kata Orndorff (See Sharp Press, 1998).

Big, Big Love: A Sourcebook on Sex for People of Size and Those Who Love Them, by Hanne Blank (Greenery Press, 2000).

The Change: Women, Aging, and the Menopause, by Germaine Greer (Fawcett, 1993).

The Clitoral Truth: The Secret World at Your Fingertips, by Rebecca Chalker (Seven Stories Press, 2000).

Early Embraces, Volumes 1–3, edited by Lindsey Elder (Alyson Books).

The Erotic Lives of Women, by Linda Troeller and Marion Schneider (Scalo Verlag, 1998).

The Essential Guide to Lesbian & Gay Weddings, by Tess Ayers and Paul Brown (Alyson Books, 1999).

Female Ejaculation and the G spot, by Deborah Sundall (Hunter House, 2003).

The Femme's Guide to the Universe, by Shar Rednour (Alyson Books, 2000).

For Yourself: The Fulfillment of Female Sexuality, by Lonnie Garfield Barbach (Signet, 2000).

Gay Old Girls, by Zsa Zsa Gershick (Alyson Books, 1998).

The Gay Report: Lesbians and Gay Men Speak Out About Sexual Experiences and Lifestyles, by Karla Jay (Simon & Schuster, 1979).

Good Vibrations: The New Complete Guide to Vibrators, by Joani Blank with Ann Whidden (Down There Press, 2000).

The Good Vibrations Guide: Adult Videos, by Cathy Winks (Down There Press, 1998).

The Good Vibrations Guide: The G spot, by Cathy Winks (Down There Press, 1998).

The G spot, by Alice Kahn Ladas, Beverly Whipple, and John D. Perry (Dell, 1983).

The Guide to Great Dates, by Paul Joannides and Toni Johnson (Goofy Foot Press, 2001).

A Hand in the Bush: The Fine Art of Vaginal Fisting, by Deborah Addington (Greenery Press, 1998).

Is It a Date or Just Coffee? The Gay Girl's Guide to Dating, Sex, and Romance, by Mo Brownsey (Alyson Books, 2002).

The Joy of Lesbian Sex, by Emily Sisley and Bertha Harris (Simon & Schuster, 1986).

The Lesbian Erotic Dance: Butch, Femme, Androgyny, and Other Rhythms, by Joann Loulan (Spinsters Ink, 1998).

Lesbian Passion: Loving Ourselves and Each Other, by Joann Loulan (Spinsters Ink, 1987).

The Lesbian Polyamory Reader, edited by Marcia Munson and Judith P. Stelboum (Harrington Park Press, 1999)

Lesbian Sacred Sexuality, by Diane Mariechild and Marcelina Martin (Wingbow Press, 1995).

Lesbian Sex, by Joann Loulan (Spinsters Ink, 1984).

The Lesbian S/M Safety Manual, by Pat Califia (Alyson Books, 1998).

Naming the Violence: Speaking Out About Lesbian Battering, edited by Kerry Lobel (Seal Press, 1986).

Our Bodies, Ourselves for the New Century, by the Boston Women's Health Collective (Touchstone, 1999).

Outing Yourself: How to Come Out as Lesbian or Gay to Your Family, Friends, and Coworkers, by Michelangelo Signorile (Fireside, 1996).

The Persistent Desire: A Femme-Butch Reader, edited by Joan Nestle (Alyson Books, 1992).

The Phallus Palace, edited by Dean Kotula (Alyson Books, 2002).

Pleasure and Danger: Exploring Female Sexuality, by Carole S. Vance (Routledge & Kegan Paul Books, 1984).

Sapphistry: The Book of Lesbian Sexuality, by Pat Califia (Naiad Press, 1988).

Sensuous Magic 2: A Guide to S/M for Adventurous Couples, by Patrick Califia (Cleis Press, 2002).

Sex for the Clueless: How to Enjoy a More Erotic and Exciting Life, Marcy Sheiner (Citadel Press, 2001).

Sex for One, by Betty Dodson (Crown, 1996).

The Silent Passage: Menopause, by Gail Sheehy (Pocket Books, 1998).

SM 101: A Realistic Introduction, by Jay Wiseman (Greenery Press, 1998).

The Survivor's Guide to Sex: How to Have an Empowered Sex Life After Child Sexual Abuse, by Staci Haines (Cleis Press, 1999).

Susie Bright's Sexual Reality: A Virtual Sex World Reader, by Susie Bright (Cleis Press, 1992).

Susie Sexpert's Lesbian Sex World, by Susie Bright (Cleis Press, 1990).

Tickle Your Fancy: A Woman's Guide to Sexual Self-Pleasure, by Sadie Allison (Tickle Kitty Press, 2001).

The Ultimate Guide to Anal Sex for Women, by Tristan Taormino (Cleis Press, 1997).

The Ultimate Guide to Cunnilingus, by Violet Blue (Cleis Press, 2002).

The Ultimate Guide to Pregnancy for Lesbians, by Rachel Pepper (Cleis Press, 1999).

The Ultimate Guide to Strap-On Sex, by Karlyn Lotney (Cleis Press, 2000).

When the Earth Moves: Women and Orgasm, by Mikaya Heart (Celestial Arts, 1998).

The Whole Lesbian Sex Book, by Felice Newman (Cleis Press, 1999).

[Organizations]

AIDS Coaltion to Unleash Power (ACT UP)
(212) 966-4873
www.actupny.org

The Bisexual Resource Center
(617) 424-9595
www.biresource.org

Children of Lesbians and Gays Everywhere (COLAGE)
(415) 861-5437
www.colage.org

FTM International
(415) 553-5987
www.ftmi.org

Gay and Lesbian Alliance Against Defamation (GLAAD)
(323) 933-2240
www.glaad.org

Human Rights Campaign
(202) 628-4160
www.hrc.org

Lambda Legal Defense and Education Fund
(212) 809-8585
www.lambdalegal.org

Parents, Families, and Friends of Lesbians and Gays (PFLAG)
(202) 467-8194
www.pflag.org

San Francisco AIDS Foundation
(415) 487-3000
www.sfaf.org